Halfway Home

* MY LIFE 'TIL NOW *

Ronan Tynan

A LISA DREW BOOK
SCRIBNER
NEW YORK LONDON TORONTO SYDNEY

🌢

A LISA DREW BOOK/SCRIBNER
1230 Avenue of the Americas
New York, NY 10020

For information about special discounts for bulk purchases,
please contact Simon & Schuster Special Sales:
1-800-456-6798 or business@simonandschuster.com

Designed by Colin Joh
Text set in Galliard

Manufactured in the United States of America

9   10   8

Library of Congress Cataloging-in-Publication Data
Tynan, Ronan.
Halfway home: my life 'til now/Ronan Tynan.
p. cm.
"A Lisa Drew book."
1. Tynan, Ronan. 2. Singers—Ireland—Biography. I. Title.
ML420.T97 A3 2002
782.42'092—dc21
[B]   2001049662

ISBN: 978-1-5011-1244-7

To my father, Edmond, and mother, Theresê,
who believed in me and always held a lighted candle
of success in their hearts and helped me throw
the discus of life that little bit farther

On a hot July afternoon in 1999, I stepped from a yellow cab onto the corner of Thirty-fourth Street and Eighth Avenue and faced the imposing structure that is Madison Square Garden. Later that night, the other two Irish Tenors and I would perform the fifth concert of our whirlwind American tour for the first time inside the Garden's enormous round walls. The sidewalk bustled with people. The heat and noise peculiar to New York City in summer seemed to bounce up at me from the pavement. But as I entered the arena, the air cooled and a hush greeted me. I had never in all my life seen such a place, and my immediate thought was, "Holy God, have I come through the wrong door?" Some of the best musicians in the world had performed on this stage, the greatest athletic battles had been played out in the center of this stadium, and here was I. When the manager brought me on stage, I felt a tremendous charge. With its impressive array of lights, scaffolding as tall as a skyscraper, and sea of empty seats, Madison Square Garden oozed power. The building itself seemed to speak to me, challenging, "Come try me."

That night the arena was full to capacity, the orchestra was in place, and the splendid lights illuminated the stage in all colors. Then my heart began pumping madly, not a state conducive to smooth singing. Before walking out in front of the crowd, I said a silent prayer to my father, who had passed on two years before: "It's you and me, Dad," I said. "Let's go." The orchestra started up the first notes of "The Minstrel Boy" and John McDermott, Anthony Kearns, and I walked out. We all wore crisp tuxedoes, mine characteristically roomy. With my swaying gait and solid build, I looked more like a rugby player than a singer. Swaggering slightly on my two artificial limbs, I made my way to the center of the stage and, with John and Anthony, began to sing.

The crowd was in ecstasy from the start. When I sang my first solo,

"I'll Take You Home Again, Kathleen," I looked down at the people in the front row. They had tears in their eyes, and my heart went out to them. I thought, "My God, what kind of a state will they be in by the time we finish?" When, after over an hour on stage, the piano floated the first bar of another of my solos, "The Town I Loved So Well," I had found my composure. In came the bass notes, and I began a seven-minute test of stamina.

For any person, standing singing for so long can be tough, but as a double amputee, for me it's an even greater physical effort. There's nothing out there to lean on, only yourself. But the love I felt from the crowd made me forget my fatigue completely. I thought to myself, "Right, if you tell the story the way it was meant to be told they'll be in rapture." And so it was. I couldn't feel the pulse of the music in my feet, but I felt it deep in my heart. And as I always do when I sing, I bared my soul, putting myself naked before the public to be judged. My soul and my voice were one and soared out to the audience with ease. I felt not only the rhythm of Phil Coulter's beautiful song, but its true sentiment, which begins with the innocence of childhood memories, moves to describe growing up, shifts forward into anguish and despair, and comes back in its final verse to a hopeful longing for peace.

Strange to say, my own life story follows a similar arc. It's a life that, from the start, has not been all about singing. Yes, I am a singer. But I am also a horseman, an athlete, and a doctor. I am a son, a brother, and a friend. I can sing as I do only because of the life that I've led. With each decade I've found myself in very different, ever more challenging arenas, but the many stages of my life have always intertwined. I have moved from one stage to the next as if on a wild steeplechase, keeping my eye fixed straight ahead and above me. If there is a single line connecting all the episodes and main events of my life it is this—a gift both given and received. Give a little, you'll get a lot, my grandfather used to say, and over years and many obstacles, he's been proven right.

When I finished my song at Madison Square Garden that night, the applause of the crowd rose up to meet me like a thunderous warm wave. Fifteen thousand people stood and clapped. I'd given my all and the shouts, screams, and tears the audience gave me in return were the greatest rewards a man's soul can have. I drank it all in, wondering again how in hell I'd ever made it from my family's small farm in Ireland to this wide stage.

Halfway Home

* CHAPTER 1 *

My mam says that I launched myself into the world with a ferocious racket, giving a high-pitched wail as if someone had hit my bottom with a wooden spoon. This is no surprise to me, as I've never been shy about expressing myself and Mam's wooden spoon was a utensil I would become quite familiar with in my childhood years. While I may have come into the world loudly, I didn't come alone. My twin brother, Edmond, arrived just before me. As a child, I often wondered about our birth, but never asked, as I didn't want to upset Mam by having her recall a traumatic event. Edmond died within a year of our arrival. For most mothers, giving birth is a happy occasion despite the final moments of labor and delivery. Judging by the outcome, however, our birth was quite a sad event in Mam's life.

When I was twenty-one, I finally plucked up enough courage to inquire. On a cold day in May 1981, my mam and I left at the crack of dawn for the town of Knock to make the pilgrimage. She was dressed in her best blue suit, her made-up face firmly set and her still-dark hair swept back off prominent cheekbones. Mam had once made a promise to God that if I ever walked and had a perfectly normal life, we would walk the 170 miles from home to Knock in thanksgiving. Despite her promise, we were driving not walking. "God grants rewards for mortifications and we won't get half the deal going by car," she lamented, driving at a snail's pace. I laughed and told her, "We may as well be walking for the speed you're driving at."

Surprisingly, when I finally got the nerve to ask my mother about Edmond and me, it was as if she had been waiting all those years for her chance to tell the story, no rehearsal needed. With her eyes fixed firmly on the narrow road in front of her, Mam told me she had been hospitalized at the Coombe in Dublin the six weeks before my twin brother and I were born. She was under observation owing to her increased weight and high blood pressure. Her pregnancy with Edmond and me had been fraught with problems. Mam said she got absolutely huge and her legs swelled terribly. She often had to climb the stairs on her backside, as it was too difficult to walk. Every precaution was being taken to ensure that this set of twins be brought into the world safely, particularly because the year before, Mam had given birth to another set of twins, Thomas and Vorneen. Shortly after this birth, Vorneen had died due to prematurity and for a long time it was touch and go with my brother Tom as well.

On May 13, 1960, a magnificent bright afternoon, Mam said she had her first set of contractions commencing labor. She was all on her own at hospital in Dublin, since Dad hadn't been able to find anyone to help milk the cows and was seventy-five miles away at our farm with my brother, Tom, and sister, Fiona. Mam was under the care of Dr. Charles, who had attended her the previous year. After fifteen hours in labor, delivery began. Edmond came out first. He was a small baby, weighing five pounds and one ounce. Delivered without difficulty, he looked perfectly well to all in the delivery room. But at two in the morning on May 14 when I made my noisy entry, an unearthly silence came over the room. The midwife went to my mam and, putting her arms around her said, "The little fellow has a problem with his legs, but don't worry, he'll be fine." Dr. Charles cradled Mam and told her she was marvelous. The trauma of the year before came sweeping over her, and Mam cried bitterly, fearing the worst.

As in all hospitals of that time, priests were at hand to offer their help consoling mothers under difficult circumstances. Mam vividly recalls her priest coming to visit shortly after the birth and saying of me, "That little fellow will make you very proud, and do you know, with lungs like those he will surely sing." Little did either realize how that prophecy would be borne out.

Later, my parents would be told that I had focamelia, a bilateral congenital deformity below the knee. I had partially developed tibias and only about a quarter of my fibulas on both legs. In laymen's terms, this means that my legs were about a quarter shorter than they should have been and both my feet were splayed outward. I had only three toes on each foot, which I eventually named Curly, Larry, and Moe on the right, and Tuppeny, Fuffo, and Jinks on the left. I came up with these names from watching television shows and reading Enid Blyton's books about goblins. As my mother had taken no drugs during pregnancy, it was speculated that my deformity resulted from my position in the womb, being a twin. Turning her eyes from the Knock road for the first time since she'd begun her tale, Mam looked at me and said, "God alone knows."

After a few weeks, all three of us were released from the Coombe. Edmond was taken home to our farm in Johnstown, and I was immediately taken to Temple Street Children's Hospital, where many babies who had deformities or other serious complications were sent. It was decided that this way, if deemed necessary, corrective surgery could be carried out at any time during the first eighteen months. The first three years of my life would be spent at Temple Street. I still don't understand why I stayed there so long. No surgery was performed on me, as nothing could be done about my condition at that time.

My own recollection of the place is fragmented and filled in with the help of my dear sister, Fiona, who sometimes seems to remember more about my life than I do. Two years older, Fiona told me she was often put in charge of me when the family came to visit. My sister had the freckled face of an angel, and I adored her from the start. She recalls that I was quite a rowdy toddler, forever babbling and chatting with everyone who came into the room. She told me that if by chance the family were to come and visit me during feeding hours, they would hear me from the end of the ward making a tremendous racket, screaming for my food. "You loved your food then," she tells me, "and you're a living testament to it today." Fiona also remembers that I had a little friend in the cot beside me named Orla and that many of the nurses used to fantasize that Orla and I might get married, as we used to pull ourselves up on the bars of our cots and chat incessantly. I do remember Orla's curly hair and her little tan dress. She hung on to the bars of her cot and affectionately gaze down at me, even when I tried to steal her biscuits. God bless her, she was the first woman ever to tolerate me.

Unbeknownst to me, when I was eleven months old and in Temple Street, my fraternal twin, Edmond, contracted viral pneumonia and died. It wasn't until I was four and Mam thought I could understand that she told me that I'd had a twin. It's odd, but even before Mam told me about him, I carried a picture in my mind of a beautiful baby with blue eyes and sandy hair. I have no idea if that's how he looked and it's hard to explain, but somehow I feel that I've never been alone, that someone's always been watching over me.

I don't think Mam felt the same sense of protection and I believe the events of those years nearly broke her. I can't fathom the loneliness and heartbreak that both she and Dad went through in the years 1959 and 1960, suffering the loss of not one, but two children. Yet her response to the hardship was to become fiercer than ever and she squeezed all her will into her living children. I've since been told that when Edmond got sick, Mam was so desperate and fraught she wouldn't let anyone touch him. When Edmond died, my mother made one promise to herself—that I would walk. She wanted me to have a normal upbringing like Tom and Fiona. This pact she made with God.

CHAPTER 2

*L*ike the refrain of a favorite song, the innocence of my childhood on the farm still pulses in my memory. At three, I was brought home from Temple Street. It was a wet November day when Mam and Fiona came to collect me. As a young baby I was always bundled up by Mam when we went out, even in good weather. My legs were never shown, I suppose so that no one would see a difference between me and any other baby. Still, I had not been out of hospital much as a toddler and when I arrived at the house, my grandfather would say of me, "He's a hardy little lad, but terribly pale. Sure, that'll all go out of him when he steps outdoors."

On the day I left, Nurse Maureen carried me out to the car. Fiona walked in front of us lugging a little wicker basket full of my baby things across the car park, a wash of pink in her lovely dress. Mam had put her blue raincoat over Maureen and me and was rushing ahead to open the car door. When she took me from Maureen's arms, I bawled at leaving behind my nurse. With her large, gentle hands and familiar smell of Johnson's baby powder, this lady had been with me every day since my birth. Frail, saintly Sister Aquinas, head of the ward, also came with us to the car and Fiona remembers her whispering to Maureen about Mam: "Sure the poor woman, she thinks he'll walk," she said. In the years to come, Mam would often take me back to visit Sister Aquinas and Maureen and both women kept soft spots in their hearts for me.

From the backseat of the car I stared at the world as it passed outside my window. Temple Street was in North Dublin and from Fiona's description to me later, the city looked to me dull and drab, overhung as it was with buildings, its big old houses with angular slate roofs floating by unattached to ground. In those days, the trip from Dublin to County Kilkenny took more than three hours, and though not far from the capital in distance, Kilkenny was entirely different in character. Situated in the midlands of Ireland, the county was almost all farms. Known for fine race horses and dairy production, the prosperous land stretched out in acres of rolling green fields, which were lined with stone walls and spotted with sheep and the occasional ruined castle. After the town Nass, the dual carriageway ended and we continued onto a narrow, twisting road walled in by wild hedge.

Our family farm sat at the foot of Spa Mountain, a great green hill crisscrossed with grey stone walls the whole way up. The house, Donoughmore, stood and still stands at the crossroads of the Spa and the Kilkenny Roads. Our rectangular home was covered entirely in thick green ivy, which was always neatly trimmed. In between the outer wall and the front door my grandfather, Pappy, kept beautiful half moons of green lawns paneled by flower beds. Ours was a tidy house with a big Victorian door that was brushed with so many coats of white paint, it had become textured with bubble marks. The S-shaped brass knocker always kept its shine and an old iron foot cleaner shaped like an "H" stood scraped with mud next to a much-used wire mesh mat that lay at the threshold of the door.

I had been home for weekend visits during my first three years, but was only a little familiar with my new familial environment. Compared to the bright whites and gleaming surfaces of the hospital I'd known up to then, the inside of our house seemed very dark. Looking back, I realize that while the family were trying their best, it had been a hard few years and a sort of gloom rested over the place. When I first came home, I was carried up the wide white staircase and brought to Fiona's room, which had green linoleum and a red lampshade. I was put next to her bed into a blue cot with shiny steel bars at its side, and covered up with a thick eiderdown quilt. In retrospect, it later dawned on me that this must have been the same cot where my poor twin, Edmond, had spent his first year.

Dad, Pappy, my brother, Tom, and our housekeeper, Lizzie, were relatively new faces to me. Straightaway, I loved the warmth of Dad and his smell, earthy with a hint of silage from his work on the farm.

Dad would often hold me before the huge mirror in the sitting room. "Who's that?" he'd say, pointing at my reflection, then, pointing to himself, "This is Daddy." Well, who else would he be? The image in the mirror revealed a gentle man, about five feet four, with neatly kept black hair, big ears, and a mild expression in his blue eyes. I loved to smell Dad's hair and wrap myself around his neck, basking in his straightforward love for me. And whenever I saw myself reflected in his eyes, I always felt ten feet tall.

Lizzie, my mother's housekeeper and nanny, was immediately put in charge of me. She was a small, elegant lady with short jet-black hair and the most beautiful dimples when she smiled. Aside from all those great qualities she had a wonderful nature and the whole family's trust. Spending a lot of time talking to me and dressing me up she must have thought that I was a live doll that responded at every interval when chatted to and was able to cry and pass water when the mood came over me.

I remember the kitchen, as I spent most of my time there. There was a big, red, painted wooden table situated in the center of the room. The floor was stone and quite cold, which I knew firsthand as I spent most of my time down on it. A big old Aga cooker was situated beside the back kitchen wall, with its bottom oven door almost always left open. The wooden clothesline hung from the ceiling above the Aga. Every time Mam would hang the fresh laundry on the wooden frames she would let the ropes controlling the line all the way down so the clothes enveloped me with the clean fresh fragrance of laundry detergent. Occasionally, the laundry left wet patches on my face. This always threw me into a frenzy of laughter. Mam was tickled pink by my reaction. I realized, even at that tender age, that the best place to sit was near the cooker.

Several darned woolen socks belonging to Pappy and Dad used to hang from the silver bar of the range. On most occasions the socks stank to high heaven, which not only got up my nose, but also infuriated my mother, who used to take her fury out on the culprits. Of course, they never paid any heed.

Pappy was my father's father. A distinguished man, well respected in the community, Pappy always wore a black suit and white shirt. I can remember him saying to us, "Wear your best coat and hat, and look prosperous, even when you are at your worst."

As children, we were all fond of him. He was particularly fond of Fiona. I was always attracted to my grandfather's shock of white hair, and when lifted into his arms, batted my hands against it. "Good pet," Pappy would say, giving me a beamy smile. Each evening at six o'clock after saying the Angelus, a prayer of devotion to the Blessed Virgin Mary, Pappy would sit down by a turf fire in his special chair and religiously read the newspaper from cover to cover. If I disturbed him on these occasions he'd get a twig from the garden and chase me around the mahogany dining table yelling, "Come here, you little cur, you!"

Aside from Pap and Dad there were many other new faces. Mrs. Ringwood, the resident cook, always wore an old blue Irish wrap apron with little flowers trimmed with red material at the edge. A strange smell exuded from her. It wasn't exactly repugnant, but it sure didn't draw me to her either. Then there were the two workmen, Martin Tobin and Jerry Burke. They were really funny characters.

Off in a corner would be my brother, Tom. Quiet and watchful, with a small, thin face, dark hair, and big ears like Dad and myself, he must have been eager for a playmate when I first came home. He was obedient and well behaved, and he waited to see what sort of companion I'd make, staring at me rather than chatting with or touching me as Fiona did. Shy, with knobby knees and elbows, and beautiful hands with long, tapered fingers, Tom took after Dad. He was a slight fellow in his youth and I remember him being given half a pint of Guinness every night to build his strength.

Each morning I awoke to the incremental shriek of our two roosters and the bawling of the cows and calves that heralded mornings on the farm. The barley crusher with its massive cogwheels pumped like a steam engine. The machine spat out crushed barley onto the ground, and the scrape of our two workmen's shovels accompanied its steady breath. My father and Pappy would be up and out early herding the cows, feeding the other animals, and making repairs to tools and buildings as needed. As a toddler, I'd pull myself up by the bars of my cot and begin adding my own noises to this chorus. After all my time confined at Temple Street, I absolutely hated sitting alone, and cried to be outside at the heart of the action.

Once downstairs, I absorbed the inside world from a little pen with mesh sides that Dad had set up for me in the front kitchen. The faces of my brother and sister appeared to me across the mesh, only to disappear when they ran outside. I'd listen to the shush shushing of Mam's scouring brush against the stone floor and the bustle of her skirt as she moved from room to room. These soft sounds were punctuated by the occasional sharp word Mam spoke to Lizzie, who always answered, "Yes, Mrs. Tynan." Mouthwatering smells of stew, bacon and cabbage, tapioca pudding, and brown bread poured from the blue Aga cooker. With enough whining on my part, my mother or Lizzie would lift me from my pen and set me down by the warmth of the cooker. But I would soon get into all sorts of trouble pulling pots and pans from the scullery, which soon drove Mam mad. She'd pull out the wooden spoon and through clenched teeth, yell as she whacked, "You're ungrateful, untidy, and always underfoot!" These words didn't fall on me alone. If Tom and Fiona got in her way, they'd make the acquaintance of the wooden spoon as well, and the sound of this instrument was added to the orchestra of home.

At a certain hour every morning, trouser legs would begin to flash around the kitchen sink as Dad, Pappy, and the workmen, Jerry Burke and Martin Tobin, washed up for tea. I loved the people around the house, and the constant bustle of activity. Lizzie was a gem, and Jerry and Martin were with us for years. They were hardworking young men, and good with children. Martin had tough, tight skin over his hands and a ready smile for us kids. Jerry was sandy-haired with a poker nose, and always bent down to ruffle my hair and call me Mickey Finnegan. Both workmen addressed Pappy with genuine respect, calling him "sir." They called my father, who worked hand in hand with them, Edmond. My mother was always "Mrs. Tynan." I knew from an early age that Mam wished for better than the lot of a farm wife. She was a very determined and focused woman, and, though I loved everything about the farm, I suppose I was too, in my own way.

When I first came home, heedless of the hospital staff's predictions, Mam tried everything in her power to stimulate me to walk. She must have seen my frustration at sitting in one place and certainly her goal was always for me to be as normal as possible in the eyes of the world. I had a great fondness for colored soaps and Mam tried to tempt me by leaving block soaps on the kitchen table to see if I would walk from my place by the cooker to get them. But instead of walking, I would crawl, grab the soaps, and begin gnawing on them, making myself quite sick and adding to my reputation for having an insatiable appetite. Something would have to be done with me.

After a few months at home, I was bundled up for a ride back to Dublin. Dad drove and Mam sat in the passenger seat. Both were wearing their Sunday best—he in tweed jacket, checked shirt and tie and polished leather shoes, she in a smart suit and high heels, her wavy hair done up and her makeup carefully applied. As we set out on the Dublin road, there was apprehension in the car. We had to make several trips to the clinic in Dublin. This wasn't too easy for us because it was a three-hour drive in an old, unreliable Ford Prefect. This car was the cause of many major arguments between Mam and Dad. She constantly referred to the frequency with which it attended Osmond Bennett's garage for spare parts. She was obsessed with her belief that Dad's driving was always the cause of the car breaking down. "His big, flat feet won't clutch the car properly," she said. But I can tell you it sure kept Ossie in business.

On this ride back to Dublin we were headed for J. E. Hanger and Co., a warehouse in an industrial part of the city for a company that manufactured artificial limbs. Dad turned around to me and with his free hand patted my bundled knee. "You're going to get new legs today, Ronan," he said. "No, don't say that to him, Edmond," Mam interjected sharply. She knew there was no certainty they'd be able to help me, whereas I think Dad had the innocent hope that technology might make my deformity go away. Dad was more apt to accept things as they came, or didn't. Mam, on the other hand, had a fierce will and often assumed the worst.

As we pulled into Hanger, I bounced with energy in the backseat. "Now, be good," Dad said softly. I knew even at that young age to behave myself in public. I remember the company was down a dark and narrow back road, but that did nothing to dampen my mood. I don't know if I understood what was happening, or simply enjoyed the adventure of going someplace new and seeing new faces. Once inside the clinic, all was clean and bright. I was introduced to Mr. Tom Hodgins, the head prosthetist. A smallish, well-set man with a very harsh voice, Tommy spoke to us a mile a minute. From the very outset, my mother and Tommy didn't get on well. Perhaps it was his insistent manner, or perhaps it was hers. But even she hung back when the mysterious process got under way.

First, I had to be measured up so that my natural height could be ascertained. Tommy and his assistant, Tony, laid me down on a table on a large piece of hard white paper. Then Tony drew an outline sketch of my entire body. They also measured me hip to knee and knee to ankle with a measuring tape and metal calipers, which felt cold against my skin. This double-pronged instrument made me nervous, but I never said a word. On the many subsequent visits I made to be fitted with new limbs, I would always keep quiet as well, awed by the ritual of it all.

From their measurements, Tommy and Tony were able to determine what my height should be. Next, they laid steel rods from my kneecaps to my toes and wrapped my little feet in cellophane. The rods were to make sure they didn't cut into my flesh when the mold was cut. I was put into the casting chair, a contraption that resembled an electric chair. Here, they cast my legs in plaster of Paris, wrapping my limbs tightly with the warm plasters to get a mold of my leg shape. Once this was done, we went home and waited while J. E. Hanger commenced making my first set of artificial limbs.

I remember asking my mother why I needed the limbs and why I was different. Six weeks had passed and we were again driving to J. E. Hanger for the first fitting of the limbs they'd made for me. It was a beautiful bright day and I could taste the excitement in the car. At the wheel, Dad hummed a cheerful tune. Mam told me that my new limbs would help me be more like Fiona and Tom. "To help you walk like the rest of them, Ronan," she explained, "you are going to need these aids." When I asked her if I would need them the rest of my life, she paused and Dad stopped humming. "Yes, Ronan," Mam said, "you will. To get around, you will."

Inside the clinic at Hanger, Tony gently placed me between two small rails and began to attach my new aids. Artificial limb technology at that time was not what it is today and my first limbs resembled a clunky pair of knee-length, ladies' lace-up boots. First, Tony directed my feet into leather booties, which were like little socks attached to the inside of the boots. Reinforced with steel rods at the sides, the boots had platform heels that were inches thick, making up for the height I'd been missing. To keep my feet in place, each bootie rested on three lined-up rivets that stuck up from the platform and were cushioned by layers of chamois cloth. The aids were far more intricate, yet far less substantial than those made today. Tony tightly laced each boot up the sides of my legs to further hold the braces in place. Then he lifted me up into a standing position, supporting me lightly at the waist.

"Now hold on to the bars, little man, and put one foot in front of the other," Tony said. I reached up and gripped the bars, pulling myself with his help further into a standing position. This was the first time I had ever stood upright. Though not completely without assistance, I felt fantastic, as if some great force were propping me up. This sensation of being held up would recur at different times throughout my life when I overcame physical challenges, but this was my first taste of that feeling and I grinned from ear to ear.

I could sense Mam's eyes bearing down on me and Dad's hands itching to reach out and help. "One foot in front of the other now," Tony repeated. I took a breath and shifted my weight to my left foot. Then I lifted my free right foot, heavier than lead in the braces, swung it out, and set it down on the shiny floor beneath me. Haltingly, I shifted my weight to the right foot, feeling the cushion of the bootie and the chamois at my sole. Tony's hands lifted me a little at the waist and I moved my left foot forward the same way, wobbling in my hips and knees a bit, but still smiling broadly. In this awkward way, I took four glorious steps.

I sneaked a look at Mam and Dad, who were standing to one side, clasping each other's hands. Both my parents were overcome. Dad was beaming, his eyes red. Mam gripped his hand tightly with both her own. She wore a look of great pride, both in me and, I think, in herself for bringing this moment to pass. Years later, when I asked him about the first time I stood, Dad told me it was one of the most precious moments of his life.

On that same day I received my new legs, Dad decided that he would buy Fiona and Thomas a little toy car. It was red in color, a smaller version of the black Prefect, but requiring fewer visits to the garage. It had pedals, a steering wheel, two front seats, and was about four feet in length. He did this so that Fiona and Tom wouldn't feel left out of the picture. The little red car thrilled them and was worshiped by both. It was given several polishings and more attention than any of the dogs or cats on the farm.

Tom and Fiona were none too keen to let me into it, as even at the tender age of three and a half I had a very curious nature. As usual, I persevered and got around Dad to let me drive it. To this day, I'm not sure what part of the car fell apart once I was in it, but the reason for its demise was the weight of my limbs on the push pedals. They just fell apart.

It was an eventful day and there were a lot of tears. Dad and Mam cried tears of happiness when I stood up between the parallel bars. Fiona and Tom cried tears of helplessness as they watched me destroy their new car. The realization struck both of them quite hard that Ronan had come to play.

CHAPTER 3

In spite of the excitement of having new limbs, when we got home to the farm I was only able to balance by holding on to the kitchen table and taking small steps. This didn't exercise the muscles in my legs very well, nor did it suit my taste for greater mobility. As a solution, Dad decided to make a tiny push carriage with wheels on its base that I could use for assistance in walking, pushing it along with my legs. This little wood walker he crafted gave me my first sustained taste of independence and freedom.

When no one was around to assist me, I learned how to lift my push carriage over the threshold of the back kitchen door and get myself outside. Once out, I lifted my face to the air and breathed in the smell of the farm. Dense with the scent of animals and silage, the air also held the earthy smoke of neighbors' turf fires. Out I rolled into this fascinating new world.

Life on the farm was a kind of symphony to me. Each animal had its part and the movement of all of us around the place took on its own pattern. As I became better acquainted with the beasts of our farm, I felt myself more and more a part of nature and of the life around me. Pushing myself around the farmyard in my carriage, I was able to get acquainted with all the animals—the cats, ducks, calves, and turkeys that roamed our property. I got my face licked by Nip the sheepdog and learned that the piglets were kept separate from their mother so the enormous sow wouldn't crush them. I loved to imitate the animals' sounds, talking back to them with the same attitudes they displayed to me, and Pappy used to comment on my natural way with them. I became particularly great friends with a pure white duck named Snowy. We were quite attached to each other. As I appeared each morning to feed her, Snowy paraded up in all her plumage, producing great remonstrations that I answered back in my own language. Perhaps because they were simpler and more predictable to deal with than certain people, I loved and respected nearly all the animals. The Bantam hens, however, were another story.

We had two types of chickens on the farm, the Rhodinan hens and the Bantam hens. The Rhodinans were lovely and docile, with white and red feathers and nice, plump bodies. The Bantams, however, were scrawny black and grey creatures. When Fiona and I went to feed them, the Bantams would hop over, knock the Rhodinans out of the way, and scarf all the oats. These miserable things were so pushy they rushed at my hands one day as I held the feed and started pecking away. I raised my arms above my head and screamed. As at other times before, Pappy came to my rescue, shooing them away. "I don't know why we got them. They're the nastiest hens in the place," he complained. "They would peck the legs off you."

I learned that Pappy's words weren't far from the truth when one day, a hysterical Fiona came into the kitchen. The Bantams had pecked her shins and ankles, and she was bleeding profusely all over her white bobby socks. That was it. Nothing or no one would attack such a great friend of mine and live to tell the tale. Little did these horrible creatures realize that as soon as I had the wherewithal to bring about an end to their tyranny, I would do so.

Before the hens' day of reckoning, I had learned the profound effects of alcohol on behavior. An old man called Ned Walsh used to ride his bike past our house on his way home from the pub and he often seemed to be having endless loud conversations with someone. But I could never see anyone else present. I remember asking Dad who Ned was talking to and whether the other person was deaf and that's why Ned had to shout at him. Dad roared with laughter. "At the time of the night Ned's coming home, most of his conversations are with God," he said. That satisfied me for the time being.

Mam kept drink in a cabinet in the dining room. She cleverly kept the minerals, or soda pop, on the top shelf so we kids couldn't reach them. On the bottom shelf, though, were several bottles of Baby

Cham, a mix of champagne and minerals favored by ladies. The bottles had lovely pictures of baby fawns on the labels. One day, I was drawn to investigate the cabinet and the Baby Cham. My investigation was complete after I drank six bottles. At this point things went from bad to worse as the Baby Cham made a second appearance at our house on Mam's good Youghl carpet. Fiona, always helpful and always looking out for me, decided to clean up the mess herself. As the carpet was red, Fiona decided that red wine would be the perfect cleaning agent and proceeded to soak the affected area of the carpet with the wine. The house must have smelled like a bad bar on the wrong side of town when Mam got home that day.

Acquainted then with the effects of this drink and still plotting my revenge against the bully hens, I once again raided the drink's cabinet one day when Mam was out. I took two bottles of Harvey's Bristol Cream and a bottle of Paddy's whisky and poured their contents into the Bantam hens' feed and water. It wasn't long before the demeanor of those demons changed drastically. They became sluggish and stumbled crazily around the yard. Soon, they simply sat down, unable to move at all. I seized my opportunity and caught the creatures one by one, putting them into a tank of water to see how well they could swim. Even at that young age I had a keen sense of injustice. "You'll never peck anyone again!" I roared. Six of those hens failed their swimming test, which I admit satisfied me, my dear sister, and even Tom, who had had his share of trouble with the Bantams as well. My father and Pappy must have been secretly pleased, too. But the death of her hens had an unpleasant effect on my mother, and my rear end once again met with the wooden spoon.

I sometimes wonder whether Mam ever regretted her unflagging mission to gain me greater mobility. My new legs had brought me a freedom, and a freedom of will, that could not always be controlled. As I approached my fourth birthday, I was wearing my aids all day and getting stronger through the use of the little carriage Dad made me. But I still had not walked in my new limbs on my own. One day, Mam decided to try her soap trick, arranging different colored bars of soap on the kitchen table. Mam put me in a chair on the far side of the kitchen and told me to go and get the bar of soap I liked best. Without hesitation, I got up, walked across the kitchen floor, and picked out the red carbolic soap, taking my first unassisted steps. Mam was elated. "Come in quickly," she called outside, shouting so shrilly that everyone thought something terrible had happened.

When Dad, Pappy, and the others came in, Mam declared, "Ronan's walking!" She came over to me at the table and embraced me, giving me a big kiss. She told me I was wonderful. It was the first time I remember her expressing affection that way. Then she said, "Show them what you can do, Ronan," and made me repeat the walk a dozen or more times. The backs of my knees began to hurt terribly as I clomped across the kitchen floor. "God, this is hard work," I thought, amazed at how heavy the parts I was missing must be. Everyone marveled at my accomplishment. "Good man," said Pappy, and Dad beamed a smile at me. Fiona clapped and Tom smiled and walked along with me. It was as if everyone knew from that moment that I would be able to lead a perfectly normal life. From Mam's point of view it was high time to show the world, or at least our little corner of it, that her son was normal.

Our farm is located in the small village of Johnstown in the north of County Kilkenny. Eighteen miles from Kilkenny City and seventy-five miles from Dublin, Johnstown was and is a tidy place with a wide main street that turns into the Dublin road, its buildings few but well appointed. The main square was always decked up with lovely flowers and the biggest building was the Catholic church. When I was growing up, the town claimed a population of about a thousand people. Our family had been in Johnstown for generations. The village had a post office, a butcher, a hat shop, a garage, and five public houses, or pubs. One of the pubs is named Tynan's and it is run by a family of no relation to us.

Our family, the Rocheford Tynans, were not rich but were well respected as hardworking within the farming community in and around Johnstown. Because Pappy thought it more dignified and

Mam didn't want to mix much with local life, we kept to ourselves. People outside the house would not have known much about our business. Even when we nearly lost our herd several times to disease, we always wore our best when we went out. Like Pappy, Mam was eager to keep up appearances, but she tended to take things to extremes.

Very soon after my first steps in the kitchen, Mam decided that she and I would walk through the town. She dressed me in my danger-red dungarees and tartan shirt, put on a flowered summer dress herself, and carefully adjusted her hair and make-up. Reluctantly, Dad drove us down to the little Protestant church at the edge of the village. He let us off and Mam caught my hand. "Hold your head up high, now, Ronan," she said to me.

It was a beautiful cool day, but I labored the three hundred meters to the post office holding Mam's hand, sweating from the work of it. Once inside the doors, I reached up and gripped the countertop, which was still high above my head. Mam greeted Mrs. Con Tynan, no relation, who ran the shop. "What a nice day we're having," Mrs. Tynan said. "And not a bit too cold." Mam agreed. "And I have Ronan here with me," she said with a steel edge in her voice, gesturing to me. Old Mrs. Tynan came out from behind the counter to have a look. Astonished to behold the much-discussed but seldom-seen youngest Tynan, she gave me a big yellow lollipop saying, slowly and curiously, "Sure is this the poor little dickens?"

We left the post office and walked down the main street. Mam wanted to show the people of Johnstown that we were not to be pitied. As we walked, everyone gawked, some whispering and even stepping out of the shops to look at me like hens to feed. I didn't like the feeling of their eyes one bit. It was as if a dark net were being cast over me. I wanted to break loose of it, but didn't know how. I was as unsteady as a newborn foal on my new limbs, experiencing the still odd mix of freedom and pain that walking brought. The platforms were heavy and my splayed legs meant that I had to use my hips to move, resulting in a none-too-graceful, crooked gait that took a lot out of me. Mam fixed her gaze straight ahead and pulled me along at an unmerciful pace, nodding greetings to anyone who dared make eye contact. "Is that the little fellow, then?" one woman asked. Another exclaimed, "God bless him." Mam walked me into the butcher's and into Sharkey's, the grocery store, and we accumulated stares and a few weak congratulations as we made our way.

I had never walked so far on my own and my long boots began to chafe me as new shoes would. But Mam paid no heed of this and marched me onward. At the edge of the village, we ran into the parish priest, a tall, wizened man with thinning hair and a beaky nose. He made the mistake of asking, "Oh, is that the delicate little fellow?" as he bent his pursed face down to mine. I felt an instant aversion to him and tried to hide behind Mam's flowery skirt.

"None of my children are delicate, Father," my mother replied sharply. "And this one will not be little."

The priest straightened and we walked on, back to the Protestant church where my father waited in the car. Getting into the backseat, I settled in, relieved to be off my feet and away from the town. "My aids hurt," I whined. "Can I get out of these legs?" "You go ahead, Ronan," Dad said, staring straight ahead. "No," Mam answered, flashing a look back to me. "Wait till we're home."

We drove down the road in tense silence, then Dad ventured to say to Mam, in a terse whisper, "You shouldn't have done that to him." She didn't answer and he drove on, pointedly not saying another word. Suddenly, Mam turned to me in the seat and pointing her finger for emphasis, said tersely, "They looked at you because they never saw you walk before. And now you have showed them, Ronan."

"I don't want to go back down there again," I whimpered and Dad turned to me. With those blue eyes that drank in all my feelings, he gave me a look that said, "I know what you went through down there and I'm sorry."

When we got home, I took my trousers off and removed my aids. The sides of my knees were nearly as red as my dungarees, and the soles of my feet were raw, souvenirs of my first public debut.

* CHAPTER 4 *

With time, I would become more and more accustomed to my aids and to walking. In different ways, each of my parents' encouragement propelled me ever outward. Instead of retreating as some with my condition might have, I came to absolutely revel in the freedom of doing as and going where I pleased. Putting my parade through Johnstown behind me, I ventured farther and farther from home without fear. Though each new growth spurt caused new levels of pain from my ill-fitting braces, I would not be stopped. As I grew, my circles of movement became wider and wider. I began to explore and take in more of the world around me and in turn the world had to deal with me.

Mam knew I had a tendency to wander and wanted to be able to pick me out easily in a group. For my first year of school, she made me several pairs of long pants of red, yellow, and green material so that I could be easily seen. My roving worried her, for I was then taking the bus to school with Fiona and Tom. It was up to Fiona to look after me once at school, where I had a grand old time making many new friends. In the terrible, honest way kids do, some of the other children must have teased me about my legs, but at that stage I didn't know enough to be bothered. And, never one to tolerate bullies, I gave back as good as I got. "If anyone bothers you," Mam had told me, "kick them with those heavy legs of yours." So I did, once even coming to my older brother's aid in a school yard fight.

Always more interested in making love than war, however, in my first year at school I met a reckless kindred spirit named Collette Dwan. Collette was a lovely blond girl who, much to Sister Xavier's chagrin, used to smear yellow paint over herself, stand up on her desk, and, attempting to remove her dress, declare, "Buttercup!" I fell in love immediately.

As an older child, I started to explore the stone fences around our property and help with chores around the farm. We had about eighty Friesian milk cows, great shiny black and white heifers that were kept in the two green fields across the Spa Hill Road. In the cool, quiet morning hours Dad and I and our sheepdog Tupper would begin work. Dad gave a quick look to the eager dog. "Bring them on," he'd say and we'd watch Tupper take off like a bullet across the road. Tearing into the dewy pasture, he made a wide arc around all the cows and like magic, they'd line up single file and come to the road as docile as you please. All of this was done in perfect, crystalline silence, with Tupper never even nipping at the cows' heels. Dad and I then brought the herd across the road into the barn. One after the next, my father would pat their hindquarters gently, repeating softly, "Good girl." He always told me, "Treat the ladies right and they'll do anything for you." These have proved to be words to live by.

In the barn's enclosed reception area, we donned long plastic aprons and hosed all the cows' udders down. Then we led them to the milking parlor, eight at a time, and hooked them up teat by teat to the automatic milking machine. With the rhythm section of the milk squirting into the metal bucket behind us, Dad and I sang to the heifers with all our hearts. We sang ballads and many unfinished medleys, due to the fact that Dad could never remember lyrics. We'd let go with "Come Back, Paddy Reilly," "When I'm Calling You," and plenty of Mario Lanza. Dad collected loads of vinyl records of singers like Nelson Eddy and Jeanette MacDonald, Kenneth McKeller, John McCormack, and his favorite, Lanza, whom Dad loved for his great, powerful voice and his passion. I was honored to sing in the milking parlor with my father, whose voice was as soft and high as John McCormack's. "Don't ever scream or screech, now," he'd advise me. "You never want people to say 'Jaysus, that's terrible.'" As he was a man of few words, his advice was always given in an offhanded way, in between tasks. Anything he had to tell me was always for my good. With each passing year, he and I seemed to understand each other more with saying less.

When we came back into the kitchen after milking, Mam would give yell at us for smelling like silage. It was as if she blamed my father for running a farm. We'd walk to the sink to wash, Dad rolling his eyes to heaven. "Is there a towel, so?" he'd ask her, shaking the water off his weathered hands. "I'm not going to give you dirty things one of my clean towels," she'd start, her hard voice tightening a notch. Without a word, but with a few chagrined looks between us, we both used the putrid flannel beside the sink and stayed as far away from Mam as we could. She was prone to sudden outbursts and we tried not to do anything to provoke them.

In the evenings, Dad and I would head across the fields to gather and milk the cows and again, we left our respective worlds behind us as we sang. Singing lifted our spirits and the cows seemed to like it too. They never scuttered in the barn and their milk was plentiful and sweet. Though other members of the family might complain that we were having too much fun to be working, the bacteria count in the milk was actually lower when we sang.

It was around that time that I began my lifelong habit of singing in the fields for hours on end, just letting loose for the sake of it. I sat on the stone cemetery wall near the house and sang back to the swallows, while they scooped and dipped like kamikaze pilots. I made up my own words and tunes, enraptured with singing to all the animals around me, to nature and to God. I have always loved the sense of control singing gives me, especially when I manage a high note. But I suppose I also love the release it brings, as if the purest notes are coming through, not from, me.

Singing also distracted me from the agony my artificial limbs had begun to cause. The rapid growth spurts I underwent as a child meant that before I knew it, my feet would outgrow my boots. The leather would peel off the rivets that positioned my feet and the six screws would dig sharply into my bare soles, chafing off pieces of my skin. Severe pain became normal to me as I was growing up. I needed new aids nearly every six months.

In lieu of a full replacement, Dad would sometimes bring the legs to

Osmond, our local mechanic. A well-built man with a round friendly face, glasses, and perpetually oil-covered hands, Ossie worked magic on my aids. Amid spare parts, tractor wheels, and broken-down engines—often of our own family's unfortunate car—Ossie managed to repair hinges and take dents out of my aids, saving us a pile of money. It seems appropriate to me now that my limbs should have taken their place with the other broken-down vehicles. While the aids were my ticket to freedom, they also frequently curtailed it. As Dad and I waited, Ossie would weld on a piece of steel to reinforce the bars. The local harness maker would then put new pieces of soft leather over the spots where the rivets came through. Still, such repairs were never enough. While my parents had numerous heated discussions as to where the money would come from to pay for all the expenses, I ran all over creation, eager for more activity. No one could convince me to stay off the limbs and no one tried. Despite the costs, I never went without a pair of new limbs, a great testament to both my parents' love for me.

Although it seemed our family often struggled for money, I never felt deprived. On Christmas of my eighth year, Fiona and Thomas were given bicycles and I got a Mechano set. While I enjoyed piecing the sticks and cogs together in odd formations, I quickly realized that my brother and sister had received a form of transport I longed for. All I could think about was how much independence they had over me. They could cycle anywhere they wanted to go, or at least all around the yard, up our short drive, which we called the Rocky Road, and a little ways up the rutted back road to Spa Mountain. I begged and begged Dad to get me a bicycle for my birthday, never thinking I might not have been given one due to my legs. I wanted one just like Tom's, a Raleigh chopper with big white wheels. Dad sighed and promised he would get it for me and I breathed easier. Dad's word was gold.

In spite of financial difficulties brought on by an epidemic of brucellosis in our cows, when my next birthday came, Dad was true to his word and bought me a black bike from Sharkey's in Johnstown. In an effort to help me balance on the bike, Dad had affixed large grey training wheels with red centers. On the night of my ninth birthday, he propped me up on the hard seat. It was seven o'clock in the evening in the middle of May. The bare lightbulb above the back door cast a circle on the cement where we were standing and the line of Spa Mountain could just be made out against the night sky. "I'll hold on to you, Ronan," Dad said, a touch of anxiety in his smooth, soft voice. "You just try and manage it yourself. Pedal like you've seen Fiona and Tom do."

I followed his instructions and we were at it for about an hour, the bike wobbling back and forth between the two training wheels. I couldn't balance and at one stage was thrown down on to the pavement, grazing my cheek. "That damn wheel!" Dad cursed the bike, nearly beside himself as he rushed over to help me. But I got back up and, painful as it was pushing all my weight into the pedals, I persevered. Finally, Dad let go of the bike again and I was suddenly balanced, cruising expansive circles in and out of the light.

The sensation of freedom was fantastic. I was over the moon and so was Dad. When he finally got me off that bike, I hugged him hard and told him he was the best father in the world. "Ronan," he said, his soft voice dropping to a brimming whisper, "you're great."

I soon mastered cycling and, feeling like a king, spent many hours roving mile after mile around the wide green Kilkenny countryside. Sometimes I'd don shorts and, shamelessly playing the role of the poor disabled lad, beg for chickens, ducks, and even horses from neighboring farms. On one particular occasion I arrived at the Walshes of Boundregeen, which was about ten miles from home. Mrs. Walsh, having fed both myself and my sheepdog Rover our lunch, gave me a Muscovy duck and drake. I brought them back in the basket on the carrier, which was on the back of the bike.

The drake, which is the male, had to be the ugliest bird I'd ever seen. I let him into the duck house with all the others and quite soon he was jumping up onto the backs of the females. I honestly had no idea why the drake was doing this to the females but I was angry at such behavior and decided the only treatment of such a cruel duck was to leave him out in the back haggard and let the fox deal with him.

Two weeks later, Pappy asked me if I had seen the drake. I replied, "I sorted that drake out. He was trying to gang up on the others, so I got rid of him." After I described the male's behavior, Pappy said, "Go in to your mother." I sauntered in and said, "Why was the drake jumping up on the ducks?" "So the duck will lay eggs," she said. "But why? How does that make eggs?" "Ask your father," she told me. I met Dad later that evening while he was milking the cows, because I knew he couldn't run off. "I've been asking everybody why the drake jumped up on the back of the ducks and everybody tells me to go to everybody else for the answer." Dad said, "What did your Mother say?" "She told me to ask you," I said. "In time you'll learn all about it," Dad said. "But it's important for the duck to have the drake so every few months they have a family just like your mother and I." I suddenly realized what was going on and concluded that I was an accomplice to a murder. I was devastated and decided that a trip to the confessional was the only way to make amends for such a terrible deed. So on Saturday at 7 P.M. I went to confession in St. Kieran's parish church and told Canon Scott I had played a major part in having the drake killed. He asked, "Why did you do that, son?"

I began to cry and sobbed, "I thought the drake was ganging up on all the ducks, but it was only after I put him out in the haggard for the fox that I asked Dad why he did that. I learned from Dad that that was the way the duck and drake had a family. I killed the father." Father Scott seemed to go into some type of convulsion in the confessional. I wasn't sure if he was having a fit, blowing his nose, or upset over what I had told him. He burst out, "Say two Hail Mary's and all will be forgiven," and roared laughing.

When I got home, Dad and Mam were in the kitchen. They asked where I had been and I told them I had confessed to helping to murder the drake. Dad said, "You did what? You did *what?*" Mam went into the pantry roaring with laughter. Both of them were rolling around the kitchen. Dad sent me in to watch television and told me,

"Everything will be fine." They could still be heard laughing from the sitting room. I had no idea what was so funny.

Not one to let anyone lower in authority than Him stand in her way, from the time of my birth, Mam took a keen interest in everything to do with my legs. I was placed under the care of Dr. James Maher, who had quite a reputation for corrective surgery in infants and young children. The Mahers were a respected family from County Tipperary and at that time, doctors were revered and woe upon anyone who should stand up to them or argue with their decisions. Ordinary people were not expected to have an opinion when it came to their own children's health and well-being. But when Dr. Maher met my mother, whose drive and determination I fear I've inherited, he realized that he would not have the last say when it came to my future. A good-looking, well-spoken woman with a commanding manner, Mam was very sure of herself. Dad would often say two things of her: "She has a fine set of legs" and "She'll hold her tongue until she gets a chance to lash it, then, boy, will she lash it."

When I was ten, Dr. Maher would advise Mam and Dad that I should have my deformity corrected. So, in the middle of August 1970, I became a patient at St. Vincent's Hospital in Dublin. Both my parents were quite concerned about the upcoming event. Were they making a decision for me that might end up making my life more difficult? Should they interfere with the way the good Lord had made me?

When I arrived at the hospital I was put into an adult ward, as there were none for children. I suppose my early familiarity with hospitals had worn off by then and the ward was a frightening place, with ten or twelve occupied beds in rows, and no curtains dividing them. When I came through, there were quite a few murmurs from the other patients. "The little fellow shouldn't be here," someone piped up. Mam and Dad had gone back home to run the farm and I was quite lonely. I became withdrawn for the first few hours, but true to form, soon became acquainted with all the nursing staff, domestics, and other patients. In the mornings, the old man in the bed next to mine would lean over and whisper conspiratorially, "One of our number died last night, you know." This gave me nightmares and I would jump into a little cupboard by the nurses' station, wrap myself in the cardigans they stored there and sleep until one of the ladies led me back to bed.

Early in the mornings, I was awaked by the distinguished Dr. Maher and his team, a clump of interns whom I referred to as cronies. This was a word Mam used when describing some of Dad's relations. The cronies were all obsessively interested in what surgical procedure they would carry out and treated me as an object incidental to my condition. I didn't understand a word of their lingo and was subsequently left in my ignorance until late one evening when another doctor appeared on the ward. A burly man, Dr. William Quinlan had a massive head of dark hair and a great smile. He seemed very friendly, so I sauntered up to him as he was writing his notes and asked, "What does amputation mean?"

It was the only word Maher and Co. had used again and again throughout all their conversations. Quinlan paused, lifted me up to his table, and looking me kindly in the eyes, explained in the simplest way possible: "They're going to take off the crooked bits so that you will get new legs that will make you run faster and you will be able to ride ponies really well." I thought this was great, but asked would the procedure hurt? Dr. Quinlan talked to me as my father would have, reassuring me that I wouldn't feel a thing.

From this point on, with my parents unable to visit me often, Dr. Quinlan and I became fantastic friends. Every morning I would go down to the doctor's residence and wake him up. Some days he would bring me down to the seaside at Dun Laoighre pier. I would sit on the beach, dipping my little toes into the water while he swam. For the six weeks that I was in the hospital, Dr. Quinlan was my hero and the greatest friend a young boy could have. It was my relationship with him, along with my years of experience in hospitals, that would later inspire my decision to become a doctor.

One Friday, I was brought in a wheelchair down to a lecture theater and asked to get up, walk around, and show off my limbs to an assembled audience of doctors. I was barefoot, wearing a track suit Mam had bought me. The floor felt cold and everything smelled of ammonia as I walked obediently back and forth in front of the mass of white coats and blank faces. Mam had come for the occasion and stood to the back of the lecture theater behind the doctors. She wore a grim expression, her eyes darting shrewdly between my audience and me. When the doctors asked me to take off my pants, I did so without hesitation. All the doctors present began a long and intricate discussion about my condition while I stood there waiting, barelegged.

Later that evening, I was surprised to see Mam and Dad at my bedside. "Get your things together, Ronan. You're going home," Mam said in her steely way. I was thrilled but confused. One minute they were making plans to amputate and the next minute Mam and Dad were taking me home. Years later, again facing the prospect of amputation, I found out from Dad that Mam had argued with Dr. Maher. He was keen to remove the lower half of my legs, but Mam was not convinced. Fearing it might go wrong in some way, she worried the operation might stunt my growth and felt I had spent enough time being trotted around hospitals. Dad told me that my mother said to Maher, "Ronan is our son and when he is old enough he will make the decision, but not until then. There will be no experimental surgery carried out on him."

I would feel the impact of Mam's choice for years to come. In retrospect, I thank her for having the strength to leave the decision to amputate to me. In the years ahead, I would be in and out of hospital, suffer excruciating pain, and push against barriers to my freedom with every ounce of strength I had. Still, I never cursed my legs. The condition I was born with, despite the many stops and starts it has caused me, has also taken me places I might never have ventured otherwise. Had I not the cross to bear that I did, and had I not made my own sort of pilgrimage in bearing it, who can say whether I'd ever have been rewarded with all I've been given?

So, for better or for worse, Mam's fierce determination forged me as sure as any other force in my life. When he told me of her argument with Dr. Maher, Dad said with more than a touch of admiration, "That's Mam, and if you cross her, all the demons from hell won't save you from her wrath." It would be many years before I fully understood the impact of Mam's decision on my life. At the time, I simply packed my things and Dad and Mam took me home again to Kilkenny.

Mam and Dad took me to visit Mr. Hodgins in Dublin to discuss a new pair of prostheses. As I had taken to wearing shorts during the warm weather, Mam wanted my new limbs to be more aesthetically pleasing in appearance. She also wanted them lighter in weight, so I could get around more easily. As it turned out, this would be my final visit to J. E. Hanger & Co. as a child, for Mam had a major row with Mr. Hodgins. She told him that she would take me all the way to Queen Mary's Hospital Roehampton in London, where, she said, "they have the professional experience to deal with cases such as Ronan's."

It took nearly six months more to get everything arranged to go to London and during that period, I was growing at a phenomenal rate. The artificial limbs were just too small and I removed them as often as I could for relief. But finally Mam and I started off to London to have my new limbs fitted. On earlier trips we went by car ferry from Dunlaoighre Harbor in Dublin to Hollyhead in Wales, and then by train to London. After two years of traveling by this tedious method, Dad decided it would be better to fly to London directly from Dublin. This would save both time and money. My new prostheses were called metal twelve's. Metal cylinders, they fixed into a hinged ankle joint on a polyurethane foot. The legs were definitely more pleasing cosmetically than my old "boots." However, a small gap had to be opened through one cylinder for my left foot, as my deformity was becoming more and more pronounced on that side, my foot splaying outward more than ever. This increased my discomfort while walking, cycling, and running, but I wouldn't let up, pushing myself harder and harder.

Not only did I expand my physical range as a child but I also continued to exercise my voice. I found that, oddly enough, the two different things gave me a similar pleasure. From the age of eight to twelve, I attended the Christian Brothers School in Thurles. At Christmas, we were all made to attend the annual Christmas concert and the younger boys were to be part of the chorus for the show that the senior boys put on. The chorus master, Mr. Vincent Brennan, was an elegant, soft-spoken man with a beautiful, mellow singing voice. My first year at the Brothers, he asked all of us boys to sing individually, to hear whether we could carry a tune.

When it came my turn, I stepped up to the piano and asked what I should sing.

"Anything you like, son," he told me.

Just as I would were I in the milking parlor with Dad, I belted out a rendition of the drinking song from Lanza's *Student Prince* album, singing, "Drink, drink, drink to eyes that are bright and sweet as the bloom on the tree."

Mr. Brennan laughed with delight. He liked my voice and it probably tickled him that one so young would sing of things presumably so far from his experience. In this way, I got my first big break, the solo in the Christmas concert. Considerably more reverent than the song I'd auditioned with, the solo was "Mary's Boy Child." I would stay after school to practice with Mr. Brennan and he began teaching me other new songs as well. I remember him positioning me at one end of the classroom while he stood at the top and listened to me sing "By Killarney's Lakes and Fells." To this day, I've not forgotten the words to the songs he taught me. A true gentleman, his was a classroom in which I never fidgeted, nor longed to be elsewhere. Brennan was also the first to tell me I had a natural gift. "God gave you that voice to share with the world," he said.

The night of the Christmas concert, Mam fed me a hot honey and lemon drink with a raw egg in it for my throat. There were forty of us lined up on the stage, all wearing white shirts, red ties, and dark trousers. The stage lights were very bright while everyone sang together. Suddenly, they were dimmed, signaling the moment for my solo. My little friend, Jim O'Brien, shone a torch light onto a spot on center stage. The torch had been engineered with a stencil cut out in the shape of a star. So nervous I thought I'd wee my pants, I stepped from the line of boys out into the starlight.

The piano started, softly and sweetly, like new snow falling, and I began the same way, "Long time ago in Bethlehem, so the Holy Bible says . . ." Looking out into the audience, I couldn't see a thing, but I felt their eyes and their attention all there with me. My voice rose and fell over the words of the song, and images of the story it told filled my head. ". . . Mary's boy child was born on Christmas Day." My voice at that stage was a perfect treble and as I sang I felt I was gliding effortlessly up a lovely white staircase. When I finished, the audience erupted.

Afterward, I made my way off the stage with the others and down into the crowd. People came up to Mam and Dad and me, full of praise. "Ah, what a little angel," they said. Even the bishop came up and gave me a pat on the head, calling me marvelous. Mam beamed and Dad was particularly proud, perhaps thinking that all the singing we'd done in the milking parlor was bearing fruit. I didn't understand that I had a good voice then, or even what that meant. I reveled in my parents' pride, but I felt something else, something that took me beyond their ambition or love for me. Though I stood in one place, when I'd sung, I had the sensation of moving into another realm altogether. I had also had my first taste of praise from an audience and that too satisfied me deeply. As I stepped from that small stage onto myriad and greater stages in my life, I would carry with me both the love from the crowd and my own insatiable hunger to move freely and in my own way out into the world.

Mam was always of the opinion that if you didn't hail from a *gaeltacht* (Irish-speaking) area, you had to be abysmal at learning and speaking the language. So she decided it was necessary for the three children to go to Irish college for the three weeks of June that year.

On the advice of Tom's fourth-class teacher, Murris O'Cleirigh, we were sent to Colaiste Lurgan in Spiddle, County Galway. Mam suggested that we hire a mobile home to live in in order that she could mind us for the three-week duration. I was the only one out of the three of us that voiced my disapproval of this. The lads in school had told me that none of their parents was going to watch over them and they were getting pocket money and food. But much more important, they were all going to be living together. I really envied them their first taste of freedom away from home and of course here were all the little Tynans unable to fend for themselves, like little piglets always protected by the mother.

We didn't have much of a democracy in the Tynan household and my disapproval was met by a quick clip across the ear, followed by, "If you don't behave you won't be going at all." Well, that soon shut me up. A holiday away from home, irrespective of who is in the driving seat, is a hundred times better than none at all.

We arrived in Spiddle having driven nearly four hours in horrendous weather. It seemed to do nothing but pour down on top of us. I thought if this is an augur for the rest of the time, we're doomed. As it turned out, the gloomy weather was the perfect backdrop for our temporary home.

The place was a mile down a small narrow lane, which appeared not to have seen sight of mechanical traffic for years. The hedges on either side were so overgrown that they kissed each other forming a canopy over the road. The center part of the lane way was so thick with grass that a farmer would have been able to cut two crops of hay from it. As usual, I couldn't keep my opinions to myself. I wondered if, by chance, we had gone down the wrong lane. This comment was greeted with complete silence so I took it for granted that no was the answer. At the end of the lane, in a secluded plot, was our mobile home. Fiona had read the occasional murder mystery to me at that time and where we were located would have been just the ideal setting for one of these awful events.

Thank God we brought Fatso, our black cocker spaniel. At least we had some canine protection should any unwanted stranger appear. Every morning Mam would have us up at the crack of dawn, washed and ready to go to college. We would walk the mile or so up the lane, which was more like a wilderness. It had one major plus. The smells from the wildflowers were magnificent. It was as if one had just stepped into a florist shop; it was spellbinding.

At eight-thirty each morning the yellow school bus would appear tanked full with kids of all ages. More often than not there were no seats available, as we were the last stop before arriving at the school. Tom and I were in the same class. Fiona on the other hand was in the senior girls' class.

Pretty soon we all made friends, even Tom, who was very slow to mix. He always took his time about choosing a friend but when he did they usually got on famously. I was often left on my own when his friend would appear, not that it bothered me as I had plenty of people to visit.

By about the second week we had plenty of callers to our mobile home in the oasis. They really enjoyed visiting our hideaway, as Mam always would have plenty of biscuits and oranges for the small guests on their arrival, which thrilled all of us to bits. From what I recall this was one of the only times that I remember Mam being really relaxed. She really enjoyed being out in the wilds of Galway, taking Fatso for walks and I suppose having loads of time for herself. The most notable change: She stopped arguing with us and we all seemed to be less stressed. Despite our location and the distance that had to be traveled to get anywhere, we were really beginning to function as a happy family, which was sweetened even more by Dad's visits on the weekends.

Every year the Galway region organized their own *Feis Ceoil* (singing competition). It always took place in the college, as it was the only place around with a big hall to cater to the general public. My brother Tom was tone deaf, so he was given a dispensation by Mam. However, Fiona and I were put under starters orders to get our entry forms and show those Galwegians that the finest singers in the country more often than not lived outside the stone wall district of Ireland.

I entered the under-twelve section. The only rule in the competition was that every competitor had to sing in Gaelic. I had learned a beautiful lullaby called "The Connemara Cradle." It compares the tranquility of the countryside resting among the lilies with a little baby sleeping softly without a care in the world. Dad and Mam both loved this song, so it was the obvious choice.

My competition started at three o'clock on a glorious Sunday afternoon. At the time it seemed to me that every young fellow from God knows where had entered the competition. To add to the sheer number of competitors, each appeared to have brought not only their parents and other relatives but half their neighbors as well for moral support. On top of that, some of them appeared quite tough-looking, which set the fear of God in me just being there. I could only imagine how those poor wretches were feeling themselves.

I was tenth to sing. Everybody was seated in the hall either on old wooden benches or cast-iron seats. Comfort was not a priority. It was also very apparent that the local talent had gathered in one area of the hall while the rest of us were scattered, like weeds in a field, all over the place.

Each competitor was announced from the top of the room by the judge. He was a very portly man, aged about sixty, wearing a checked shirt and tweed suit. The suit had a waistcoat that was unbuttoned on the bottom half, presumably due to the enormity of his belly. When my turn came I was a little shy about walking up in front of the rabble. Recognizing that Mam would have murdered me if I didn't walk out, I wisely chose to cast my apprehension aside. When I reached the judge's table, he asked me what age I was and then asked what I was going to sing. His facial expression was very soft and I felt a lovely gentle nature from him. I relaxed almost immediately and replied willingly. He gave a smile and said in Irish, *"Ar aghaidh leat,"* which means, "on you go." My voice was crystal clear and for those few minutes of song it seemed second nature to me to be singing and entertaining. I enjoyed every second of my short performance. When I had finished even the natives clapped, which stunned me, as they hadn't been clapping for too many, not even for some of their own. I sat down next to Fiona, who was beaming at me and said that I was brilliant. Dad gave me a wink. That was enough for me; once he thought I did well, as far as I was concerned I had won. He was the best judge in my book.

We sat there for a further hour and a half. God, I was bored out of my mind. We listened to nearly the entire repertoire of Irish songs. I took a glance over at Dad, who by now had dozed off. Mam brought him around with a sharp elbow into the side as the judge got up to announce the result. He spoke for about twenty minutes in Irish. He spoke so quickly that I hadn't a clue what he was saying, until my name was called out as being the winner of the under-twelve competition. The whole family was elated; even the locals gave a good cheer. Dad left for home shortly after the *Feis* as he had a long journey ahead of him.

The college was finishing by the middle of the following week. I think Tom and Fiona were a little sad to be leaving as they had made good friends. As for me I couldn't wait to get home to see the farm and go fishing. Mam had promised to buy me a fishing net for winning the competition. On our way home I spotted fishing nets for sale in a little shop in Oranmore twenty miles into the journey. I shouted at Ma to stop. She nearly had a heart attack as she thought we had run over a cat or missed a traffic light, which she had a habit of doing. I was always a little suspicious that Ma was color blind. But on this occasion there were no lights and when she realized that nothing sinister had happened, the relief was evident on her face. Based on her startled reaction, I thought I had blown my opportunity to get the promised gift, but luckily all I got was a cautionary stare.

Oranmore at that time consisted of several pubs and one or two tourist shops. It was in one of these that I bought my net. Fiona and Mam had gone into the shop next door that was full of Waterford Crystal decanters and wineglasses of every shape and size. I strolled into the shop as proud as you like, not a care in the world, and delighted with my new purchase. Having no idea how long the pole and net were I began swinging it around to get the feel of it while I looked for Fiona and Mam. Unfortunately my sweeping movement managed to catch about ten crystal wineglasses that were on display and drove them into next week. For a split second there wasn't a sound to be heard in the shop as the glasses were displaying their gymnastic skills somersaulting and pirouetting before they made their ungraceful landing onto the ceramic floor, shattering like a shower of hailstones all over a road. I looked over to Mam and Fiona; both their faces had turned ashen. At that moment I wanted desperately to run away but I was stuck to the floor and my jaw opened well beyond its normal capacity. Harsh reality was fairly swift in its approach. The owner of the shop, while fully sympathetic to the situation, was adamant about being paid. The damage was in the region of 100 pounds. Mother held her composure till we got into the car. World War III then erupted.

Fiona and Tom sat like mice in the car while Mam went out of her mind with rage over what had happened. She cried the whole way home repeatedly saying how hard it was to make ends meet, how many sacrifices she and Dad had made particularly for me. This was a cruel blow as I was only too well aware what kind of a financial drain I had been on them but only God knew how desperate I was feeling. Later Fiona told me that she had seen a sign on the wall of the shop that said "Nice to handle, nice to hold, but if I'm broken consider me sold." Boy, did this statement pack a huge punch.

Eventually Fiona suggested that we say the rosary. I think she had two reasons, first, to stop Mam from continually scolding me, and second, to get us all home safely as Ma was driving like a lunatic.

When I got home I disappeared like a fallen star without a trace. I decided to camp out with Rover the sheepdog in his tiny little house. I must have fallen asleep for I awoke to the frantic shouting of my name. As soon as I saw Dad I ran over to him. He put his arms around me and said, "They're only glasses. You're not hurt and no one has died. What does it matter?" I started to cry and through my sobbing tried to explain what had happened. The whole episode had been relayed in graphic detail to him by Ma. Mam had calmed down considerably by the time we returned to the house but I could still feel she was fairly devastated about the whole day. There was no doubt in both our minds that this day would never be forgotten.

✳ CHAPTER 5 ✳

Growing up, religion was to the fore in our house. Every Friday night, at eight o'clock, the whole family would kneel on the landing of the stairs in front of the picture of the Sacred Heart to say the rosary. "Hail Mary, Full of Grace, the Lord is with thee," we'd begin, progressing slowly. I'd stare up at the wall at the colorful picture of Jesus, with his soft wavy hair and sorrowful eyes and his hand held up in a gesture of forgiveness. The crown of thorns that drew beads of blood from his forehead and the other ring of thorns around his heart, also drawing blood, particularly transfixed me. This picture was mild, though, compared to the one in my grandfather's room. Pappy's showed the whole of Our Lord's thin body, His hands and feet punctured by nails. Jesus' anguished eyes followed me in that one, terrifying me to the extent that, if ever I had to go in to Pappy's room, I'd race straight out.

The three mysteries recited in the rosary are the joyful, the sorrowful, and the glorious. For some reason, our family seemed to recite the sorrowful mystery more than the others. More important than reciting the right words was the way in which they were recited. Devotion had to be demonstrated. If the proper reverence were not shown, Dad would interrupt the prayer to give the culprit a quick clip to the ear. Usually giddy as hell during these sessions and unable to sit still, I often came away with my ears quite red. The whole prayer lasted an endless twenty minutes followed by a litany of "Sister so and so and Saint such and such look down on us." As the minutes dragged on, I nearly burst my skin with impatience to be elsewhere.

Still, all those prayers must have served me. In the difficult years of adolescence, I would many times ask for the blessings of Mary and her Son. And I must say that these two seldom let me down, even when I let them down, or failed to turn the other cheek.

In 1971, at the age of eleven, and as my siblings had been before me, I was sent to board at an Irish school for a year course. As I said my excited good-byes to Mam and Dad and the others at the farm, I had no idea what I was leaving behind. Going to school simply meant the purchase of a lovely new Antler suitcase for me, along with a tuck box for my cakes and biscuits. The school, Trabolgan, was situated in Whitegate, West Cork, and though it was my first time away from home, I was thrilled to be there. At the time my brother and sister were off at other boarding schools and all I knew was that I would no longer have to bear the brunt of Mam's rages, which seemed to be getting worse as we all got older. Trabolgan had about fifty lads from all parts of Ireland. It was a friendly place and I made plenty of pals there. Initially, my only problem was that my aids were becoming more and more of a hindrance.

During the annual school sports I realized for the first time in my life how much my disability impeded me. At Trabolgan, there were medals to be won in every possible discipline, but I won nothing. It was impossible to find the sport where I could be competitive. Frustrated with my lack of agility, I often pushed myself too far. The strain of trying to keep up with the rest of the lads at sport soon became too much. Up to this point I had been in a little world of my own and my family's making and had yet to face the cruelty of the wider world.

One day while playing football, I felt a greater amount of discomfort than usual in my foot. Stepping out of the game, I went to the edge of the green and sat down next to a big chap who was also sitting out. Upon unlacing my boots, I found that the three exposed rivets on my left aid had dug two or three centimeters into the soles of my feet, becoming lodged there and drawing plenty of blood. The lad next to me could hardly bring himself to watch as I yanked the rivets out. "My God," he said, "that must hurt." "You're not joking," I replied with a grimace. To me it was par for the course. The pain had become part of my daily life, one of the crosses that I had to bear.

Principal O'Riordan, a kind, sympathetic man who could see the toll my disability took on my spirits, was on my side. He decided to organize an event for everyone in which I might really shine: a fifty-meter dash sack race. This simple sack race would be a defining moment of my life, one that showed me how important it was for me to be able to compete on a level playing field.

Principal O'Riordan and I discussed how I could do my best. "Why don't you take off the limbs?" he suggested. "You'll be faster because you can put your toes in both corners of the sack." It was worth a try. On the day of the race, we all walked down to one end of the long football pitch. Excited, I selected my burlap sack, sat down at the edge of the field and took off my prostheses. It was always a relief as my feet and legs met the fresh air and came unchained from the limbs. I got into the sack to try it out, but without my limbs it was too long and I had to get up again and choose a better size. Finally satisfied with my bag, I practiced my technique a bit and lined up at the start with the others, sweating with nervousness.

The whistle shrieked and I tore away as hard as my legs would go. I moved like a bullet, the rough material of the sack scratching my bare feet, my legs pumping like pistons. Carried on surges of adrenaline, I felt great. With ten meters out of fifty to go, there was only one lad out of the twelve in the race who was still caught up with me. I pumped and pumped but couldn't shake that lanky bastard. I had him right in the corner of my eye and he was gaining on me. I pushed my legs to their limit to no avail. Horrified, I saw my rival pass in front of me. With a moment's lapse in concentration, I saw my first place position disappear as he jumped across the line before me.

Stumbling across the line myself, I went numb with defeat. I had desperately wanted to win on my own merit and had come so close I could nearly grasp how it might feel. While I concealed my disappointment, on the inside I was absolutely screaming, "Why, God, are you so damned unfair?" I wondered if I would ever win anything in my life. I held the tears inside until I got to the edge of the field, but then the dam burst.

I was numbed by the whole event and I felt that I would never succeed in sport of any kind. Thankfully, that numbness was only a transitory event in my life. Mr. O'Riordan came over and gave me a big hug and said in Gaelic, *"Ta chroi mor agat"* (You have a big heart). At the time, I felt a fat lot of good that did me! But I also realized that in his heart he wanted me to succeed and win the race. I know that although I had come in second, I had come in second on merit, without any allowances in the race being made for me. Once I accepted that, I was delighted with myself. This became the basis of my future determination to succeed in sport without any allowances being made for my disability.

Despite Mr. O'Riordan's empathy, at the time I thought a big heart sounded good, but it didn't win me the race. But the challenges in the years ahead would prove me wrong, demanding as they did all the heart I could muster. This was especially true at De La Salle College, a prestigious boarding school in Waterford, where I was sent at age twelve to join Tom. It was there that I learned that it was one thing to fail in athletics and quite another to fail to be accepted by my fellow students.

When I started at De La Salle, Tom had already finished his first year. In his first year Tom had earned the reputation of being diligent, extremely well focused, and a good worker. Conversely, my report card from the previous year in school read, "Ronan has bundles of ability, but he can be distracted very easily and doesn't achieve the standard of which he is well capable." Though it thrilled me to be getting out into the world and farther away from home, I felt I would never be able to live up to the paragon of Thomas Tynan. Still, Mam had her sights firmly set on De La Salle for both her sons and De La Salle it would be for me.

My brother and I had always been like chalk and cheese. To me, Tom seemed meek and obedient in those years and was, to my mind, overly methodical. In his eyes, I'm sure I was a reckless, undisciplined fellow, always making trouble for myself unnecessarily. In the years at De La Salle, Tom used to drive me mad by writing letters home reporting on all the minor infractions I had committed. Instead of an ally, he became a stranger to me then, as I suppose many siblings do at that stage of life. In those years, we avoided each other as much as we could, pretending we came from totally different families.

On a wet September day, Mam and Dad drove us both down to De La Salle in the old Ford Escort. As usual, before even reaching the iron gates of the school, Tom and I were at each other's throats about something trivial. Pulling up to the drive, we faced a massive five-story stone building. Its blue-trimmed windows looked back at us like blank eyes and we quickly shut our traps. A stern, solid monk named Brother Ameddy met us at the car. The approving way he greeted Tom made my stomach sink; I felt I had the deck stacked against me from the start.

As I walked up the stair entrance with my family, I encountered my first problem at De La Salle. There must have been thirty stone steps leading to the main door, with no rail for the last few. Gorgeously outfitted, the rooms inside had grand furniture, high ceilings, and floors waxed to slippery perfection. But we had to climb what felt like a hundred more stairs to reach my fourth-floor dormitory room. On leaving, Mam gave me a lipsticky kiss on the cheek and Dad squeezed my shoulder, unable to bring himself to speak. I unpacked my new tartan rug, rested on it at the edge of my cast-iron bed, and looked around at all the other lads doing the same. We boarders slept fifty to a dormitory, which was in turn divided by partitions into smaller areas of sixteen beds. All the beds had blue cover panes and only two feet separated one bed on either side. Suddenly, I had a sinking feeling, as if I were back in the hospital. None of the fifteen other lads around me spoke, and while usually gregarious, for some uncharacteristic reason, I didn't speak either. I suppose all of us felt a bit choked up at being left by our parents.

De La Salle was like a small village, with a total student body of well over a thousand and a rigid social order based on survival of the fittest. We all took a class placement exam in the great study hall, which had imposing wooden doors with shiny brass handles and rows and rows of wooden desks. Surprisingly, I did very well on the exam and was put in the top stream. My class of thirty-one was a combination of boarders and day pupils. I got on better with the day pupils than the latter group. As boarders, we all breathed the same stale air, ate the same food, and snored or sighed in the same room day after day after day. Familiarity bred contempt.

At first, no one made a remark about my legs, but fairly soon after we settled into a routine, I began to be picked on. Friends were hard to come by. This new world had a coldness about it that did not encourage camaraderie. I've always had a great sporting nature and played football and hurling, a Gaelic sport similar to field hockey, with everything I could give. Still, I was not welcome on the teams. Once, in football, I was out on the pitch at a practice game. I was thrilled to get possession of the ball until a big cocky player from the other team ran up to me and dead-legged me, kneeing me so hard in the thigh I had to sit out. In hurling my reception on the pitch was not much better. The message was clear. In the eyes of those great sportsmen, I was worse than an eyesore; I was useless. Almost always the last picked for any team, I began to feel dreadfully insecure. The so-called best and brightest would not accept me because of my imperfect legs.

My teachers at De La Salle were the usual mixed bag of inspiring and irritating, but they seldom stepped in to defend me against bullying. Needing my sister more than ever, I wrote sorrowful letters to Fiona, who comforted me in letters back as best she could. But Fiona was far away in her own boarding school at Galway and I soon enough realized I would have to take care of myself in this wilderness.

Because Trabolgan had been so friendly, I had not anticipated how much I would miss home at De La Salle. Sometimes in the evenings I would sit on my bed and, thinking of Pappy and Dad and the animals at the farm, come very near to tears. I missed the sounds and smells of Donoughmore and yearned to watch the cows line up in the field in the morning and sing a few bars of "The Scottish Soldier" with my father in the milking parlor.

But singing was no refuge for me at De La Salle, though at this preadolescent stage, my voice sounded sweet, soft, and pure. Early on in the year, while we were all in choir, the director Mr. Boyer's ears pricked up and he began circling the group. "There's a beautiful voice here," he said. I hung back a bit, not wishing to be singled out as different yet again. But I was soon enough discovered, to the point that older people from the town would stop by our school chapel to listen to me. I wasn't doing terribly well in my other subjects, but Boyer encouraged me to sing, even advising music as a career. Boyer's praise of me just gave the other lads ammunition and they used my talent against me, making fun of my still high voice to the point that I nearly lost my will to use it. Mam, too, discouraged me from taking singing as seriously as I might have. "Singers live by their wits," she worried, "and that doesn't put too much bread on their tables!" As a result, I spent my early years at De La Salle in near silence, deprived of the nourishment singing for my own pleasure had once brought me.

The troubles I had were made worse by the progressive failure of my artificial limbs. Between the endless stairs, my rapid growth, and my tendency to overexert myself, my aids couldn't take the wear and tear. In the first year at the school, I had to travel to London four times when the limbs broke down, interrupting my studies and my ability to adjust. To make matters worse, I also began to have more and more pain, along with mysterious and debilitating spasms in my lower back.

One day in French class, just as the boy next to me was asked to decline the verb "to be," I experienced a jab at my back and a dark haze came over me. My arms and legs felt as if they were being pricked and my whole body went numb with pins and needles. The room went completely still for me as my ears filled with silence. I stood up from my desk and said to the teacher, "I'm sick." Brother Clemention was a slightly stooped man with steel grey hair and an angular jaw that he often clenched before reprimanding us. But all he said then was, "Are you able to go out?" I answered that I didn't know.

Up to this point in my life, I had had a few of these attacks and could feel when one was coming on. They worried me greatly, as there seemed to be no pattern to them, but I didn't like to talk about them for fear I'd be seen as making excuses or asking extra favors. Sometimes, I could feel the spasms coming in enough time to take a position that wouldn't aggravate things, but more often, the attacks would strike like a rocket with no warning at all, tormenting me mercilessly. One minute, I'd be talking. The next minute, all of a sudden I was gone.

On this particular occasion, my odd behavior temporarily saved my grateful classmate from the burden of the pluperfect and he sat down with a sigh. At the front of the room, Brother Clemention appeared to me as a dark shape, which began to move toward me, saying, "You're pale as a ghost." My back felt as if a giant needle had been stuck in me from pole to pole and nearly, but not quite, blacking out, I had to be assisted to the sick bay, where I lay down for three or four hours before recovering. Here was one more thing that set me apart from my classmates in a miniature society where it was woe unto anyone different.

I craved a close friend dearly, but friends were few and far between in those years. Something about the visual effect of me, of my legs, seemed to keep others away from me. Still, as always in my life, there were a few angels of mercy who came through for me in those cruel years. Funny enough, they were often the simplest people, big tough lads who weren't afraid to step in and save me from an attack, or choose me for their team in the face of ridicule. Once I remember being picked eighth instead of last in hurling by a solid chap from Offaly. I was delighted, but puzzled, and asked him why he'd done it. "I know you'll kill yourself to get that ball," he said. "I'd rather have someone with your heart than someone with perfect legs and no heart at all." I told him if I didn't kill myself for the ball, I'd at least kill anyone else who got near it.

It was during this year that I began going to Mass every morning and returning to the chapel in the evenings. I had to take heart somewhere and it became a real point of solace for me to sit in the oratory whenever I could. With its glowing wooden pews, well-cared-for altar, and intricate stained-glass windows showing the incredible lives of different saints, the place was beautifully calming. I stayed there for hours, sitting before the four-foot statue of Our Lady, with her blue veil and serene face, praying to her and also asking God to please make the other lads just leave me alone. "Look, if you do this for me," I'd say silently, "I'll do anything for you." I was feeling very low, but whether it was my own toughness, which my parents had forged in me as a young child, or the guardian angel I had looking after me, in all this time I never felt alone. Even though my prayers were not answered directly, I didn't lose faith and always came out of the chapel peaceful as a lamb. But I wasn't always able to maintain this peace.

Those lads who tormented me picked on my most obvious flaw. They called me bandy-legged so often that I began to wish they'd come up with something more creative. Because of the way my parents raised me, though, I never saw myself as flawed. I never took my tormentors' view fully on board. Still, I suffered. Everything is felt so much more intensely in adolescence and it had been a time of great departures. I had taken leave of my home, my family, and my carefree days on the farm. At the worst moments, it even seemed I'd left my own happy, robust self back in Johnstown. The very things I'd so blithely given up, the routine of my family's daily life, the chores around the farm, and even the prayers recited on the stair landing, were the very things I now longed for. Still, I learned during this time that there was one thing that I would never leave behind, one thing that could never desert me. This was my own strength of character.

One day when I was thirteen or so, a thin fellow with glasses, known to us all for his family's wealth and influence, began a typical project of calling me names. This was during a break between classes. "How do you stand yourself, bandy legs?" he began, moving on to other brilliant labels like "crooked legs" and "false legs." Surrounded by his cronies, this little imp was absolutely drunk on his ring-leading powers. "Why don't you shut up?" I told him. But he wouldn't let up and once we were all out on the football pitch, I went after him.

There must have been a hundred lads gathering like flies, all of them chanting, "Row, row, row, row." I got in the first blow and then, as if it were a boxing match, put my two fists up and faced the chap. I waited for an opening and then, with all the strength I could gather, punched him straight in the nose. The force of the wallop I gave him traveled up through my arm and made me even more unsteady on my legs. But I found my balance and tore into him again, beating him with my hands alone, though I could have done more serious damage with the limbs he so despised. None of this chap's friends stepped in to help him. He was down on the ground, bleeding, when Brother Ameddy came pushing through the circle of boys that surrounded us.

"What on earth is going on here?" he demanded, as the crowd went silent.

Breathing hard from the fight, I replied slowly, in a hard-edged voice, "I had to take a stand." Brother Ameddy looked at me and didn't say a word. Sick to my stomach with what I had been forced to do, but nonetheless defiant, I walked up to the line of boys, which parted to make way for me, and marched the long, laborious way back up to my room.

"I had to take a stand," I repeated softly to myself as I lifted my sore legs up one stair after another.

✳ CHAPTER 6 ✳

*D*uring my teen years, horses became my salvation, helping me to stand, if not on my own two feet, at least on their four. They were my friends, my teachers, and the best solution that I could come up with to address my limitations. Horses had always been part of life on the farm. Pappy proudly told me that our house had once been a stopping point on the national Bianconi coach line and my grandfather's bold and meticulous character had been defined by horsemanship, first in the cavalry and then in the North Kilkenny hunt. My own career as a horseman began with coaxing our little white pony, Sunbeam, to canter in the field opposite my house and progressed to riding thoroughbreds into wider and wider arenas. Through horses, I gained range of motion and confidence and was finally able to realize my competitive dreams. I rode over green pastures and down country lanes and horses eventually took me to different parts of the country and throughout the world for competitions. Though I nearly died trying, on horseback I learned to overcome the obstacles my legs presented.

The road to believing I could be a good horseman was not easy. When, at the age of ten, I first began attempting to ride, I wished there were someone who could show me how to ride. I wanted Pappy or Dad, both experienced riders themselves, to step in and teach me. Dad had done very respectably in local races and hunts. Pappy was a master of the hunt and he and his horse Bugle Boy were known all over as having a nerve of steel. But how could Pappy or Dad find my balance in the saddle? I learned I had to find it myself.

Dad's and Pappy's advice to Tom or Fiona—"Use your heels," "Feel the horse in your feet and calves"—could not apply to me. To their credit, Dad and Pappy knew this and just let me persevere, rarely passing comment on my riding. Once, Pappy told me I had a natural seat in the saddle. This was quite a compliment as Pappy was a man who never praised unless it was deserved. But at the beginning, this comment didn't help me to stop and start, or turn the pony where I wanted him to go. Getting the pony off the ground to jump, my ultimate dream, was more difficult still. No one taught me. I had to look inside myself, learning how to communicate with the horse through trial and error, fine-tuning a technique that was all my own.

When I first began, I made up my mind that our little white pony, Sunbeam, was going to be brought out of retirement and made to earn his keep. I found a horse bridle and shortened it with a leather worker's knife. I dug out Pappy's old cavalry saddle, a huge monstrosity made of dark brown leather, and much to Mam's chagrin, soon had Sunbeam outfitted for his new occupation: carrying me to points unknown.

I used to rise early in the morning, saddle up the pony, and ride off up the road to Bergins Racing Stables, about a half-mile from the house in the direction of the Kilkenny road. I loved the clip-clop of Sunbeam's hooves on the road, the rhythm of his body under mine, and the height I had up on his back. Every Sunday evening, while the rest of the family was inside the dark house glued to "The Riordans" on television, I was out trying to gallop Sunbeam. I'd take him to the field by the cemetery and, as the air grew cool and the light dim, I'd press my body into his, nearly welding myself to him with the intensity of my desire to take off.

One Sunday evening as the blue was just dying in a crisp autumn sky, I pushed Sunbeam as hard as I could to break from the trot into the canter, digging my heels deep into him. As usual, my aids were hurting me terribly and the muscles in my legs were tender, but I was getting stronger every day. Managing to get Sunbeam to the corner of the field out by the graveyard, I started driving him like mad. This time he seemed to know I wouldn't let up or give in to tiredness. I also had a little plastic bag, which I waved noisily in the air to inspire him. Just when I thought he'd never go, much to my joy and surprise, between the bag and my overtaxed heels, Sunbeam suddenly took off across the field.

Oh the freedom! I was out of my mind with delight, never having felt anything like it. My heart pumped like the bellows of an organ as we raced across the blurring green field. Like a boat on a wave, my body rose and fell in the saddle and I imagined myself jumping the stone fences for miles and miles across the country. We'd be over the Atlantic in no time flat at the rate we were flying. Though I couldn't feel much of Sunbeam's body through the rods in my aids, what I did feel was the rhythm of his glorious movement. It was this rhythm I joined him in, hanging on for dear, dear life as we pushed forward, going like the clappers. After years of having my movement restricted by pain and fatigue, I had finally found that by connecting my body to a little white pony I could keep going and going as long and far as I chose.

My first pony shows were at the local gymkhana in Johnstown, a sort of annual fair day with an amateur dog show, rides, dice-throwing games, and horse jumping by the local children. The gymkhana was attended by the whole community and nearly every young rider I knew in Johnstown had his sites set on a jumping trophy. The first two years I went, I took Sunbeam. A decent hunter pony, Sunbeam was unfortunately no show jumper. Year one was a disaster. Sunbeam stood paralyzed at the edge of the ring and wouldn't move. I was eliminated, a great embarrassment before all the local tribes and scribes, who always had an opinion when they saw me out in public. Their attitude, though never spoken to my parents' faces, seemed to be "Why don't you hide the 'delicate' lad at home?" Dad was livid at Sunbeam for letting me down, but his attitude to the townspeople was "Sod the begrudgers." Unwilling to give up jumping or to suffer another defeat before the hometown crowd, I concocted a plan to get a decent mount.

A dun-colored Connemara pony, thirteen two hands high, Billy Jim took orders from no man. Still, I convinced Dad, who was worried about my safety, to let me have him. Once I got the okay, I promptly started trying my best with Billy Jim. When I approached him, he'd fiercely run me out of the paddock unless I was carrying a bucket of oats for him. With enough oats, though, I was soon able to ride Billy. When I did, I found he was a good hunter with a lovely curve in his tail and great spirit. I wanted to try show jumping with him. When I told Dad I wanted to practice jumping Billy, he looked at me skeptically. Finally, he said he'd buy me the raw materials to build a practice course, but that if I was really serious, I'd have to build it myself.

For six weeks during the summer of 1974, my fourteenth year, I went out into the orchard field every day. The apple trees along its edges offered scant relief from the hot sun as I skinned and painted the poles Dad purchased for me for the jumping course. I drove the uprights two feet into the hard ground of the orchard field near the house and cut cups for the poles out of old rubber tires. When Dad saw my motivation, he agreed to soften the landing places for the ponies by plowing up the hard ground there. When I finished, Dad looked out at the sparkling course I'd built around the twelve apple trees in the field and said, "It just shows you what you get when you persevere."

I registered both Billy Jim and Fiona's new dark grey pony Moonbeam with the Show Jumping Association of Ireland. Aware that some might discourage a disabled boy to compete in a potentially dangerous sport and wishing to look as legitimate as possible, I persuaded Dad that I needed the appropriate attire to compete. This consisted of a black show jumping jacket, a white shirt and tie, a pair of jodhpurs and black riding boots. With my uneven gait, I particularly stood out among other competitors when I walked a course of fences to see what lay ahead of me. Also, my artificial limbs were highlighted by the breeches, making me horribly self-conscious. But once I was up on the horse, I forgot the eyes of the world and felt like a whole new person.

The first show I took Billy Jim to was in Thurles. I had never been to pony clubs, and despite my homemade course, hadn't a firm grasp of the finer points of show jumping. If truth be told, I was reckless. My philosophy was simple: You saw the fence and you jumped irrespective of which leg the pony was leading with. Dad had told me, "A good rider will fall at least seven times on his first outing." By that definition, I was already excellent.

When we arrived at the show, there were hundreds of other competitors already present in the field. I hadn't a clue how to enter the competition, but I knew if I found Tom Farrell, whose father, P.J., had racehorses in a trainer's stable where I used to go riding, all would be sorted out, as they were very familiar with all the procedures. As luck would have it, we found a parking space just two horse boxes from Tom's box. I jumped out of the Jeep not even realizing that Dad wasn't finished parking. I nearly broke my neck as I tripped up. I was always very impetuous and couldn't wait to meet Tom. P.J. and Dad went off and did the entries. When I returned from meeting Tom, Fiona and I got the ponies ready. Sizing up the competition, I looked around at the other horses; their manes and tails were all much more neatly done than I'd managed to plat Billy's. He had monstrous thick black hair and although I had worked my thumbs ragged trying to braid it, it hadn't come out very well. "Don't worry," Fiona soothed, "the others may look nice, but do they have the heart of Billy Jim?" At the moment I was less worried about Billy's heart than his brakes.

Dad had put me into the novice pony class. He then took me off with P.J. to walk the course. P.J. went into great detail about how many strides between the fences and to watch out for the dogleg between fences two and three. I hadn't a clue as to what he was talking about. Dad didn't either, even though he gave P.J. his undivided attention and nodded in agreement. I was more concerned with remembering the course.

When I returned to Fiona, she asked what P.J. and Dad were talking about. I told her they were talking about "dog's legs" in the course. We both thought this was hilarious. Fiona asked, "Where the hell is that?" Within about twenty minutes I was to learn the significance of P.J.'s warning. I also forgot to mention that Billy's steering wasn't too good either!

After ten minutes of practice jumping, both P.J. and Dad felt that I was ready to take on the course. When we walked into the ring for the first time I was concerned about the effect of the colored fences on Billy. At home we used only plain wood poles and I feared that the colors would spook him. Irrespective of all the variables presented on this day, I had an innate determination to succeed and drive forward. As Dad and my brother Tom said to me, "Thank God you have no reverse gear."

The judge for the ponies at that time was a very kind man called Paddy Power. He had a great reputation for giving young kids a chance to get acquainted with the whole show jumping scene. Paddy introduced me over the loudspeaker. "Next to jump, young Ronan Tynan, on his little dun pony Billy Jim." Up to now, no one made an issue of my disability. This pleased me to no end, as I was competing on an even sporting field with all the other competitors. I didn't want it any other way.

The judge rang the bell and off I went, with the determination of a top class international show jumper. The first fence was made up of two rustic poles and bales of straw underneath as a filler. We cantered down with no problem, cleared the jump, and my confidence was building. Fence two was a blue and white vertical situated down by the corner of the arena. At this stage Billy was getting keen and progressed from a nice show jumping canter into a slow gallop, but could I hold him? Not a hope. He jumped it and we were flying. We turned from fence two to three, which was the dogleg. It got this description due to the angle at which the fence was situated. I tried to take a check on Billy but to no avail. Billy had other plans, which did not, as it turned out, include fence three. By now the slow gallop had quickened quite considerably and we were tearing straight up the arena in full flight with me shouting, "Stop, Billy!" But the more I shouted, the faster he went. "I'm dead," I thought. The colorful fences and faces of the crowd blurred by. Billy had veered off the course and jumped the rope that surrounded the ring.

When he finally slowed down we were at the top corner of the neighboring field, where Billy stuck his big gob into the grass to feed.

Heart pounding, I dismounted, unsure whether I wanted to punch Billy or hug him. It had been the spin of my life and despite my fear and disappointment in my performance, the buzz was incredible. Dad and Fiona came running up to me, patting me on the back and asking if I was all right. They were clearly relieved that I was unscathed after such a traumatic ride. Dad was savage with the pony whereas Fiona looked at me and waited to see my reaction. We both laughed and got a good kick out of it. When she described what it had looked like from a spectator's viewpoint, we rolled around the place, as did P.J. and Dad.

Then Dad began complaining about Billy Jim. When I tried to defend the poor pony, Dad told me I was feeding him too much oats. "Oats sends them cracked," he said. I only nodded, plotting how I could school him better for the next show, trying to contain my joy. "I don't know which is worse," Dad sighed, "you or Billy Jim."

On the car ride home, Fiona and I had a good laugh about wild old Billy Jim, but Dad said sternly, "No more shows until both rider and pony are well schooled." He softened the blow with offers of ice cream and it was agreed we wouldn't breathe a word to Mam about these shenanigans. For my part, I vowed to reapply myself to fine-tuning my technique as soon as the sun rose the next morning.

When we arrived home, Mam as usual had a fine meal prepared. It had been agreed among the three of us that the details of the discussion at dinner would be tailored so that Mam didn't hear about some of the more intriguing events of the day. Dad had already made up his mind that Billy's show jumping days were over. No matter what I said, I couldn't convince him to give the bold Billy a second chance.

The majority of that summer was spent in schooling another horse, Moonbeam, for the next Johnstown gymkhana, which was held about half a mile from our house. For this show, I brought Sunbeam out of his retirement so that I would have better chances to get a ribbon.

There was great excitement among the local people, as there was one competition specifically designed for the children of the area. I had major designs on the annual trophy that was given in this class.

However, my cousins and half the kids in the parish had the same idea. Well, as the saying goes, "Nothing ventured, nothing gained." Unfortunately, my appearance in the show jumping ring was much like the first two. Everything was going fine until Sunbeam had a last second change of heart at one of the jumps. While Sunbeam was able to stop his forward progress by digging in his heels, I didn't have that luxury. My body continued the jump quite nicely, but without my horse. It would have been bad enough if the momentum had allowed me to sail over the fence, but I wasn't that fortunate. No, Sunbeam had left me short and I was catapulted into the fence. For about a minute, I was on another planet. When I came to, I looked up and saw that I was surrounded by swarms of locals with wrinkled wide-eyed faces of concern, wondering if I had been shot, or worse still, whether I would be able to speak after such a horrific fall. But God, as everyone knows, had other designs for my vocal skills.

At this stage, Dad seemed to have lost all patience with our equine stock and vowed that he would sell the whole lot as they were of no blessed use. I knew that he was just annoyed that once again they had let me down in front of our neighbors. He also knew that I had put in an incredible amount of work up to that point. I know that some of the locals thought that Dad was irresponsible for allowing me to ride such wild ponies. Little did they know that my riding was all Dad ever worried about.

Mam, while she loved us riding in the hunt and the hullabaloo that went with it, didn't like show jumping. Both Mam and Dad couldn't wait for September to come and for me to return to De La Salle College. As the end of the school holidays approached, I tried every trick in the trade to get out of going back there. Of course, I used my legs as the main reason, indicating that heavily competitive sports were breaking the steel bars and more important, there was no one in Waterford like Ossie to fix them. I was full sure that I was in business, but on the third of September, all three suitcases and tuck boxes, which held snacks and homemade cakes, were made ready and packed with school uniforms, towels, toiletries, and other things I would need at school.

By the age of fifteen I had convinced my parents to send me to a school in Kilkenny. Though I told them they could keep a better eye on my study habits if I were closer to home, my real motive was to be as far away from De La Salle and as close to the horses as possible. When I wasn't neglecting my studies to train my newest pony, Black Jet, which Mam had bought for me, I began to notice that dear old Pappy was losing his health. Well into his eighties, Pappy had supervised the local hunt, calling out all twenty-six hounds by name and bestowing honors on the winners. But those days had passed. Pappy had always been a robust man who, between chores, offered plenty of advice about the hunt and horses. Now he seemed to be fading in his eighty-fourth year. He was always meticulous about his appearance and methodical in his actions, but became unable to care for himself as well as he used to. Every morning Dad brought him breakfast, taking care of the things Pappy couldn't do for himself. Their bond was like Dad's and mine and it broke my heart to see Dad worry so about his father. By late winter of 1975, Pappy took to his bed.

On the Ides of March, Pappy was taken by ambulance from the house. All three of us were home and poor Fiona, the closest to him next to Dad, was nearly weeping. As they carried him out by stretcher down the stairs, Pappy lifted his gaunt face up from the stretcher, pointed a finger, and said to us all, "You will never forget this day." That evening, an eerie tranquility settled into the house. Dad, who was feeling very low, spent most of the evening outdoors working. The rest of us couldn't help be reminded of Pappy at every turn. I went into the dining room and stared at his moon-shaped chair, where years earlier I'd knelt at his footrest. But instead of laughing at the old images of Pappy chasing me when I disturbed his rest, I felt like crying and quickly left the room.

My brother and sister went back to boarding school and I continued as a day student at St. Kieran's in Kilkenny, not far from the hospital where Pappy stayed. During lunch, I'd borrow a bike and visit him. In April, after he had been operated on, I went in to see him and was met by an older nurse, a firm, kind woman who told me it might be best to let him rest. "Why, what's wrong with him?" I asked her. "Well," she paused, taking a slow breath in. She admitted he'd been diagnosed with liver cancer and that it had spread to his bowel.

I went into my grandfather's room. He lay against the white sheets, his pallor yellow, the bones more prominent than ever in his face. There was a cloying smell about him, the so-called sweet smell of death. "Well, pet," he said, his bright eyes shining up at me. Images of Pappy working around the farm, brushing down the horses, and dressing up for the hunt rushed through my mind. Was this the same man? I couldn't find much to say, but I sat with him for a little while and squeezed his thin hand. When it was time for me to go, he pointed to a tin of biscuits on the windowsill. "Take those, Ronan, I won't be eating them," he said. Not one to refuse sweets, I took the tin. Then as I was walking down the corridor, for reasons I can't explain, I set the tin down on a side table and walked on.

A couple of weeks later, on the ninth of May 1975, I took Black Jet to her first show of the year in Rathowney, County Laois. Dad took me in the tractor and trailer, the only means of transport he could muster. Working my fingers to the bone, I'd managed to plat Black Jet's mane and tail perfectly with red and white ties and between this and the white star on her forehead, she looked resplendent.

More important, she was on fire that day and jumped superbly. I felt I could make no wrong move on her. After years of meticulously counting strides between fences and calculating my moves, I had finally become the boss in this partnership and earned my right to act a lunatic. "If I'm sharp enough," I thought, "I can win it." That day, it also felt as if a great force had swooped down to steer us both. Surrounded by colorful banners and ribbons, with our plastic number pinned on the bridle, Black Jet and I won our first proper registered competition. After years spent trying to win at any sport in school, the feeling I had was indescribable. I was fifteen years old and had finally won something. I felt I must be made of great stuff after all. Dad was thrilled and gave me a big hug when I dismounted. It was the first time I had seen him happy since Pappy's illness had set in.

We left the show at about six o'clock that evening, towing Black Jet. I sat beside Dad on the tractor and leaned against the mudguard, my hand around his shoulder for support. We had come onto a straight stretch of road when suddenly a magpie flew in front of us. As the black and white bird dipped across the road, I went cold all over and squeezed Dad's shoulder. Something inside me said that Pappy had passed away.

When we arrived in the yard, the phone was ringing. "Daddy," I said gently, "I think it's not good news." Dad leapt from the tractor and nearly broke down the big white door of our house to get in and answer the phone. I followed him in and watched his face fall as he gripped the receiver tightly to his ear. The news was as I had feared. Pappy had died. With uncanny timing, it was as if, in departing this world, my grandfather had given Black Jet and me a bit of his magical nature.

Many people loved my grandfather and his funeral was a grand affair, with a massive cortege of cars. When we came to Donoughmore, the hearse paused to give Pappy his last farewell to our family house. All the dogs started barking in what seemed a paying of respects and Dad broke down and sobbed. Mam tried to console him, but I knew that part of him had gone with Pappy.

In the days, months, and years to come, I would often remember how Pappy had said to me, "Remember, Ronan, time waits for no man." These words would become a kind of touchstone for me. After he died, I wanted to waste none of my precious time on earth. I threw myself ever more deeply into riding, becoming better and better. Nature has a funny way of making you pay for what you want. You have to give life an awful lot before you're given more back. I practiced harder than ever. Trying everything I could to make myself faster and more streamlined, I even took to riding without my legs, using rubber boots, or Wellies, for riding boots.

Though I was embarrassed at first to show the world my disability, my mounts rewarded me for lightening their load by giving me better performances. I soon progressed from winning on ponies to winning on horses, competing in point-to-point races with my first horse, Jacko, then My Time and Cora Lady. When I rode a race, hemmed in on every side by twelve other riders all aiming to jump the same fence that lay ahead, there was no thought of my disability. My heart, head, and hands would be spinning with excitement, but I had learned that if my mind were all over the place, my horse would be too. So I learned to tame my recklessness just enough, racing and jumping ever more beautiful horses. Over time I was holding my own in fierce competition at a national and eventually international level.

Riding taught me I could compete on a level playing field, as long as I was willing to persevere. I learned to trust my own instincts and technique. Rather than riding by touch, as others do, I ride by attuning myself to the horse's rhythm. In these and other ways, I found that for me riding is like singing. Through much trial and error, I have finally discovered the key to riding well. When I ride, the horse and I become one. I feel the animal's power under me and am transformed. On the horse, I have four perfect legs instead of two imperfect ones. I gain speed, nobility, beauty, and freedom. Most important though, for the time I sit in the saddle, I leave all troubles behind.

CHAPTER 7

*I*n the middle of my teenage years, I had become even more independent. I was constantly champing at the bit of responsibility my mother tried to place on me, more eager than ever to explore the wider world outside my family. Heedless of any risk or restriction, I jumped fence after fence powered by pure adrenaline. I was to strike off on my own on visits to hospital in London, nearly tore the face off myself in a riding accident, and finally buckled down in school only to fall madly in love with a woman as wild as I. In these years before I took off for university, I seemed to be moving a million miles a minute.

Mam constantly harped on the importance of education, but I was interested in other things. I had taken to yelling back at her to leave me alone and there were more and more explosions between us. For her, school was a means to an end and the end was not to wind up a farmer like my father. I had done poorly on my intermediate certificate, the exams taken by all Irish students at the age of fifteen, but this didn't scare me. As a day student at St. Kieran's in Kilkenny, I began cutting classes to work for a local horse trainer named Mick and barely maintained passing marks. Though I'd soon have to reform my wastrel ways, my true interests lay in horses and, increasingly, in the opposite sex.

Convincing my parents it would save money, I started traveling on my own to London to have new limbs fitted. Every six months or so, my dad and mam would drive me up to the airport in Dublin. Mam would usually complain to Dad about one thing or another the whole way. Dad would try to ignore her, singing his favorite car song of the time in that light, sweet voice of his, "Oh I want to go to heaven in an old Ford car, but the Lord he said she won't go that far." When I left them in the airport, he slipped me a fifty-pound note and told me to be careful. I walked down to the passenger lounge feeling lighter than air, vowing never to put myself under another's thumb.

Taking off in the plane from Dublin, I truly felt I had come of age. As a young man of fifteen, heading across the water with a fifty-pound note in my pocket, my parents left back on the ground behind me, I felt a little like a god myself.

Once in London, I would take three red double decker buses to Richmond and check myself in to Bishop's Hotel, where my mother and I had always stayed. Bishop's was like a castle, with steep steps leading up to it and the unlikely songs of birds filling the air outside it. An Irish family called the Doyles ran it. The first time I went without Mam, Mr. Doyle asked, "And where's herself?" When I told him I would be coming on my own from then on, he handed me the room key saying, "Good man." I felt I'd been given the key to a magic door and though it only opened on the same small hotel room where I'd stayed since a lad, the room suddenly seemed to me a Xanadu. In the evenings, I'd go out to Sherry's restaurant and treat myself to plenty of strawberry flan and milkshakes. In the mornings, I'd head for hospital and the usual ordeal.

Given the frequency of my lumbar spasms and the severity of the splaying in my feet, the doctors made it very clear that before long something would have to be done to correct my deformity. My condition put too much pressure on my back and pelvis. My uneven gait was becoming accentuated and I continued to have terrible pain where the prostheses contacted my flesh. By correction, the doctors meant amputation. Time was running out on this score and though I knew that one day soon I'd have to face the music, I put it to the back of my mind, not wanting to consider what that might mean to my freedom.

One day in early November of my sixteenth year, my friend Tom Bergen and I took my big Irish draught Jacko and another horse out to the fields to teach them the steeplechase. Still green, Jacko was nonetheless quite willing. As I raced him down to the first fence, he suddenly found the use of his legs and took off into a galloping rhythm. Once over, he was flying. Recklessly, I decided to let him go on and see how much push he really had. But when I went to pull him up, there were no brakes. I then realized that Jacko's tongue was over the bit. There would be no controlling him. Still three fields away from the road, I wasn't too concerned. I continued to gallop through the second field and then through the third. I realized the danger we were in as we neared the road. But I recalled Pappy's advice: "Stick with your horse. Sit tight, for the horse will always avoid injuring himself." Jacko was headed for a big ditch that separated the field from the lane and I reckoned that he wouldn't attempt to jump it.

I was wrong. Souped up on adrenaline, Jacko took on the ditch with great valor and we rose into the air like a linked pair of falcons. But as he jumped, poor Jacko realized that he would land on the hard road and at that instant, he tried to turn away in midair. As he turned, I fell off him face first into the road, which had recently been tarmacked and stoned.

When I opened my eyes, I was covered in blood and had a horrendous pain in my side. Good old Jacko was unhurt and went galloping up the lane. My friend Tom dismounted and came racing over the ditch to help me. When he saw my face, he went pale as a sheet. I had a gash that ran from just below the septum of my nose to my upper lip, and on from my lower lip to the midline of my chin. My nose had distorted to the right and my jaw wouldn't close. Blood filled my mouth and the pain was excruciating. When I put my tongue down, I found that it went through the floor of the mouth and into a gap that had opened between my bottom teeth and the skin below my lip.

Tom gasped, "Jaysus," and raced on to find help. I picked myself up and started home, leaving Jacko to fend for himself. Too numb even to cry, I was in so much pain I couldn't think straight. Jacko arrived home ahead of Tom and me, prompting Dad to look for me. He and Tom met me coming up Tournreek Lane, the blood still pumping out of me. "Jesus Christ, Ronan, what happened?" my father exclaimed, reaching out to me, but I wasn't able to answer him. He helped me home and, after some pressure had been applied to my aching side, he, Mam, and I got into the car. We drove at top speed up to St. Vincent's in Dublin, Mam repeating the whole way there, "Your beautiful face is destroyed."

I am well known among friends and family for my uncanny good luck. Unfortunately the good luck usually kicks in after something terrible has happened to me. In this case, when we arrived at St. Vincent's, we learned that a visiting German plastic surgeon had just operated on a young girl who'd been in a terrible accident. The surgeon agreed to operate on me and, for two solid hours, I went under the knife to get my face remodeled. The following day, I was completely stitched up and felt like a giant bruise. I couldn't talk or, for that matter, open my mouth, but it seemed then that, with the exception of a scar above my lip, the surgeon had saved me.

It had been six years since my last extended stay in a hospital. Mature man that I was, I no longer felt the need to hide in the nurses' cardigan cabinet. I was put in a ward with six other fellows, all from Dublin and all of them characters. The two opposite me were in their early twenties. After two to three days, these yokes spent most of their time trying to make me burst my stitches. One of them, a slim, blondy brown-haired fellow, had a thick Dublin accent and a big, infectious laugh. His girlfriend used to come in and visit him. She wore short mini-skirts and gave him big sloppy kisses, which we would loudly encourage. Behind her back, he'd be giving us all the thumbs-up and then he'd ask me if I wanted a squeeze from her. I had little experience with women at this point in my life, but I thought this girl was beautiful. Before I could even answer, she'd gamely come over to me and give me a big, painful hug. When her boyfriend started joking, I used to have to hold my face so as not to put any tension on it, for the jabbing sensation was terrible.

Like a baby, I was fed through a straw for two weeks. When Mam and Dad came to visit, all she could talk about was how beautiful my face had once been. Dad, on the other hand, said that once the stitches were out everyone would realize that I'd lived through something and had the scars to prove it. Sure enough, when I came home to Johnstown, I was greeted with the refrain, "We heard your guts were all over the road." My love for riding was not assailed by the fall. On the contrary, I went right back to clandestinely working for Mick and was back in the saddle training Jacko for the point to point, which is a three-mile steeplechase. I put him on a high daily protein feed of oats, molasses, beet pulp, boiled barley, two eggs, and a pint of Guinness, and rode and groomed him every day. We came in third that year in the Thurles race and Dad won a hundred pounds on me.

On April 5, 1977, the North Kilkenny point to point was held in Gowran Park Race Course. I was seventeen at this grand occasion and was a different competitor, having coupled speed with skill. I had also found two great new mounts in Cora Lady and My Time. My Time had more pace than Jacko ever did and could be a very serious contender. And sure enough, we raced like blazes coming in second in this prestigious event. The master of the hunt, Jack Murphy, presented me with a trophy and there were plenty of pats on the back and well wishes for next year's race. I felt like a king, but the best reward came when Dad gave me a hug and said, "You're great!" After the euphoria of the race, he and I prepared to go home. Brushing down My Time, he stood beside me and without turning from his task, asked, "How's school?"

Quite taken aback by his question—normally we would be discussing how the race went and the tactics employed—I answered slowly. "It's okay," I said, "but I'm not overkeen." Dad then revealed he had been talking to Mick, the trainer I'd been working for, in the parade ring. Mick had mentioned that I was a great worker and very good around horses. So the secret of my truancy was out. I was speechless. After five minutes that seemed like an hour, Dad put down the brush and spoke. "Now firstly, Ronan," he said firmly, "you will never be able to be a professional jockey. You're going to be too heavy for that. Secondly, your legs won't survive the hardships of farming."

Here was Dad finally saying out loud what I had always known. Much as I admired him and loved helping on the farm however I could, I wouldn't be following in his footsteps. Though his words could have been Mam's, the way he delivered them was typical Dad and I took it all in as sweet medicine. He went on to say that I needed a profession that would give me a secure income and a lifestyle that would maintain my interest in horses. To my surprise, I agreed with him. "Here's the deal," he said. "We'll keep this our secret and you can finish school early this year, freeing you up to race, but you must repeat your fifth year as a full-time boarder at De La Salle in September." More amazed than ever with his evenhandedness, I promised I'd live up to my end of the bargain. I felt strong enough to face De La Salle after all I'd been through and besides, since I'd be repeating some time in school, I reasoned my classmates would be a set of fresh faces. I thanked Dad for his understanding.

Like a shooting star burning brightest before it fades, I had tremendous success jumping My Time and Cora Lady that spring and summer. Cora and I, in particular, became a great team. Dad and I went to several shows together and unlike days past, ribbons and trophies were frequently mine. But in September, the shoe dropped and I returned to De La Salle to buckle down.

I lived up to my end of the bargain and my last two years there were much better than my first. I had more confidence, for one, and I had my goal firmly in mind. My brain is the most disorganized piece of apparatus going, but it was as if I took all the calculation I'd used to hone my horse-riding technique and applied it to my studies. With a major mountain to climb, I worked hard, but there was no doubt that God was on my side. Preparing for my Leaving Cert and University Matriculation exams, three weeks of nationwide tests that determine entrance to university, I would suddenly get a wild idea that I needed to study particular aspects of biology, for example. "I don't know enough about earthworms," I'd say to myself one day, then study up on them. The next day it was hormones. And it was eerie, but when I took the exams, every single odd angle of the subject I'd studied showed up in the questions. Again, it was as if someone over my shoulder was watching out for me.

By the time I was eighteen, my good old friend Tom Farrell had his driver's license. He took to borrowing his sister's old Renault 4 van so that we could go to the discos in Kilkenny. Every weekend, Tom and I would take hours to dress up in our most stylish outfits and then head out on the town. My look consisted of flared trousers called "parallels," which I bought very wide so my legs didn't show. Besides these flares, I used to wear loose, collarless shirts that were usually striped or patterned. With this getup and the plentiful hair I'd got from having it permed on a dare, I suppose I looked like a hippie. Just before I headed out, Dad would slip me a five-pound note. "Have a great night and be careful," he'd say. "Be good, and remember who you are!"

Every Friday and Saturday, Tom would drive into Kilkenny city to a disco. My previous experience dancing had been at the *ceilis*, Irish dances put on at the summer schools Tom and Fiona and I had attended in Galway as children. I loved to dance and would do my best with jigs, reels, hornpipes, and many set dances, which often involved swinging your partner until you both nearly collapsed. I usually chose a girl much bigger than myself so that when it came to the swing, it was like being on a turbo-powered merry-go-round. Her size ensured that I got the swing of my life. Often times my feet never touched the ground. Although dancing used to make my limbs tender as hell, for the length of time I was out on the floor, I felt nothing but euphoria, encircled as I was by great music and big women. I took this same spirit, coupled with the added incentive of finding a woman, into the discos with me.

Tom and I met loads of girls at the Rose Hill, which was one of our favorite spots. The inside of the disco boiled with bodies, flashing purple lights, and a mirrored ball that spun to the rhythms of Genesis, Phil Collins, Blondie, and the Village People. You could nearly see the perspiration coming off the bodies, which, flinging about, also released a cocktail of perfumes and hormones that could anesthetize an army. It was at the Rose Hill that I met my first love, a girl called Kathleen. She was a receptionist in a hotel and, boy, was she the ticket. She was five feet five, with strawberry blond hair and hazel eyes behind her glasses. The first time we met she wore a pinstriped shirt and blue jeans and cowboy boots. Kathleen was a very free spirit. She had a great sense of humor and we got on superbly well. We'd slow dance to our heart's content at the discos, sweating like horses but clinging to each other madly.

One night, just before Tom was to pick me up from home, my parallels split down the middle. This was not an unfamiliar catastrophe in my life, as my limbs tended to strain whatever trousers I had on. I stitched my parallels up quickly with white thread. Tom arrived and off we went. Once under the neon light of the disco, Kathleen's white pinstripes were glowing and flashing and so was the seam of my pants. "What's this?" she asked, and laughing, reached out and grabbed my backside. The trousers split again. Right in the middle of "Hello in There," we had to rush out to the van for cover. As it turns out, this was not a bad place to be.

The extent of my sex education had been observing the ducks and the hens on the farm. So, like many good Catholic boys of my time, I had to do a fair amount of stumbling in the dark before I finally figured things out.

Kathleen didn't seem to mind. She and I soon became well known as an item around town and when I was eighteen and nineteen, we spent a lot of time together. When I wanted to see her during the week, I used to borrow a god-awful slow Honda 50 motorbike from a neighbor. Of course, I had no license or insurance, but that didn't bother me, for love was in the air. Sometimes I would arrange to meet her at the Kittler's Inn in Kilkenny. Because I couldn't arrange to get the bike in time, or had to wait for an hour or so watching telly with the family so they wouldn't suspect anything, I might be as much as two hours late, my stomach in a knot the whole time. When I finally arrived, there she would be sitting around, a little teary-eyed, thinking that I had stood her up. But I wasn't like that. If I made a promise I kept it and I was mad about her. Big-hearted girl that she was, she loved everything about me from bottom to top. The feeling was mutual. There was nothing I couldn't talk about with her. She'd always tell me I was gorgeous and we'd discuss ourselves, our families, and our futures. Once, lying in our favorite field outside Kilkenny, I asked her if she wanted to work in the hotel forever. Rather than answering, she shot back, "Well, what do you want to do?"

It was a question very much on everyone's lips at home and at school, but I resisted being tied by it. "At this present moment in time," I answered, "I have no idea." I told her that eventually, I thought I'd like to become a doctor. That dream had never left me since meeting Bill Quinlan and through all the years I'd spent in hospital. But at that moment, in a green field with Kathleen, hidden by stone walls, eventually seemed a very long time away to me.

At that age, I don't think that I really understood what love was. But I sure as hell knew that I really liked Kathleen's company. After one particular night on the town, I returned home around 5 A.M., just as the sun was rising. I knew Dad would be awake and when I walked through the kitchen door, he greeted me in his pajamas. He smiled and asked if I had had a good night. "I sure had!" I answered, a little too quickly, I suppose. I told him that I felt I was in love with this girl and would like to marry her. Dad looked at me and laughed himself silly and then said, "I hope you have behaved yourself last night!" "What do you mean?" I countered. Turning bright red, he said, "You know exactly what I mean!" "I'm a good Catholic lad. What could I possibly get up to?" I replied, a twinkle in my eye. "I know you," he said, looking straight at me. "You love to try things out." I turned and made myself a cup of tea, changing the topic of conversation. Though I could talk to him about almost anything else, I reasoned that what my father didn't know about this aspect of my life couldn't hurt him.

As it turned out, the pending changes in my life would make my relationship with Kathleen short-lived. After secondary school, I would be heading out into a new life and despite my pleas, she wouldn't wait for me. First love passes too quickly and I was too young to realize what the passing meant. Still, I don't think either of us had any regrets.

When the results of my University Matriculation exams came out, I had qualified for university, having done particularly well in the sciences. My hurdy-gurdy approach to life had worked for me in the end.

If I continued to apply myself, I knew I would be able to forge my way in the world without my parents having to support me. I would be studying Science, not Medicine, as I hadn't applied for any other course. Mam and I had a reconciliation of sorts and Dad was very proud as well. Excited and a bit apprehensive, I said good-bye to my parents, Kathleen, and the horses. At the age of nineteen I went off to University College, Dublin, and my next adventure. I had left my old life in Kilkenny behind.

CHAPTER 8

*T*hese were supposed to be the most carefree years of my life, but fate would dictate otherwise. In Dublin, I threw myself into the wild life of a first-year student at UCD. I loved the bustling atmosphere of the modern campus, but spent most of my time in pubs with the new friends I made. In those first few months in Dublin, I felt the world was my oyster. I sold my parents with the story that I could make my classes more easily if I didn't have to wait for the bus and Mam and Dad bought me a red Honda 90 as a reward for my hard work at De La Salle. Never one to restrict myself to a vehicle's intended purpose, I reveled in maneuvering the motorbike up and down the grey streets of Dublin, far from any lecture hall. Always in search of greater freedom, after six weeks, I decided to move from the room I was letting with a family into a flat with two lads.

On the night I was to move into my new flat, I headed up the Stillorgan motorway, which was still slick from a recent rain. Fiona drove ahead of me, her car full of my moving boxes. She slowed down at one set of traffic lights, let down her window, and told me to go ahead of her, as she wasn't sure of the way. I was doing about forty when I passed her, coming up on a second set of lights, when out of nowhere another car pulled out into the intersection ahead of us and stalled.

I had no time to react. Fiona was in the left lane beside me and if I crossed into the right lane, I would be hit by oncoming traffic. Just before colliding with the car's passenger door, I prayed, "God, please help me." The bike skidded. My left arm and leg smashed against the metal door and I was hurled into the air. The next thing I knew, I had landed in a sitting position on the roof of the car, oblivious at first to any pain. I could hear Fiona's voice reading the riot act to the older woman who had been driving. This poor lady, alone in the car, had got out and was wandering aimlessly in the road like a chicken with her head cut off. The lights from oncoming traffic glared off the wet road and the sound of tires sucking pavement throbbed in my head. I began registering my injuries. The pain in my left arm and leg was excruciating. When I reached down to touch my leg, I realized my prosthesis was no longer part of me.

Within minutes, Fiona and I heard the mechanical, singsong tones of a siren and the ambulance arrived shortly afterward. The poor paramedic got the shock of his life when he found me on the roof with only one leg dangling. "Oh, Jesus, he's lost a leg," the panicked man shouted to his team. Fiona had been looking for the limb. She found it very battered at the edges of the road and brought it over to me. The paramedic was much relieved. He and his team loaded me into the ambulance and Fiona and I rode to the emergency room, both still in shock but relieved no one was critically injured. Through my pain, I remember being impressed with the ambulance ride, as I had always wanted to ride full speed through red lights.

Upon examination at the hospital, it was determined that my left wrist had been fractured and I had lacerations on my left hand. I also had back injuries, which would make themselves better known in the weeks to come. I left for my new flat with a cast on my arm, a few stitches, and a left prosthesis much worse off for its close encounter with God. The limb was so torn up I had to use crutches to walk, which I hated. When I looked it over, I saw that the main frame of my prosthesis was at least still in one piece. I used tape to hold the sidebars temporarily and as soon as I could, took it into a local garage for some reinforcement welding. But such solutions were temporary and very soon I had to go to England for another fitting.

In the weeks between my accident and my visit to Queen Mary's Hospital in London, my back and legs had started to give me an unusual amount of pain. Used to spasms, I began having different sorts of attacks, sharp jabs, and stabbing sensations that knocked me out for days. The frequency and intensity of these attacks were worse than ever. Combined with the fact that my motorbike had been absolutely shattered to pieces and that my social life had improved dramatically since I'd moved into the new flat with the lads, I essentially stopped going to lectures. I reckoned I had my own biology, chemistry, and physics to deal with.

I traveled to London in February to get new limbs and to have a consultation about my worsening back pain. I was trying out my new limbs between the walking bars, when my two orthopedic surgeons came in. "Mr. Tynan," one doctor said, pronouncing each word in the Queen's impeccable English, "your deformity necessitates that we amputate both of your lower limbs. The pressure on your back is progressively more intense." Looking down at my chart, the other one added, "Your back simply will not tolerate the pressure much longer. If nothing is done, you may end up in a wheelchair." Having coldly dropped the bomb, both surgeons walked out of the room and I was left on my own. Though the news was not entirely a surprise, I had not expected to have it delivered in so stark a manner. I had so many questions swirling in my mind, but there was no one there to answer them. I gripped the handrails of the walking course with white knuckles, fighting off my sense of loneliness and isolation.

That evening, my friends met me at the airport and we went straight to Maddigan's pub. John, Frank, Paul, and Pat were all fine friends, but it was hard for me to confide in any of them about how churned up I was feeling. I knew the amputation would streamline me and relieve the pressure on my back, but I couldn't just be happy about it. I was afraid. The surgery did not seem to me merely a simple solution to a chronic problem, as the doctors had presented it. I worried about how losing the legs I did have would curtail my freedom or alter who I was in some essential way. It's not that I adored the legs God had given me. On the contrary, more than once I'd cursed them or my aids for getting in the way of my happiness. Still, my legs, such as they were, were a part of me.

If the truth be told, I turned to beer for comfort and escape from worry. That night at Maddigan's, we consumed an inordinate number of pints. Ready to extend the party at our friends' Paula and Claire's on Raglan Lane, we jumped into Frank's minibus and tore off. Nearing

Raglan Lane, we stopped at a set of traffic lights. A popular song of the time, "Too Hot in Here," was blaring on the radio. Suddenly, I felt that I would burst out of my skin if I didn't get some relief from all the pressure I was feeling. Without a moment's thought, I stripped down to my jockey shorts and leapt from the van.

The black sky was studded with stars and the cold night air felt good against my skin. The lads came chasing after me, but I ran like a comet and they couldn't keep up. As drunk as they were, I think I was powered by a different engine. Desperately running from the harsh reality I'd been dealt in London, I was racing forward on my own steam in one final burst of abandon. Somehow, I managed to arrive on Paula and Claire's front step. Feeling the cold at this stage, I pounded on their door and, as luck would have it, the girls were at home. Nearly passing out laughing at the sight of me outside in my underwear, they quickly ushered me in so that I wouldn't get arrested for indecent exposure. The lads arrived shortly thereafter and shunted me upstairs. They dumped me in the tub, visiting me throughout the night to make sure I was still alive.

I had been put on a waiting list for the amputations. For the rest of the college year I could scarcely keep my mind on anything else. I went to see the dean of the department and explained what was going on in my life. His advice was solid. "Do what you can to keep your mind occupied. Don't worry about the exams. That will all work out. If you need to resit them in September, there's no problem." I could have hugged him! I was so relieved. I had already resigned myself to resitting those exams in September.

The eve before I was to return to college for my second year, Dad and I went for a long drive. It was only then that I told him what I was going through. I wasn't able to deal with Mother anymore. He was very patient and understanding. He said, "She is just concerned that you are giving up and not focusing on making a career for yourself." While I was aware that she may have had a point on some level, her approach wasn't very compassionate. I said to Dad that I should move out from home for a while, until things improved. I knew by his reaction that this really saddened him. "Where will you go?" he asked. With difficulty, I told him that I had already been spending a lot of time with Aunt Theresa and Uncle Ralph, Mam's brother, and that I felt no pressure while with them. He said nothing for at least half an hour. Then he said, "If you feel that you have to do this, it's okay with me. But don't forget to visit, as I'm still your dad." I was so relieved and so grateful that he understood. I told him that I loved him dearly for everything that he had done for me and always would.

I also relied on parties with my friends to ease my pain and turmoil. In March, I moved in with Paula and Claire. Both girls were from the North and loved a good time. But they were also compassionate and intelligent and I was able to talk to them a bit about how I was feeling. I felt very comfortable with this group of friends, to the point that I would take off my limbs in front of them when my legs were bothering me, something I'd never done before outside of my family.

We continued to have wild times together and rather than moping around or worrying, I threw myself into the frenzy of life with as much force as I could, feeling perhaps that I had nothing to lose. On my twentieth birthday, Paula and Claire threw me the best party that I had possibly ever experienced in my life. It was fantastic! There was a shy redheaded girl in the class who was very fond of me. Although I wasn't aware of this, Paula and Claire had decided to set us up. This girl was very sweet and came over to the house for my birthday party. Of course, the lads were in on it as well. As the night went by, she and I got together. Everything was going blissfully. We disappeared upstairs for some privacy, but this was very short-lived. Out of the cupboards, closets, and through the windows came all the lads. They grabbed me and the terrified girl fled. I ended up getting showered with freezing cold water.

The party ended in the late hours of the following day. I ended up talking to John and the girls about what lay ahead for me. Everyone was in agreement that the exams were insignificant. In all their minds it was important that I had the support to get through the situation. They were a great bunch of people, but I couldn't help wondering would their feeling change toward me when I returned from the hospital, possibly in a wheelchair.

I applied to Nullamore University residence for my third term. Thankfully, I was accepted. I thought that perhaps with some order in my life I might be able to rescue some of the subjects. At the university residence I was very fortunate to become friends with a lot of great people: Joe, Frank, Bernard, Father Macken, Father Delargey, and Fergus O'Connor, who was a captain in the army at that time. This residence was run by Opus Dei. Their philosophy was that every aspect of one's work should be offered to God. All of them helped me spiritually to stay together. They were also great fun to be around. Both of the priests helped me a great deal with the many issues confronting me. Joe, Bernard, and Frank used to play soccer, which often became very heated and sometimes the occasional brawl would break out. Frank and Joe were Spaniards with Catalonian temperaments, but once the game was over, all was forgotten. Every so often, Joe or Frank would discuss the value of having God at the center of your life. This idea wasn't alien to me, but I sometimes felt that they were pushing their philosophy on me too strongly. However, I always knew it was for my betterment.

I tried to prepare myself for the upcoming amputation as best I could. Neither Mam nor Dad was able to offer much advice about the procedure, unsure about it as they were themselves. "If you have them amputated," Dad said of my legs, "they can never be put back again." But again, Dad could not and would not tell me what to do. No one seemed to understand what I was going through. Again, it was another issue I would have to master for myself.

I felt disjointed despite my friends' boisterous support. I had very few of the props I'd relied on in the past around me. Away from the familiar solace of horses, I stopped singing. Dad and I were far apart and Fiona and Tom had their own lives to lead. Though some of my isolation was self-imposed, I felt terribly alone. To make matters worse, for the first time in my life I began to think that I was not as strong in myself as I needed to be. I did pray to God and Mary as often as I had at De La Salle. That and conversations with priests at the residence hall soothed me a little. Still, I found it hard to clear my mind. I muddled through my exams at the end of term and went home to await my summons to London.

On the eighth of August, the letter came from London. By this time, I felt more spiritually and mentally prepared thanks to the lads in Opus Dei. Fiona and Mam drove me to the airport. Because the traffic was horrendous, Mam was convinced that I was going to miss my flight. She proceeded to have a major quarrel with Fiona. I reassured her that this was not going to happen, for whatever was ordained by The Man Above would happen irrespective of whatever obstacles were confronting us. At the time I found it odd that I was having to comfort and reassure my mother about my making a flight, when I was the one about to have my legs amputated.

Not yet modernized, Queen Mary's at the time was a dreary place. I was put in a special limb surgical unit with people who had had amputations. No stranger to the sight of amputees, I nevertheless kept to myself on that first day in the hospital. Everyone around me had lost something and I didn't feel like talking to them just then.

I had loads of questions for the doctors about the procedure that lay before me. How long would it take to recover? How soon could I walk? What kind of pain might I expect? But no preoperative counseling was offered me. For some reason, none of the hospital staff talked to me about anything and I found myself wishing I were having the operation back home in Ireland, or not at all. Feeling terribly alone and far from friends and family, I didn't push for answers.

At seven-thirty in the morning on August 11, 1980, I was draped in a white sheet. A blue, netted cap was stuck over my head and I was given medicine that would put me out for the operation. I fought sleep as long as possible. I remember looking at the porters' white caps as I was wheeled down to the operating theater. These men shifted me from the trolley to the table like a sack of spuds and very soon thereafter, all the lights went out for me. By twelve-thirty, the surgery had been completed and, still unconscious, I was wheeled back to intensive care.

I woke up alone in my hospital bed screaming at the top of my lungs. Never before had I experienced such pain. My legs felt as if they were in vise grips, each nerve seized with agony. The nerve endings from my toes had been embedded in the muscle of my stumps. I felt as if I still had my toes and they were being squeezed mercilessly. Was this some form of medieval torture, or purgatory on earth? "If hell is this bad," I thought, "I can't cope." In all my years of dealing with physical pain, I had never known anything like this and there was no containing me. I roared for what felt like hours before the nurses came in.

They scolded me not to bend my legs and gave me plenty of analgesia to settle me down. I was moved into isolation, in a hyperbaric room with a bright light and loud mechanical vent at the head of my bed. On morphine, I began to feel some relief and was able to sleep. By that evening, I rang home and told everyone I was through the operation. Mam and Dad must have sensed something off in my voice. They made plans to fly over the following afternoon.

By the time my parents arrived, an infection had set in and I had become quite ill. Unable to speak, I lay in bed with a drip in my arm, moaning from pain. In the evening, the nurses came in and took off the bandages to check if everything was all right. They did so roughly and without expression. When the bandages were removed, a shocking smell of rotten eggs rose up at me and I looked down for the first time at my new stumps.

Extending about a hand's length beneath each knee, the stumps were black and blue and terribly swollen. My first thought was "Jesus, Mary, and Joseph, what has that butcher done?" The surgeon had performed a disarticulation rather than an amputation. Though I didn't fully understand the distinction at the time, I could see that he'd cut off my deformed feet. But he failed to build up muscle around the base of my stumps to cushion the spot where the end of the stump would meet my prosthesis. He'd done the job fairly brutally as well, as evidenced by the swelling and bruising I saw. Rather than dwelling in outrage, I very naturally began to think of how much more streamlined I would be this way and of how much more easily I might walk.

It would be a long while before I walked, however. In the meantime, my bandages were redressed and Dad and Mam were brought back in to the room. We were told that the next twenty-four hours were critical and I understood that if the infection did not clear up, I would lose even more of my legs in another operation. Dad was devastated to see me so sick and put his head in his hands. I knew he felt I'd made a mistake in coming. True to form, Mam was like steel, her face wearing very little expression whatsoever. I wanted to speak to them, but was so sick I felt gagged and couldn't utter a word.

Four days later, I began to turn the corner. The infection started to clear and I became more aware of where I was. I was finally able to talk to Mam and Dad. "Well, how are you feeling, Ronan?" Mam asked. I told her I felt exhausted, as if I'd been run over by a train. "Are you in a lot of pain?" Dad asked. I replied that I'd gone past the point of feeling it.

That was about all the conversation I could manage, but Dad was so relieved to hear my voice, he started to cry. Mam was not far behind. She wore a look I had never before seen on her face and I noticed two lines of black mascara running from her eyes. Suddenly, I felt that things between us might finally mend. I told my parents everything would be fine. Though I knew I'd be lonely, I said that they should head on home. Reluctantly, they did so.

After nine days I was still very depressed and detested my dependence on the cold hospital staff for all my needs, but I was doing better physically. My surgeons had never once come to visit me, but the nursing staff told me that I was ready to be measured for my new prostheses and I didn't argue. A bitter old man with stiff Brylcreem'd hair, my prosthetist was matter-of-fact to the point of insensitivity. I had thirty-five sutures in each of my legs and they had not yet healed before he shoved my stumps into cellophane and plaster of Paris. When I asked him to go gently, he answered accusatorily that if it hurt so much, maybe I wasn't ready. I told him that was his call and he kept going. The next step was to fit me with pre-legs that would properly align my legs in the finished limbs. The pre-legs were the actual size my new limbs would eventually be, but weighed about ten pounds owing to the metal jigs that gauged alignment.

One day, the prosthetist left me in the small, overly bright fitting room with these pre-limbs and hurried out without a word of explanation. I stared at my stumps and the clunky pre-limbs and did what seemed natural to me. Sitting on the floor between two wooden walking rails, I began trying them on. I pulled the white cotton mesh socks over my stumps and, guiding the ends of my legs into the pylons as best I could, took a look at myself in the large wall mirror. I had lost twenty-five pounds in the weeks since the operation and would lose thirty more by the end of my six-week stay in the hospital. In the fluorescent light, I looked at the dark circles under my eyes and my pale skin. I appeared absolutely whipped. The massive pre-limbs did not exactly complete a pretty picture. With them attached to my stumps, I reminded myself of some sort of broken-down robot.

Fighting back tears of anger and self-pity, at that moment, I made up my mind that, if I couldn't change the scene, I could change the way I acted in it. I took in a deep breath of the clinical air. Whatever I do in my life, I told myself, I will succeed at it. I knew at that moment that I would make myself fully independent of everyone so I would never, never be a burden.

With these thoughts sharp as lasers in my head, I pulled myself up and stood, putting tremendous pressure on each stump. I felt as if knives were digging into my tender flesh, but leaning on the handrails, I took a few steps forward. My arms were shaking with the effort and I was absolutely exhausted just from standing upright. As usual, I was like a bull in a china shop, trying much too hard. But with each step, I took heart, thinking, "I'm going to make this work." Change is painful at times but it had always been a part of my life. I realized that I could not become what I needed to be by remaining the way that I was.

Through work, help, and encouragement, I succeeded in making this change and blazed my own trail, as Dad had once told me I would do.

Still, my legs felt terribly sore and swollen. When the prosthetist returned, he was livid that I had tried to walk. "What are you doing?" he exclaimed. "You've pushed the process back two weeks." He sat me down and, removing the pre-legs, showed me where the suture lines had strained open owing to my attempt to walk.

I didn't say a word, but looked the man fiercely in the eye as if to say, "But I've done it, haven't I? And no one can take that away from me."

When Fiona arrived to visit she got the shock of her life when she saw me. She tried very hard to conceal her concern, but her face was transparent and her emotions were like the patterns of flowered wallpaper in summer, faded and sweet with natural sincerity. Her eyes were quite full as if at any second she would break down, but I knew it was important for both of us not to let that happen. During the short time she visited we discussed how I would manage when I returned to college, or whether I should take a year out to recuperate. I quickly dismissed that idea as I knew I would go mental at home doing nothing.

Every second day I would go to physiotherapy. This involved a lot of weight lifting and aerobic exercises to prevent my muscles atrophying further from inactivity. Fiona decided to come with me to see what was involved. When she saw me get into my tracksuit she was shocked at how much weight I had lost in such a short space of time. All my clothes had become very loose fitting and even for me who was used to struggling with being overweight, this loss had gone a little farther than it needed to go. Fiona strongly suggested that I give up the physiotherapy. She felt if I kept working at this level I would be emaciated in another couple of weeks and have energy to do nothing. Fi has been looking out for me since I was a child and she continues to do so, even to this day.

Mam and Dad came to see me one more time before I returned home. Some weeks prior to their visit I was given a wheelchair. This was a real eye opener for it was the first time since I was very young that I needed assistance other than my prostheses. I had become very dependent on others, which made me feel extremely insecure and very unhappy.

When Dad and Mam arrived they both entered my room wearing generous smiles, seeing me sitting out on the armchair and looking a lot brighter than on their last visit. However, I did catch Mam's look of surprise when she caught sight of the wheelchair in the corner of the room. I knew she didn't want to deal with that, looking at me in the wheelchair. That wasn't on her agenda. There was no way around it and we all had to accept it. Dad didn't bat an eyelid. He brought the chair over to me, fumbling trying to put the brakes on so it would be stable enough for me to sit in it. I was so delighted with his reaction that I nearly cried. He gave me a hug and said, "In a few months you'll be flying around on your limbs. Trust me, I know what you're made of." Once again he came to the rescue. I always knew that we had a special relationship but now I was even more grateful to God that nothing had changed between us.

He was proud of me no matter what way I was. Mam, on the other hand, was most definitely uncomfortable seeing me in the wheelchair. While I now realize that she too was proud of me, I felt then that she was proud of what she knew I could be, not necessarily what I was at the time. That's why she couldn't accept the wheelchair, much less me in the chair. I was saddened by her reaction but I never let my feelings be known.

Dad decided we should visit Windsor Castle, as he had never been there and always wondered how the other half lived, protected by their great fortresses from the outside world. Windsor Castle is a great testament to the buildings of that era—solid, powerful, and magnificent in its stature, set in manicured gardens outside London. As I gazed at this monstrosity the thought ran through my mind that they must need an army to keep the place maintained.

It was a glorious day with the sun pouring down its rays on my whitewashed complexion. I seemed to draw a fair amount of attention, with people looking at me with sympathetic gazes. God knows I must have looked pitiful and it seemed as if people were wondering if I had just been taken out from some terrible orphanage.

What really bothered me was the fact that I was spending the best summer in years in London trying to rehabilitate my body. I was missing out on all the opportunities with the horse shows back home. I quickly came back to reality when I noticed the huge stone step Dad was trying to negotiate with me in the chair. His breathing was quite heavy, sounding like a concertina being pushed to its limits. He had been wheeling me around for some time and I knew he hadn't the energy to tilt me back to let the back wheels go down first. The inevitable happened; he pitched me forward and I fell out of the chair onto my three-week-old stumps. The fear of God went through me as I was about to impact the aged stone. I implored God to protect me and not let me suffer more hardship. He had come through for me so many times before. Luckily I didn't feel a thing. God had worked a little miracle. Dad on the other hand nearly lost his mind with the fright of seeing me fall out of the chair. I quickly jumped back in and reassured him that there was no problem. By the time Mam caught up with us, we both carried on as if nothing had happened. We were old hands at that for years. The less said the better.

CHAPTER 9

*B*y the twenty-fifth of September the powers that be in the hospital decided it was time for me to return home. I didn't need to be told twice. I was on the phone like a bullet to arrange for my return. Dad suggested collecting me but seeing as Fiona was living in Dublin at the time, it would be easier for her. I knew he wasn't happy but gave in anyway.

I was transported from the hospital to the airport by ambulance, which was an interesting experience at rush hour in London. I had a feeling the driver wanted to get there in double quick time so he had the siren blaring at high pitch. There was no doubt in my mind that he was taking full advantage of his position and in the process scaring the living daylights out of the other drivers. I was hurled around in the back like a rag doll, barely managing to hold on to the side of the gurney, which seemed very solidly anchored into the van. I knew that getting to the airport on time wasn't a life or death situation, but apparently it was to the driver. He seemed to want me out of London as badly as I wanted to leave. On arriving I was escorted by an Aer Lingus official to a private waiting room where I was extremely well looked after. I got on the plane at 8:30 P.M. and was given three seats to lie completely outstretched. This was great for me as I was still having a lot of pain when my legs were in flexion for any length of time. The flight to Dublin lasted an hour and once all the other passengers had disembarked a wheelchair was brought for me. For some strange reason I wanted Fiona and my friends to at least see me walk. First impressions are so important and I just needed them to see that my decision was the right one. I wanted the reassurance and the approval from the people who knew me best.

So when I drew near to the exit door at the arrival area I got out of the chair. I instantly felt as if I had an attack of vertigo. I was in quite a lot of pain, as the stumps were still very tender and unaccustomed to taking any pressure. But once again my pride made me move past the pain—to take the consequences for just a few precious moments of glory.

I was greeted with great fondness, teary eyes, and hugs of affection from Fiona and my old friends from the hostel. It was so good to be home. For a few moments no pain registered, just pure joy.

Bernard grabbed my bags while Fiona and Joe got the wheelchair. It seemed like old times, back with the lads. Little did I realize that my need to walk at that moment would cost me dearly down the road.

When we arrived back at the hostel I was really exhausted. Once again, for some daft reason, I wanted to go up the steps on my own. Fergus O'Connor, who was the new director of the residence, greeted me. Fergus looked at me with surprise, knowing full well that I was trying to put on a brave show. I knew he thought I was pushing myself too hard to display my new disposition. But thankfully no one passed any comment.

Fergus thought it would be best for me if I took the room next to Dr. Frank Bravo just in case I had any need for medical assistance. As my first weekend back home approached, one of the lads in the hostel was invited to a twenty-first birthday party and asked me if I would like to go. I couldn't wait as I had been wondering to myself how I would get on with the fairer sex. I felt much more confident about my new appearance and I knew my walking and posture had improved considerably. The only problem I envisaged was lasting the night without getting too tired or sore. I was also fully aware I wasn't ready physically to wear the limbs for any length of time, but that didn't matter because I was now on a mission. Nothing was going to prevent me from getting answers to these very important questions. Would girls still be attracted to me? Would I be able to slow dance without walking on their toes as I had so often done in the past?

I decided to stuff the inner liner of my prostheses with foam. I was sure by doing this it would take the pressure off the lower areas of both stumps and I could dance the night away without feeling a thing. God how desperate this desire had become. Although the plan was well thought out and I achieved my goal of meeting and dancing with some serious-looking girls, it ultimately backfired on me. Oh, I got all the right answers to my questions. I was on air for two hours—euphoric would be a mild description—and I felt I had been given a new lease on life.

By midnight I was like Cinderella. I had to get back because my legs were on fire. Brendan drove me home and I hobbled up the steep stairs. Each step taken was more torturous than the previous one, reminding me of my stupid sacrifice for vanity. By the time I finally made it to my room, I was so tired I just fell into bed and despite the throbbing in both the stumps, I chose not to look at their condition too closely for fear of the worst.

All was revealed early the following morning. I felt completely washed out, barely able to get out of bed let alone consider putting on my limbs. My stumps were in tatters, red raw as if I had gotten sunburned. Worse were the apparent water blisters that had appeared on the pressure points. To put it mildly, I had made a right dog's dinner of both of them and I had only myself to blame. Sitting on the side of the bed I began to get really upset for I knew whatever progress I had made over the last few weeks, it was now going to be a marathon with regard to getting mobile again. I got a bottle of methylated spirits and rubbed it into my ragged limbs hoping beyond all belief that God would perform another minor miracle and take this cup of suffering away. In my heart of hearts I knew that what had happened was self-inflicted. God wasn't responsible, but, boy, did I want to blame someone other than myself.

When I eventually got down for breakfast using the crutches, Fergus, Father Delargey, and Dr. Frank Bravo were seated at the table. They all greeted me, however Frank was looking more suspiciously at me and asked, "How are you feeling?" I responded that I was washed out. I was experiencing a strange wet sensation in my left leg. He sprung up from the table, driving cutlery and food all over the place. Poor old Delargey had his coffee greet him on his lap. Fergus and

Frank immediately lifted me upstairs back to my room. A little fright-ened by all the commotion, I wondered why all the fuss. As the pros-thesis was removed, I saw my left stump was covered in blood. As Frank had suspected, the suture line had opened up and there was a large amount of clotted blood in the base of the socket. At this point I had become quite weak and before I knew it Fergus and Frank took me to the hospital. Fergus had some experience driving at breakneck pace and did so again this day for me. I was brought to the Meath Hospital where I was kept for a few days. When I eventually returned to the hostel, Fergus greeted me with a gentle smile and said, "I think the dancing will have to wait for a few weeks." I put my head down just like a dog after been scolded and said, "I think you're right."

From that day forward I used a wheelchair exclusively. It was during this phase of my recovery that I experienced what life was really like for people totally dependent on that form of mobility. What became most apparent were shops, university, and almost all pubs—let alone buses or taxis—were inaccessible to wheelchairs. Establishments dreaded to see you coming for they knew that you needed special assistance.

I remember one particular incident in a well-known clothing store in Dublin. John, a friend of mine from my first year in college, wheeled me into the shop to buy some shirts. He maneuvered me with great skill through the different intricate pathways barely avoiding the shop-pers as we went by. I got a great kick out of this, first watching the alarm and annoyance on people's faces as their apparent routine was interrupted, and second, noting their uneasiness when they realized it was a disabled person who was causing all this needless disturbance. My fun ended abruptly when I went to actually purchase my shirts. The assistant who was serving me only addressed John as she had established eye contact with him, even though I spoke to her. Blood began to boil in my veins and I projected my voice a little stronger, but this still didn't get the required response. I couldn't figure out whether she was ignoring me because she thought I was simple or whether she just didn't want to talk to an alien. However I soon reme-died the situation. Jumping up onto my knees I shouted, "It is me who

wants to buy the blasted shirts, not him. I'm the one who will be paying, so talk to me." A sudden shock came over her bespectacled face
and her eyes stared to fill. In the meantime some of the other shoppers
had stopped to see what the commotion was all about. Poor John was
beside himself with embarrassment. As for the other poor soul, she just
disappeared into the wilderness of linen and cotton.

Frustrated and angry, mostly with myself, I got John to get me out
of the store. Talk between us was at a minimum until we got back to
the car, then John let fire. "You cannot blame other people for the lack
of understanding about your situation. Be willing to give people a
chance to learn about the difficulties involved. Don't fire off willy-
nilly. People don't enjoy someone being nasty or inconsiderate, irrespective of whether they are in a wheelchair or not."

He was so right; that outburst wasn't like me. Thankfully it was
John who showed me how I needed to change my attitude. It wasn't
till months later that John revealed to me that his own father had been
in a wheelchair for most of his life.

Within a few weeks I became distraught. I was depending on everyone to give me lifts to college or just to go to the bathroom. I wanted
very much to drink myself into oblivion, but I realized I didn't have
the money or the capability to get to the pub.

After a while I realized charity can only put up with so much begging and the generosity I'd been shown was beginning to wane.
Understanding the situation quite clearly, there was only one person in
the whole world I could call to come to my need—Dad.

On a cold dark October morning in the depths of depression I rang
Dad around seven. He was always up at this time getting ready to milk
the cows by seven-thirty. The phone rang for ages and I wondered if I
had missed him. But being a man of routine I knew that couldn't be
the case. Eventually he picked up. He knew straightaway that it was me
and his intuitive nature told him that things weren't going so well. My
voice was trying to be solid without breaking down, explaining as best
I could how desperate my situation had become. Before I even got
into the sordid details, Dad piped out, "I will buy you a car and that

will ease some of your situation." I started to cry and said, "I'm costing you a fortune but I have only you to turn to. What would I do if you weren't there for me?" He replied, "Some day you will be there when I need you and until then it is my turn to look after you as best I can." I told him that I loved him, to which he replied, "I know that."

Realizing that a car doesn't run on air, I started to investigate what grants were available to disabled people. Some years back I had had the great fortune of meeting a young man from the National Rehabilitation Board named Marius Cassidy. Marius always championed the cases for many young physically challenged people. A small stocky chap with a good strong Northern accent, he was very keen to help me in any way he could. He successfully negotiated a Disabled Maintenance Allowance for me. This meant that I was able to afford to have the car and not be asking Dad for money for its upkeep. Things were looking up.

By Monday afternoon of the following week a brand-new metallic green Volkswagen Golf appeared, coming up the driveway of the residence. I was looking out the window of the study at the time. Lo and behold Dad stepped out of the car and I knew straightaway it was for me. I jumped into the wheelchair and went at breakneck pace to meet him. As he opened the door I greeted him with a massive smile and jumped up on my knees to give him a hug. "You're the best in the world," I said. He laughed, hugged me, and said, "And that's your birthday present for the next five years."

Within a few weeks I was attending all my lectures and no longer felt as dependent on other people. My whole life had changed in one fell swoop. There was definitely a light at the end of the tunnel thanks to that great father of mine.

On May 14 I reached the ripe age of twenty-one. By this time my rehabilitation was going very well and I was now able to wear my limbs continually throughout the day without getting sore or fatigued. As was customary for twenty-first birthdays in our family, we all would go out to dinner. Both parents carried out this tradition, which was seen as the final step to coming of age, marked by receiving a very valuable watch. Tradition was once again upheld by the family and to my amazement Dad produced a Rolex watch. I hugged him and whispered in his ear, "The car was more than enough," to which he smiled and said, "You only reach twenty-one once, it's all downhill from here."

After dinner was finished everyone seemed to be in a massive hurry to get me back to the residence. I was a little surprised for I was planning on having a drink with the family celebrating this momentous occasion. On returning to the residence I noticed quite a few cars in the car park, which was a little unusual, but I didn't think any more about it. As I opened the front door, I was quickly escorted down to the dining room by Fergus and Bernard. Once I entered I saw the place was thronged with friends and relatives. I was overwhelmed. I looked around and I saw Dad had purchased about six crates of beer and other liquor so that my party would become a night to remember.

The lads decided to give me the bumps by using a blanket. I was placed into the middle of it without my legs, and about ten of them proceeded to lift me up and down by pulling at the edges of the blanket. I was scared to death when I became airborne; the higher I went the harder they pulled. To say I was having an out-of-body experience would have been an understatement. Finally they got tired and Humpty Dumpty was put back together again. Relieved, a little out of sorts but thrilled with the whole uproar, I got into some serious drinking. By 4 A.M. there were a few diehards left. As for me I couldn't even remember when the family went home let alone find the directions to my room. Once again Fergus looked after me and got me to bed. The following morning I woke with a serious thumping in my head. I felt as if half the zoo had been given a license to run riot there. No one reprimanded me for I think everyone was feeling a little fragile that morning.

Summer exams that year commenced on the sixth of June starting with physics, followed by math, and ending with chemistry and biology. God is good and his angels can be serious performers when called upon. Everything went as planned. I passed.

I had finally given nature her time to heal me and she in return gave me back my mobility with a little more maturity on top.

CHAPTER 10

On a beautiful Sunday in mid-August 1981, Mam was seated in her solid mahogany armchair with the *Sunday Independent* spread across the matching mahogany dining table. As she was reading the career section she came across an advertisement by the National College of Physical Education. Two places were being offered to disabled students for the course beginning in October 1981. This was the Year of the Disabled, and Thomond College's contribution was these two teacher-training positions. Once she had read all the details she started to discuss her findings with the whole family. "I think I have found a course that really suits Ronan, studying physical education and science." Dad, Fiona, and Tom perked up and started to offer their two pence worth. It seemed as if I didn't have much of a say in this matter. Dad became extremely enthusiastic and looked at me with a keen sense of hopefulness. "You've always loved sport. This is truly a fantastic opportunity for you. It couldn't be better. You're wasting your time just studying pure science. At least having physical education with science, you'll have the best of both worlds."

With their approval, Mam sent for an application form that very evening. Within three days the application arrived and she sat down with me to fill it out. I think looking back on it they were more excited about this course than I was. Once again, Mam was looking beyond who I was to who I could be and in this situation at this time her vision was supportive and on point.

However, at the time I had a nagging doubt in my mind about it. Whether it was the physical component or being in a college where the majority of students were at the top level of their sport, I wasn't able to explain my feelings.

The entry requirements stipulated that every disabled candidate had to have the same academic qualifications as all other entrants. Additionally, they had to have a standard of athletic mobility that was sufficient to fulfill the demands of all the courses' practical components.

I decided from the moment the application was sent that I needed to start getting this carcass of mine into some sort of shape. Funny enough, I didn't have a doubt in my mind that I could reach the standard of motor acceptability, but I wondered if I had enough willpower to sustain me for the four years of course work. I started to swim daily to get aerobically fit. I was also running a mile a day, which caused my stumps to sweat profusely in the prostheses because of the woolen socks I needed to wear to protect them.

When I'd finish training, my stumps were in ragged shape. They were very raw and tender but I was determined to succeed. I continued to demand more from myself than I ever had before, irrespective of what the consequences might be. Every evening I would put mentholated spirits on my stumps in order to toughen them up. I figured if it worked for the horses, it would work on me. After a few weeks things were looking much better and I felt more optimistic about my upcoming physical challenge.

The Wednesday scheduled for my interview opened with a magnificent bright morning. The birds had been holding their general assembly since five-thirty, as they regularly did on the farm. I had been tossing and turning all night thinking about my forthcoming interview. My bed looked as if a hurricane had struck; the sheets were at one end of the bed in a knot and the woolen blankets were on the floor.

I got out of bed at seven, took a bath, and then put on my new navy blue suit, which Mam had bought for me, along with a nice crisp cotton shirt and a red silk tie. There was no doubt in my mind that I certainly looked the part. But I wasn't so sure about feeling it. I then proceeded to pack my sports bag with my new gear, which smelled unbelievably fresh. I arrived down for breakfast to find that Dad had prepared the usual bowl of porridge. He was all chat and commented on how well I looked in the suit, but remarked that I might have overdone it on the aftershave. After breakfast he gave me his usual hug and told me that this college didn't have any idea of what a great athlete they were about to get. I drove down to Limerick on my own and spent a lot of time thinking about what questions I could be asked and whether the college authorities would think I was suitable. I became so involved in my thoughts I didn't pay any attention to the direction I was going. Just before I took off down to Cork, I came back to reality and panicked the life out of myself as I thought I would end up late for my interview. Thankfully I had plenty of time; once again my guardian angel was watching out for me.

Thomond College is situated about one mile from the city of Limerick, by the river Shannon. The building is quite unique in its design, with angles all over the place, and covered from top to bottom with wooden slats. It has won several prizes for its architectural design. God only knows why. It always seemed to me that style ruled over function with a lot of wasted space inside. From the moment I walked through the glass doors, I got a strange feeling about the place, watching the other able-bodied students looking so fit and active. I just didn't feel I was going to fit in and this feeling never really left me. My interview was at 11:15 A.M., and encompassed three different stages. First was an oral interview in English, then an interview in Irish, followed by a mobility test. When I arrived, there were several candidates waiting to be interviewed, including some army cadets. They were dressed in the traditional army uniform, which definitely set them apart from the rest of us. I dared to put myself in the same category as the others as you could not tell anything about me from just seeing me standing.

The first interview was with the heads of the PE Department and the Education Department. This interview went really well. The head of Education concentrated mainly on my academic background and wanted to know my literary interests. The head of PE was particularly interested in my equestrian activities. The second interview was in the early afternoon, and was carried out in Irish. As I liked Irish in school, there was no difficulty with this.

Finally, I had to do the mobility assessment. This resulted in me changing into a tracksuit. I was far from being a stunning athlete but I had made the effort and I felt I wasn't going to make a show of myself.

However, it is difficult to keep up your self-esteem when you watch all these potential Olympians.

The sports psychologist, rugby tutor, and the swimming coach carried out the sport assessment. I was asked to run around the gym, take a basketball, dribble it down to the basket, and attempt a shot. That was just about my limit! I had tied two shoelaces from the knee straps of my prosthesis to the belt around my waist so that my legs didn't fall off during the rigorous activity. After the mobility test, I was in a lather of sweat.

Once I had completed the motor section of my assessment, the swimming coach took me to the pool, where I swam three lengths. Upon completion she commented, "Well done." But she added a little sting at the end with a remark about my large belly and that I could do with tightening it up. Well, that was it. I was convinced that I had blown my chance. After I nearly passed out during the motor assessment, the swimming instructor had concluded that I could nicely substitute for the Michelin Man. To say I was slightly depressed would be an understatement.

I changed back to my suit and proceeded to walk toward those panes of glass, which were acting as doors. As I was walking out, the sports psychologist saw me. He gave a gentle smile and said, "Well done." I was very grateful for his words, even though I thought that they were intended to console me.

On Tuesday of the following week, I received a letter from the admittance office of the college offering me a place commencing October 5. All the family were delighted for me, particularly Dad. He felt that this course was perfect. It suited me a whole lot better than the previous one.

While I was really looking forward to starting my courses, in the back of my mind I still had a needling doubt regarding my suitability for this course. More important, how would other students in the class perceive me? There were fifty students who were top-level athletes from every walk of sport accepted into this course each year. I happened to be one of the lucky ones that year, but one of only two who were disabled. While I loved sport, I feared that the others wouldn't accept me or the other disabled student who had been admitted. I decided to visit Aunt Theresa and Uncle Ralph. As a child I used to visit Ralph and Theresa with my family during the summer months to go fishing. I was extremely fond of both of them but particularly close to Theresa. Unfortunately, they were unable to have children so I always felt like the son they never had. On this occasion I wanted to thrash out with her my worries and concerns about this whole ordeal. I just felt so unsuitable, but I couldn't tell my family because I didn't think they would understand. More important, I didn't want to disappoint Dad.

Theresa said, "Look at all the disabled people who have represented Ireland in sport, and have brought glory both to the country and to themselves. I'm sure that you'll excel down there. Who knows, you might even represent your country one day in the disabled section." She always had greater wisdom and insight than anyone I knew. Little did we both realize how right she was.

CHAPTER 11

My first day at the college was eventful to say the least. During the orientation talk we were introduced to all our lecturers and shown the amazing sport facilities. When I looked around at the other students in the class, they looked so very fit and sporty. And there I was among Ireland's elite standing six three or four and at least twenty pounds over the national average for my age group. Was it me or had I just come through the wrong stage door? Trust me, at that moment I really felt oversized and underactive.

I will never forget my first introduction to dance with Dr. Anne Leahy. She was an extremely kind woman. She was always dressed in wine-colored leggings and a mauve leotard. That was the external presentation of her artistic nature. Behind the fashion was a caring, compassionate individual who was willing to accept people as she found them.

The theme for that day's class was space awareness. There was no question that I needed loads of space due to my size. Both ladies and gents wore blue leotards. What a sight! M&Ms wouldn't have looked out of place in this group. All I can say is that if you've ever seen the dancing hippo in *Fantasia,* you have a pretty good idea of what I looked like. Dr. Leahy asked everyone to remove their shoes and socks. I sat beside a chap called Pat O'Reilly and said that this was going to be fun. Pat was confused but when he saw my custom-made feet his jaw dropped, as did everyone's in the group. Dr. Leahy wasn't fazed by what she saw but apparently had not been told of my disability. Clearly, this dancing hippo was different. By the end of the class, we got on famously. Anne, as time went on, was delighted that one of her students was different from the rest. With her strong spiritual awareness she never had to question people's idiosyncrasies.

The next few weeks were filled with similar experiences, particularly with gymnastics and outdoor pursuits. Although I never really managed to execute those quiet landings in gymnastics, I became particularly good at performing inverted Ts on the ropes. Putting my heart and soul into the physical education side of the program, I was reaching new heights that were far beyond what a boy with my disability could ever have dreamed. My marks never reflected all the effort I put into completing the tasks set for me. I was regularly reminded that this was not a college for disabled students. If I wanted to be treated differently, then I should have entered a college that provided a course for disabled athletes. As I expected, my legs didn't tolerate all the activities, resulting in plenty of episodes of skinned stumps.

After about six weeks I visited Aunt Theresa and Uncle Ralph to tell them how things were going. By this time I had settled reasonably well into the course. Most evenings after the classes, all I was fit for was the bed. I was just whacked out; I couldn't wait for Fridays so I could relax and have a few pints.

Because I owned a car, it was possible for all of us to go out in the college area to pubs like Durty Nellie's and have some fun. I used to sing quite often while we were at the pubs. Songs like "Danny Boy," "Only Our Rivers Run Free," and some good old dirty rugby songs that drove the place wild and encouraged more drinking. That earned my buddies and me many a free pint.

By the end of the first semester I returned to visit Ralph and Theresa for the Christmas holidays. I told them that, as I had feared, I didn't feel I fit in at Thomond. I had more friends at the hostel where I lived than I did at school. It was difficult for me to connect with young people whose lives revolved around their physical accomplishments. I had become unhappy with the school and the course. Theresa advised me to give it a chance, as I had only completed one semester. By the start of the second term, we had commenced athletics. This encompassed track and field events and I started to really excel in this area. I had thrown shot put, discus, and javelin in school from the ages of twelve to seventeen. Now it dawned on me it might be possible to compete in the Amputee Games. I recalled what Theresa had said about all the amazing achievements of these athletes. The head of the college and P. J. Smith, the professor of sports psychology, ran this athletics course. P.J. encouraged me and, from that moment on, I became determined to compete at the highest level possible in this area.

By the end of the second term, I set about finding out more information regarding the Amputee Games. I wrote to the Irish Wheelchair Association, as I was aware that this group was in charge of such sporting events. Jimmy Byrne ran it at that time, one of nature's finest gentlemen and a fair man in every way. There was very little information available about competitive amputee sports, so I subsequently wrote to the British Amputee Association in England. I found that the BASA games were about to be held in May 1982. I set my target to enter this competition but, as usual, there were a few hurdles to get over. I knew that I needed prostheses that would be more suitable and durable for sporting activities. Hanger in Belfast had available a shin that had a rotatory capability, which I was dying to get. I knew this device would give me a greater facility in the final rotation, when I would be about to release the discus.

I started training in earnest under the guidance of Patricia Holmes, a fourth-year student who had represented Ireland in swimming. Her regime was tough and I used to start early in the morning with about two hours of work building up stamina. By the end of the day I would have swum at least two miles. Trisha was a super motivator. When I participated in the college swimming competitions I fared reasonably well, mostly making the finals and on the rare occasion getting placed.

I also had to find a good discus and shot putter to teach me the finer rudiments of the techniques required. I knew simple standing throws were never going to put me in the running for a medal.

There were two people aside from P.J. who used to give me as much time as they could. Richard Shortal was one who was generous with his time. He was an intercollegiate shot putter and discus thrower and had represented Ireland as a junior some years previously and was fully aware of what was needed for an athlete to make it. I was very lucky also to make friends with a great Limerick hurler called Bernie Harti-

HALFWAY HOME

gan, who was phenomenal at giving his time, kindness, and superior skill in teaching me the basic techniques of discus and shot putting. Bernie played a more significant role when I started training in earnest for the 1984 Paralympics.

At the end of my second term, word had spread around college that I was going to participate in competitive sport. The athletic club in the college under the guidance of Joe Weafer, a third-year student, decided to organize a charity run so that I could buy the limbs with the rotators. They raised a substantial amount of money, enough not only for the limbs but also to pay for the trip to compete. I had finally found a way to connect with the other students. Once they realized that I was as serious a competitor as any of them, they became accepting of me and very supportive.

The college raised over twenty-five hundred pounds. I was amazed at how generously people gave. Local schools in the area also participated. The Limerick people went all out to help me become a serious athlete, as did the athletic club of Thomond College. I wrote to Ronny Delaney, who was at that time the chairman of B and I car ferries. Ronny himself was an Olympic gold medalist, winning the fifteen hundred meters in the 1956 Olympics in Melbourne, Australia. Ronny was fantastic, making it possible for me to have free ferry transport for the car and two passengers. One person was my coach and the other was a spare driver.

Ronny also got me sponsorship from Puma sportswear. Needless to say, I looked like the cat's whiskers with all the appropriate footwear for throwing, plus Irish tracksuits and singlets. I was on cloud nine. Unfortunately, something had to suffer and, as usual, it was my studies. I was putting every obstacle I could in front of my studies, but had it not been for finding competition I would have definitely left Thomond.

The BASA games were being held in London at the famous Stoke Mandeville Hospital, world-renowned for the rehabilitation of spinal cord injury patients. The competition took place over a weekend in May, about three weeks before my first-year exams. Richard Shortal went as the coach and my friend Aidan Murphy was the spare driver.

When we arrived at Stoke Mandeville, we were all given plastic IDs and put into a dormitory, which had six beds to a room. For all intents and purposes, it was like a hospital without the surgery units. The trip over was great fun. Richard, Aidan, and I got on superbly. I had no idea what the competition was going to be like, but even if I was a bit of a rookie, I knew that I was very competitive and would fight to the bitter end. The morning of the competition, I was up at the crack of dawn going for a jog. I was just too excited and couldn't settle down.

The first event I was entered in was the hundred-meter freestyle in swimming. I was left to my own devices here, as Dick wasn't into swimming. Now most swimmers are lean and streamlined. I, on the other hand, am not. I looked like a weight lifter. My fellow competitors in the heat were all slightly built and I was sure they all swam like dolphins. I wondered if maybe the wave that I would create might slow them down in the chop and give me a chance. I was in the first heat and Trisha always told me to pace myself for the first fifty meters. Always leave something in the tank for the sprint in the last twenty-five meters. The gun sounded and I tore off, totally ignoring what I was told to do. By the first turn I was in third place and under pressure. It seemed as if these skinny fellows had motors in their rear ends. By the last twenty-five meters, I noticed that we were all pretty close together. I dug as deep as I could as I turned to go down the final lap and finished second. Aidan and Dick were delighted with me. As usual, Dick started to joke around, saying that swimming was for girls—not a real man's sport.

The final was held about two hours later and I was positioned in lane five. It was my plan to swim in the slipstream of the chap in lane four. However, once the gun went off all eight swimmers took off like scalded cats. Once again, I was trying to be clever and keep my mind on the job at hand. By the first fifty meters I was lying in third just as in the semifinals. This time I felt that I had a little more in the tank than in the first heat. As we hit the last twenty-five meters, the other competitors were slowing down. I was wired up and used every last bit of energy in the sprint. I won by a touch! For a short length of time I was so exhausted I wasn't able to speak. Aidan was thrilled for me and Dick commented that he hoped I had some energy left for the real events tomorrow, which were starting early in the morning.

I slept like a log that night. The next morning I ate a hearty breakfast. After going through a warm-up session, I was loosened up and ready to conquer. As I was new to the amputee games, many of the other competitors were in awe of my stature and perturbed by the degree of flexibility and technique that I had under my belt. There is nothing like an extra inch or two to scare off the opposition.

There were fifteen competitors in the discus competition of which I was number five. The first was to be a standing throw. Dick and I had both felt that it was important to get a registered throw into the sector. In that way, I would set a mark. I had no idea what the standard of the other competitors was, or if I would even be competitive against them. But I would soon find out. By the end of the third round, all three of my throws had put me ahead of the rest of the field. On my fourth throw, I decided to do a one and a quarter turn. This is where I would see the benefit of the internal rotators. However, on my first attempt I fouled and nearly injured myself trying to maintain my balance. This had also been a problem at home. But on the odd occasion that I got it together, the results were quite amazing. On my final throw, I just about executed the turn and this added nearly an extra six meters to the toss. I won the event by a fairly hefty margin and in the process broke the European and World record for the discus.

Ken Day, who was the English coach at the time, reckoned that I was a force to be dealt with. Once I established a solid technique, he believed that I would be virtually impossible to beat in my category. Dick listened intently to what Ken said, and told me not to pay too much heed to the other teams' coaches. You could never be sure what was behind their advice. I didn't give too much attention to what he had said but I was chuffed at what he thought.

The shot put was the next event. Similar to the discus, I putted about two meters beyond everyone else in the competition and broke all the established records. It was the same with the javelin, but this was a much more closely fought event.

The last event on Sunday morning was the hundred-meter sprint in track. To be honest, this is what I called the blue ribbon event. I just loved to run and had developed a system of attachments from the knee cuff straps of my prosthesis, to my waist by connecting garters from the belt to each strap. This had two functions: to keep the prosthesis on while I was running; and to lessen the friction between the stumps and the socket. Too many times in the past I had suffered friction burns.

There were six competitors, so it was a straight final. I won the race in a time of 16.4 seconds. While this is nothing in comparison to the able-bodied athletes, it was a fantastic achievement for me. It is very hard for me to describe the feeling of self-fulfillment that I had after that race. I was so delighted that I cried. I tried to maintain my composure in front of everyone but was overcome. Later that evening, Aidan told me that he had prayed while I was competing. I will never forget him for that token of his friendship.

We set sail for Ireland that evening from Holly Head in Wales. All three of us were on a high. The lads were a tremendous support. I made a phone call to Ronny Delaney to tell him of my success. It would be the first of many. Naturally, I phoned Dad first. He was hysterical with delight. I could feel his excitement over the phone. God knows, he was such a great man and so full of admiration for whatever I did.

I was amazed at Dad's reaction and yet, why should I have been? He was always so proud of me and never shied from telling me. We finally arrived home and Dad was ready with a huge dinner. He raved to Dick and Aidan about how fantastic it was that I had represented the country and achieved such wonderful success. To tell the truth, I was a little embarrassed, but they both thought that it was great to see a father so proud.

When we arrived back in college, my successes were greeted with much less enthusiasm. Looking back it's clear that the students at Thomond expected physical success. It wasn't to be celebrated when it was achieved. But they never understood what I had endured just to be at the games, much less what success had cost me. There was quite a mixed reaction from the lecturers on the course. The educationalist and the science lecturers seemed more proud than did the PE lecturers, except for P.J.

I sat my exams and passed by the skin of my teeth. About a week into my summer holidays, I received an invitation to compete in Belgium at the European games. They were to be held at the Heizel Stadium in Brussels. Once again, Ronny Delaney and Puma came to help.

I was now living with Ralph and Theresa because I was more relaxed there than in my parents' home. Remembering how Mam had dealt with my amputation, I needed time to accept her reactions even though it was a very tough price to pay not being around Dad the way I liked.

I used to train on their front lawn, throwing the discus thirty-four to forty meters. My objective at that time was to reach the road, which was about fifty meters from the house. Ralph and Theresa would often sit outside and watch me train. Years ago Ralph was a very fine athlete. Theresa had once told me that with proper coaching Ralph could have been selected for the National Team to compete in the high jump. Circumstances were different then, and a farmer's son was obligated to do one thing: work on the farm. When he watched me throw he used to shout, "God help anyone that gets in your way, you'll drive them into next week." Then we all would laugh. I knew they loved me like a son. They were extremely proud of me.

I decided for the trip to Belgium that I would take Dick and my friend Tom Farrell from home. The games were on in early July 1982. We drove to Roslare and took the car ferry to Cherbourg. I decided that we would give ourselves three days, so that I would have adequate resting time before the competition. My swimming days were over, as I couldn't face the training I needed to maintain the fitness required to keep me up to anywhere near a competitive level. Furthermore, I was beefing up from doing weights, which was more beneficial to a thrower than a swimmer.

The competition in Brussels was a lot tougher than at the BASA games. The morning of the championships everybody had to register in the main stadium. That included escorts as well as coaches. Our passes had to be worn at all times around the stadium. There wasn't a hope in hell of getting into the stadium without your identity card. On the morning of the opening, Tom forgot his pass. He was sent back to the hotel to get it. Poor Tom was worrying whether or not he had lost it the night before, clubbing with Dick while I tried to have an early night. I should have gone with them for I wasn't able to sleep.

The games commenced the morning after the opening ceremonies. The discus was the first competition. At this stage, I had improved considerably in performing the one and a quarter turn in the circuit. So, I said to Dick that I would try this on my first throw. He wasn't completely in agreement with me, but decided that it was my choice. His fears were well founded. I fouled on both my first and second throws. I had no throw registered and was facing the cutoff to be allowed to enter the final stage of the competition. I played it safe and performed a standing throw. Once again, I shot into the lead and, as on so many occasions before, I asked God to help me. He hadn't let me down so far, so I knew He wasn't about to start now. On my final throw, once again, everything fell into place. The victory was sweet. I had thrown at least two meters farther than in England. In the process, I smashed my own European and World records. This was ratified by ISOD (International Sports Organization for the Disabled). I also won the shot put, javelin, and the hundred-meter sprint. Trophies and medals were presented during the closing ceremonies. I was so proud to see the Irish flag being hoisted and to hear our National Anthem being played.

When I returned home the national media had picked up on my success and Irish Television Network did a feature on me. I'm not sure whether this helped or hindered my relationship with people at the college, but one thing was for sure, I still wasn't enjoying my situation there.

In my second year at Thomond, I became quite friendly with Niall Rennick, who was in my group for chemistry. Niall was extremely talented in both sports and academia. Sad to say, he also had his own mind about Thomond. He seemed to think that it was a place where one had to conform to the powers that be or suffer the consequences. They didn't want any individual to get attention in their sport or in any other aspect of media coverage. All too well we were both learning this.

Every year, there was a major soccer tournament called the Collingwood Cup. Thomond had a very good reputation nationally for soccer players and this year was no exception. I became a fanatical follower. The Collingwood was held in early spring. Only the soccer players had been given grace to participate and take the time off. I was so involved that I was unable to forgo the opportunity of watching the lads play. I became like a mascot for the team. The tournament was on at UCD, the University College of Dublin. I went to every match, cheering and roaring until I was hoarse. Up until the semifinals of the tournament, I was the sole Thomond supporter in the stands. They progressed through each round playing with great skill and determination and it was an honor to be a part of them. I used to secretly realize some of my own dreams of playing at that level of soccer when I would watch the guys play. Niall was particularly talented, as were the rest of the squad. The camaraderie among us was very special; something I will never forget. But as I've often realized, nothing lasts forever. The final of the cup was between UCD and Thomond. Several busloads of supporters now came from Thomond to support the team. The lads played their hearts out, but sad to say, we lost 1–0. No shame on any member of the team. They were all class. They all received plaques and somehow managed to get an extra one, which they presented to me for being their supporter.

Within three weeks of the tournament, all of the college was sent out on teaching practice. This was one particular part of the course I really enjoyed. I was sent to the academy in Mallow, County Cork. Niall was sent to Clonakilty. There was one other person sent to Mallow, my good friend Bernadette. It was during our teaching practice that Bernie and I started to see each other. She was a fantastic character and, boy, did she have a sense of humor. She had long black hair and a wonderful figure. To me she looked like Wonder Woman. We both got on fabulously in teaching practice.

Every weekend during that five-week period, I would drive down to Clonakilty and pick up Niall, either with Bernie or we'd collect her on the way back. All in all, it was a trip of about one hundred miles. We would go out on a Friday night and Niall would meet Anne, another girl in our group who was very struck with him. They married some years later.

By the end of my second year, I hated Thomond. The feeling that I had always had that I didn't belong there had grown stronger over time. Trying to fit into a world that centered on physical ability was never going to work and my self-esteem was taking a pounding. All I wanted to do was leave and study physiotherapy at Trinity. I had reapplied and had been accepted for the course commencing in September 1983. As always, I discussed everything with Theresa as we would go for our four-mile walks around Muckalee, where they lived. Theresa always listened to me moan about Thomond. Then she got me to see reason. "You have two years completed, and you have only two left. This will go much faster than you think. Always look at how close you are to finishing." Theresa had a great effect on me. I was very fond of her and always paid heed to her judgment on any issue. We discussed the family problems and my position with Dad. Theresa held both my parents in great esteem and tried to maintain a neutral opinion at all times. She didn't show favoritism toward either party.

I would often take Theresa to Dublin to shop. She was a small, frail, dark-skinned lady and very, very pretty. On these trips, she used to sit in the passenger side of my car and if I was driving too fast, I would see her from the corner of my eye holding on to the seat for dear life. "Are you all right?" I would ask. "Of course, yes, it's great; we're flying along." Then both of us laughed. She made me very happy.

In July 1983, I represented Ireland at the European games in Paris. On this occasion, I decided to bring Tom once again, as well as Bernie. We turned it into a two-week vacation. The first week would be spent at the games. We would tour France in the second week. I had great success in the games. I won five gold medals and broke all of my existing records. For the first time, I participated in the long jump. The results were sent back to the media in Ireland and on returning home I was interviewed on several radio shows.

CHAPTER 12

I used to always bring a huge variety of tapes to listen to whenever I would travel to competitions. At that time, Christopher Cross and David Gates of Bread were very popular. I must have played "Ride Like the Wind" over a thousand times. I adored the album. There was one song from the David Gates album that I especially loved, "If." I felt the lyrics captured everything that had to be said about being in love. My favorite classical artists at that time were Mario Lanza, Luciano Pavarotti, and many of the great old tenors like Caruso, Gigli, and Kraus. My favorite of all was Jussi Bjoerling, the Swedish tenor.

One day as I was driving along, listening to Pavarotti sing the "Ave Maria" by Schubert, I started to sing along, as many of us do. But lo and behold, when I opened my mouth to sing, a completely different sound came out. It was much deeper and louder than before. I had stopped singing publicly some time earlier because I felt that my voice was too high. I can still recall how when I was nineteen, I could sing three octaves starting from "E" above middle "C." To me this didn't seem to be a proper sound for a man.

Once I found this new sound, I couldn't be shut up. I returned to college in September 1984 for my third year, which was also the Olympic year. I had been selected to compete for Ireland by the Irish Wheelchair Association. This also meant several training sessions during the year. I was left in no doubt by the college that I needed to apply myself to my studies and not get too caught up in competing. Niall and I got a flat together. For most of the first term we would drive up to Durty Nellie's every Friday night. I would sing Irish and popular songs, and get free drinks for both of us. When I sang "Danny Boy" the place would erupt.

I was blessed that year to have made contact with a very famous

Donoughmore House.

Mam and Dad on their honeymoon in Jersey, Channel Islands.

At age seven, my first Holy Communion. I'm on my mom's right—with Tom and Fiona.

Pappy.

At age eleven, my Confirmation. I'm on my dad's right, with
Tom and Mom.

Having completed the point-to-point in Thurles, County Tipperary. Jacko (alias Fair Dues) with me on top and Dad walking stride for stride.

Riding The Queen in the Amateur Championship in Gowran, County Kilkenny.

Tom's graduation. His degree in agriculture was the whole family's.

Ralph and Theresa,
my aunt and uncle, at my
1985 graduation from
Thomond College.

Mam and Dad at my graduation from the Thomond College of Physical Education.

Competing in the long jump in Sweden at the World Amputee Games in 1986 in Gothenburg. I jumped 5 meters 63 centimeters and broke the world record for double amputees.

Paralympics in Seoul, Korea, in 1988. I received the gold medal for the discus competition and broke the world record six times.

Graduating as a doctor from Trinity College in 1993.
With Mam and Dad.

Go for It winner, March 1994.

Placing third in the team event for Northern Ireland at the Amateur Horse Show in Arnheim in 1998.

Rosemary Clooney and I after opening night at Feinstein's at the Regency Hotel, Park Avenue, December 1999.

Performing with Patrick Healy in March of 2000 in Westbury, New York, on my fortieth birthday.

Mam and I after the first Irish Tenors concert
in Dublin in 1999.

Aidan Murphy, Tom, and I.

Tom, Sarah Farnel, and Aine Cassidy.

Dennis and Kathleen Mullins and I.

Keith Synnott on my left and Marrius Cassidy on my right.

Performing with The Irish Tenors at the Christmas hour, 2000.

Ronan, Fiona, and Tom.

Limerick sportsman called Bernie Hartigan. Bernie was a fine, well-built man, standing about six two. I was so fortunate to meet such a patient and kind individual, with a great heart. He spent hours with me teaching the finer technique of shot put and discus throwing. We trained in good weather and bad for months on end.

From the very beginning of the term I had started weight training and commenced on a high-protein diet. By mid-March, I was in great shape. I had lost forty pounds and was able to run about a mile each day. Some of the students used to keep me company, both on the track and in the weight room. Once again, as exam time drew near, Niall and I had to quell our visits to the pub. This wasn't that easy to do, as both of us were addicted to our Friday night entertainment. Thankfully, the exams went fine and on June 26, 1984, I flew from Dublin to New York to compete at the International Games for the Disabled at Hofstra University on Long Island. Ralph and Theresa saw me off at the airport. Theresa started to cry, I think because she had witnessed so many of her friends and neighbors depart to the United States, never to return. It made me a little sad, but also showed me how much she loved me.

That same year the BBC in London decided to do a sports documentary on my life. The plan was to follow me through the games and televise all my experiences. It was difficult enough to have the cameras watching every move you make, let alone have them record your emotions when you didn't want them seen.

All the athletes were housed in the Hofstra University residences. I shared a room with a young chap named John Creedan, who suffered from a disease known as Friederich's Ataxia. This is a hereditary condition causing idiopathic cord deterioration. This disease is very debilitating and causes serious problems with movement. But what I can tell you is that John was one of nature's kindest and happiest human beings. He was an absolute joy to be around.

The team leader was a lady called Carol. We didn't always see eye to eye, but sorted that all out and became good friends afterward. The team itself was made up of many inspired and dedicated athletes, whom I feel never got the proper recognition they deserved. There were over 1,700 athletes from all over the world. It was truly a spectacular event. The opening ceremonies involved all the athletes from the different countries parading just as the able-bodied Olympians had in Los Angeles a few weeks prior. It was the first time that I really focused on how hard each of these special athletes had worked to achieve such a high level of mobility and skill in their respective sports. It was no small achievement for these people to earn their place on their national teams under such difficult circumstances. All I can say is that it opened my eyes.

I had also decided to write my undergraduate dissertation on motives for participating in sport among amputee athletes. I passed around three hundred questionnaires to various athletes from all the different countries. I used the English amputees as a control group for my studies, as they were the easiest to contact. The questionnaire was translated into five different languages. The results showed that disabled athletes had the same social and psychological motives for participation in sport as those who were able-bodied. They were very aware that their performances weren't as aesthetically pleasing to watch, and therefore nowhere near as commercially interesting to the corporate sponsors.

I became very friendly with many athletes from all over the world. I trained with one particular African-American, Antoine Archie. We exchanged views on different throwing techniques and trained together for the duration of the games. This was a wonderful experience for me, as I would not have been given that opportunity unless I had established myself as a sportsman. The friendship and kindness shown to us by so many different American communities was unbelievable. Top of the list for me had to be the Nassau County Police Department. I became great friends with many of them. They eventually got me a summer job in Manhattan; their pipe band entertained the athletes at the opening ceremonies.

The games commenced the following day. Most of my competitions were in the early afternoon, but if another team member was competing, the rest of us would go to support him or her. Once the games had commenced, spectators were few and far to be seen. This bore out what most of the physically challenged athletes felt: This was not a major spectator sport for the normal fan.

I started my competitions two days into the games. First up for me was the discus, which I won and set a new world record. I also won the shot put and again set a new world record. I came second in the high jump and I won the long jump and the hundred meters. In total I won six medals, four gold and two silver, and set two new world records. At the closing ceremony I was presented with the Sir Richard Kuntzer award for the most outstanding male athlete of the games. I was absolutely thrilled and couldn't wait to ring Dad. I phoned that evening. He was so delighted that he became emotional on the phone and said he would have given anything to be there to see the Irish flag and watch me get the gold medal. He could not wait to see me. This became the first of many phone calls I made to him through the night as I became more emotional with each passing pint.

I wasn't in too fit a state after the games, thanks to the generosity of some of the thirstier pipers in the Nassau County Police Band. We had one week off before we were to return to Ireland. We returned with thirty medals in total, divided between the wheelchair, cerebral palsy, amputee, and blind athletes.

I had planned to return to the United States after a couple of days, as I had obtained a J-1 working visa. Thanks to the policemen, I had a job to go to. I became a general factotum working for the W. R. Grace Co. on Forty-second Street and Fifth Avenue in Manhattan. My years of formal education had obviously impressed the people in personnel. They assigned me a job that consisted of shredding paper. For a break in that action, I was allowed to set traps for mice and then dispose of them before any of the office staff arrived at work. The heat was intense that summer and it had its effects on my legs. I used to suffer desperately from heat rash. I stayed in Oceanside on Long Island with a very generous family, the Kinirons. I also became good friends with Tony and Maureen Jackson, who treated me like family.

During August and September, I went to study at Michigan State University to research all the relevant material that had been written on the psychology and sociology of sport. My time at Michigan State had been arranged for me by Harry Smith, who worked for the National Rehabilitation Institute. I had never seen such a massive campus. It was like being in a city within a city. I worked in the library, which was triple the size of any I had ever been in before, and had amazing facilities. I worked every hour God sent while I was there, as I knew that I could only find this material here and I would only have one chance to get it right.

I returned to Ireland about two days before the start of my final year of college. I was glad to have only one year to go and remembered what Theresa had said to me about focusing on how close I was to finishing something. That was probably the only aspect of the year that was positive. But I had also decided that I wasn't going to teach as a profession. I had taken on a design project looking at the use of storage energy in artificial feet, to aid ambulation in active prosthetic users. I sent my proposals, along with my résumé, to J. E. Hanger in London. They responded promptly, offering an interview for two different posts. One was in the area of prosthetic design, the other as a trainee for European Area Manager. The interview was to be held in May 1985. If successful, I would start on August 1 of the same year.

Niall and I once again got an apartment together. There was no doubt that the pressure was on as my undergraduate dissertation had to be completed, typed, and submitted by March. This all had to be done prior to going out on my final teaching practice. Despite the pressure, Niall and I still couldn't resist going out to Durty Nellie's, even more frequently than before. At this stage of the course most of the major teaching skills relating to the different disciplines of sport were completed. I particularly enjoyed rugby, as I played as a prop in the front row. It gave me a chance to use my strength and also to vent some of my aggression. P.J. was the instructor and was hugely into the sport himself. This helped matters, as he offered quite a degree of skill and knowledge to the teaching element. I was also very interested in gymnastics and dance, particularly working on a routine.

In my final teaching practice, one of my classes was dance. I had made up my own dance routine to the music of Michael Jackson's song "Beat It" from the *Thriller* album. The theme of the class: "Your Body Parts Aren't Part of You." I started to demonstrate the routine, which encompassed twists and turns and jumps and kickouts. During my demonstration of the kickout, my left leg flew off and nearly hit one of the girls. This was followed by complete silence as an awkward silence fell over the assembly. Then one of the more verbal girls in the class piped up, "Is that what you mean by not being part of your body, sir?" Some of the girls smiled, others were stunned by her audacity. I laughed, and took it in the lighthearted way in which it was said. As a result, all the girls relaxed and the character of the class picked up the errant missile and brought it back to me. She smiled and said, "I'm sorry, sir." "Not to worry," I said. Needless to say, the subsequent classes were full of excitement and activity. This all resulted in a super grade on my final exams.

By April most of our course work had been completed. Despite finals drawing near both Niall and I still found it very difficult to focus and discipline ourselves to get down to the books. Try though we might, we were unable to force ourselves to even do two hours of study each day.

By May all of the students had found employment in different schools around the country. I had applied to some schools to get the experience of doing interviews. I was told by one principal after an interview that while he felt I would be a good teacher, it would be too much of an insurance risk to employ me. After that I was no longer interested in applying to other schools.

I had initially taken a post with the European Commission as a project leader setting up integration programs for the physically challenged in the community. The remuneration was good. I knew that this would put me in a better negotiating position with Hanger if they were to offer me a position.

My finals commenced on the fifth of June and lasted for two weeks. I was really worried as I knew I had just done the bare minimum or maybe even less. I was relying very much on God's help to guide me to study the relevant material. I was starting to wonder how often I could ask for His help. But that's how it is when you haven't done the work. You only get away with so much before you have to pay the piper. I really hoped that I was going to play the right tune. God is good and He was certainly looking after me on this occasion. I knew up to this point of sitting for the exams I was getting through. Both the education and sports science papers were on target. However, the three chemistry areas were a horse of a different color.

Niall and I had stayed up the entire night before these papers. There was no doubt in either of our minds we were under severe pressure caused in large part by a considerable lack of knowledge of chemistry. After nine hours of exams Niall was a little more confident than me. I had a major problem with physical chemistry and it was well borne out when I saw the exam paper. There were five questions to be answered, but I couldn't understand even one of them. Finally I decided to rewrite the questions so I could at least have reason to stay in the exam hall for the three hours. The outcome was as I expected it. I did not do well with the physical chemistry, but I did well enough on the other two papers to pull myself through. Luckily my results went on the better side of the curve. Thankfully both of us made it through and graduated, two very happy campers.

I commenced working on the International Integration Project in July at Tullamore in County Offaly. It meant traveling at least forty-five miles there and back every day by car. I could not wait for Hanger to send their offer. When it eventually arrived I was ready, willing, and able to go.

CHAPTER 13

*P*rior to setting out for London I bought a new suit and trench coat so I would be suitably attired for the occasion. On my arrival in London I was met by the sales manager, a small stout man a little the worse for wear. As I went to get into the car I heard the sickening sound of thread tearing from material as the seat of my trousers split. I nearly died. Thankfully he didn't hear it. God knows no one travels with spare trousers. Luckily I had brought the trench coat for now it had a real purpose aside from the obvious.

The weather was glorious, not a day for a trench coat, but, boy, was I delighted to have it. My feeble excuse was that I had a cold, and needed to wear the coat continuously to stay warm.

When I arrived at the company's headquarters, it was like déjà vu. Their clinic I had been attending throughout the years was exactly where their offices were situated. I first met with the marketing director, Chris Kubiski, a small thin man, who was extremely polite but had a very inquiring disposition. He asked me how my finals had gone and wondered would I graduate with honors. I responded that I hadn't received any results as yet but I was confident (at least in front of him) that all had gone well. I told him I had received a top grade from my undergraduate thesis and it had been published. Those results had been posted long before we sat our finals. However, my overall results had not been posted so I was not in a position to discuss or forecast the outcome. The next interview was with Tony McQuirke, who was the prosthetic director. While certainly not as academically minded as Chris, he was very interested in my ideas of improving the prosthetic services in Ireland. He wanted to know how I would set up workshops in underdeveloped countries. I waffled on, as only I knew how. This intrigued him no end. After both interviews, they offered me two different positions in the company. One position was in prosthetic design and manufacturing, which also included training as a prosthetist. The opportunity afforded me was a four-year training scheme with quite an impressive salary.

Chris Kubiski's offer, on the other hand, was to work in the marketing section as a training export area manager for Europe; after one year I would be made permanent with all the trimmings. This post meant that I would be traveling all over Europe. Needless to say, traveling all over Europe seemed to be much more appealing than going back to college for another four years. There was only one snag that was apparent to me: Chris wasn't offering as good a salary as Tony. But the bigger picture with Chris looked more promising in terms of development.

That afternoon I met the personnel manager. The first thing he asked me to do was to take off my coat, as I appeared to be extremely uncomfortable. My face was the color of a beetroot. I told him that I had a cold and it was better that I left the coat on. However, he looked suspiciously at me. Noticing his skepticism, I responded, "I'm sure you think I have something to hide by not taking my coat off." He looked even more puzzled and replied, "Whatever you're happy with." After this great start, I thought I had blown this whole interview, but the situation improved dramatically when we discovered that I knew some of his relations in Ireland. More important, we both loved music. At the end of the interview, I stood up to say good-bye. As I turned I said, "The next time I will take my coat off, as I am sure I will be feeling better." To which he retorted, "It's best to wear dark underwear as it's not as noticeable." I nearly dropped. "How did you know?" "I saw the split in your trousers as you entered. Don't worry, it could happen to a bishop." After that encounter, we became great friends. I later found out from Chris that Roy said the sun shone out of my backside.

I returned home to Dublin that evening with the two offers from J. E. Hanger. Dad thought this was fantastic as did Theresa. Mom, on the other hand, felt that as it involved sales it couldn't be as secure as a good solid teaching post. I had put that idea well to bed by the end of my term in Thomond College. I eventually succeeded in thrashing out with Chris a little extra finance starting off, plus six months' hotel accommodation free. This gave me an opportunity to get to know London and the surrounding area so that I would become more familiar with house prices. I stayed in Bishop's Hotel for the six months. This of course happened to be the hotel that I always stayed in when I was attending the clinic as a patient. I loved this area and most evenings I walked through Richmond Park and watched people horseback riding. It was then that I really missed home and the horses. I made a vow that someday I would be in a position to have horses.

I had no sooner started in the company when Chris sent me to San Francisco to their sister company Hosmer Dorrance to learn about upper arm prostheses. On my trip I also attended a lecture given by Dr. Childers on myoelectric stimulation of muscles. I found this lecture fascinating. Once the talk was over I discussed at great length the whole area with Dr. Childers. He advised me to go back and study medicine and then progress to rehabilitation as this would be the only way for me to fulfill my desire to put to good use what I had learned. From that moment on the seeds of medicine were well planted.

I returned back from the States to start my company-trained marketing course at Slough College near London. I attended these classes twice a week and quite enjoyed them as it gave me a chance to meet new people.

After two months in London I was quite lonely. I knew very few people other than those I worked with. I eventually found a pub in Twickenham called the Swan. It was there I met a great Irish ballad singer called Donal Warren. One evening Donal asked me to sing a song. I was a little hesitant at first but then threw caution to the wind and sang a good Irish ballad. Donal was stunned and the crowd seemed to really enjoy my performance. It was then that I first thought that maybe I should consider singing as a career. This thought never left me from that moment onward.

One evening while I was there, two other people decided to sing. They were superb and afterward I met with both of them. They invited me to join their choral group, the Orchard Singers. Chris, Annie, and I became good friends. We would meet socially every Wednesday night. There were more women in the group than men. One girl particularly had my interest. She was from Holland and lived on a boat on the Thames. The boat was a great means for both of us to have a good time as we particularly enjoyed sailing up the River Thames, having a bottle of wine, and occasionally singing under the bridges along the route.

After a few weeks I became acquainted with the Hanger prosthetic design team, headed by Alan Wilcocks. They were involved with the design of a lightweight prosthesis and the development of a storage energy foot called the Quantum. This foot was designed to facilitate all ages of amputees in ambulation by helping them to have a springlike action in their foot. As I was at hand every day, some of my time was spent trying out prototypes of different feet that the boys would produce. Oftentimes, these feet wouldn't get past the first trial. Being totally active I would put quite a degree of stress on them. A lot of the time they would crumble even though they had already gone through a series of machine trials. The team also brought in feet from their competitors to examine what storage energy they had. I was always available for the trial of these before they stripped them down. When I came across a foot that had real potential, I advised Alan to order a pair. I would try them out and see if they would last for me. I also had a second motive for getting these products: I was still competing in sports. I realized that if I had the facility of storage energy in my feet, it would give me more power and flexibility in both track and field events. I really enjoyed working with the design team because they were full of ideas and they always respected what little contributions I made to their designs.

By the end of my first year I was made Area Manager for Europe. At that stage I was working in a different country in Europe every month. It was fantastic as I made many new friends from my travels, and more important, brought in quite an amount of revenue for the company. I had a superb working relationship with Chris and with Paul Jamerson, who was the Area Manager for the Far East and Malaysia. Paul was an exceptional man in every way and highly intelligent.

After a year, I set about buying my first apartment. I found a beautiful two-bedroom maisonette in Ham just outside Richmond, which was valued at 38,000 pounds. It was quite a lot of money for me at the time. With the help of the company and a small contribution from Dad, I was able to put down a deposit. It was Tudor in style and in dreadful repair, but that didn't bother me. I was so delighted to own my first home. I set about doing all the repainting myself. I decided white, being a neutral color, would be the best for all the walls. But my main priority was to have a functional toilet and shower and to have a working kitchen. I spent most of my weekends for about six weeks doing up the house. I moved into it fully on the twenty-third of May 1986. I was well pleased with myself. I never really got to know my neighbors, as I was away so much. Most of the population living around me were older. So as you can imagine, it was a quiet area.

I invited Dad and Mam over to stay for a holiday. When they saw how well I was doing they were delighted, especially Dad, who must have thought I had won the lotto. They stayed for a few days and I brought them to see a West End show and dined out at different restaurants. It appeared like a second honeymoon for them. Dad warned me not to be too hasty about getting involved with a woman for if she saw this little haven she might get very fond of it. I laughed and said not to bother his head with such stupid thoughts. They were very happy to see that the job was working out well, but little did they know that, as usual, my mind had already moved on to the next challenge.

When they were leaving Dad gave me a hug and said, "You have a lovely home and a good job; what more could a man want?" Mam said she would love to live with me, as she started to reminisce about the time she had spent as a teacher living in Wales. At that point I encouraged them to go as they had a long drive ahead of them to the car ferry.

I joined a fitness club in Ealing as I was training for the World Championships, which were being held in Sweden that year. I had been working out nearly every evening after work and was really getting into good condition. I trained at the physical education college in Strawberry Hill for my track and field events. I was constantly trying out different feet I had borrowed from Hanger to see which would give the optimum performance. Prior to the arrival of the storage energy concept there was nothing on the market for athletes. Hanger's foot was still not able to cope with the rigorous demands I was making on it, so I had to look elsewhere for a performance foot. The most important aspect of any limb is the socket. If this isn't right, you can forget about everything else because you won't be able to use the limb in the first instant. I was lucky to have several good prosthetists working with me in the company who were also very interested in sport, thus I was nearly always guaranteed a good-fitting limb.

The championships were held in June 1986. The company decided to send me to Sweden at that time, which was a blessing because it meant that I was able to save money on the flight. I had suggested to Chris that I visit Bengt Rangstrom, the president of Centri, a prosthetics manufacturer in Sweden. He lived in Upsala, Sweden, and Hanger had previously worked with him. But owing to poor service over the past years, liaisons with Centri had fallen afoul. I made arrangements to meet with Bengt during the games to try and rekindle the relationship and to see if I could get him interested in Hanger products again. Chris also wanted me to see some of the German distributors in the upper part of Germany, which was on my way. I took the car ferry and left a week before the games. I started from Dover to Ostende and then began the long haul to the top of Germany then up to Sweden. I arrived in Stockholm at the end of the week, having made three visits to different distributors in Germany along the way. I received a healthy order from one of the distributors, which was quite an achievement as I was in the home of Ottobock, the largest manufacturer of prosthetic components in the world. A phone call to Chris to relay the good news of my exploits and then I was finished except for meeting with Bengt from Centri. Bengt and I eventually met up in Stockholm and instantly became good friends. This business relationship was to prosper for all my working time with Hanger, and we have remained good friends to this day.

I arrived at the games feeling very confident as I had brought with me two storage energy feet and if everything came together during the competition, I would be very difficult to beat. The opening ceremony was fantastic. It was a display of gymnasts and acrobats performing unbelievable routines. I was now very familiar with competing on the European circuit. I had many friends from different countries all over Europe. I got along great with the German and Israeli competitors, among others. The German coach, Heinz Gulich, would even give me some coaching tips when he would be out coaching his own athletes.

Heinz unfortunately passed away as a result of a massive heart attack six weeks after the games. I was very sad, as I'm sure that all the German team was. I also became great friends with one of the German team members, Eirhart Engel from Duisburg. On several of my trips to Germany, I stayed with Eirhart and his wife, Wilma, rather than in a hotel.

The first event was the discus and I had every intention of winning; I figured that the discus was my best shot at setting a new world record. But just minutes before it was my turn to throw, one of my feet broke across the middle. Naturally, I didn't have a spare, so I thought I was through. I glanced around at all of the other athletes in the competition and tried to identify which one of them had a similar foot to the one I was wearing. As luck would have it, I found a pretty close match on the Canadian. I hadn't a clue as to the size of his foot, but that didn't matter, for all I needed was a base underneath my leg. So I asked him a question you would only hear at a Paralympics. "Could I borrow your foot for the competition? I'll give it back to you as soon as I finish my throw." To my amazement and delight, he willingly gave me his foot. As I always carry a spare set of Allen keys, we removed the feet in breakneck time from our limbs. I stood up and knew straight away his foot was different. It had tremendous energy and bounce. I needed to make the appropriate adjustments for myself to allow for the extra energy that was in the foot.

My first throw was at a stand and even then I threw two meters farther than I had ever thrown before. I was elated, for with this throw, I knew I would qualify automatically for the final. This gave me a chance to experiment with my next throws and make some real demands on the foot. All I could think of was if only I had two of these feet I could throw the discus where I could never be beaten. The Canadian watched in awe at my throwing technique and asked me if I would coach him after the competition. I replied that it would be my greatest pleasure to help him in any way I could to repay his wonderful generosity. Having said this, he produced a corresponding right foot to match the left he had already given me. I was over the moon and quickly changed the other foot. On my fourth throw it all came together. I threw nearly fifteen meters farther than any other competitor had ever thrown. It was unbelievable. It also shocked the rest of the competition.

For the first time in my sporting life, I was asked to do a drug test. I couldn't wait to perform this simple act. For years I had read and watched how all the major able-bodied athletes of the world were drug-tested following their competitions. It was as if this simple act somehow legitimized my achievement. I was finally being taken seriously as a competitive athlete. Needless to say, I was clean. I won the competition outright and received the gold medal. I also broke the world record, which I already held, by a huge distance. My Canadian friend benefited because beginning the following day I coached him for at least an hour a day for the duration of the games. He improved significantly. We lost contact so I have no idea how he fared after his visit to Sweden.

My next competition was the shot put, which I also won, setting another world record in the process. I competed in the hundred-meter sprint, running the fastest time I had run in my life, 13.6 seconds. I was on cloud nine, maybe even ten, and all on a borrowed set of Seattle Feet. My final competition was the long jump. I counted twenty strides from the take-off mark and then went five strides over my original mark. To say I felt like a jet going down a runway was an understatement. It was an incredible feeling. I hit the board and was cata-pulted spread-eagled into the air. I landed unceremoniously on my behind. I had jumped 5.63 meters and was ecstatic. I didn't place in the final as this competition was open to all levels of amputees.

By the end of the games I had broken four world records for my cat-egory. The next day, the headline of the daily Swedish newspaper read, RONAN THE BARBAR. When I reminisce about these events, I still smile to myself.

While I was returning home, I had a brainstorm. I decided to use the photograph, which the press had taken of me performing the long jump, as the cover photo for Hanger's component catalog. I felt this demonstrated the strength and durability of the components I was using underneath the socket of the prosthesis. I presented this to Chris, who thought it was a great idea.

I thought I would receive special recognition for this and felt sure I would receive some remuneration for my photograph. But this didn't happen as company policy gave Hanger the right to use any aspect of your work while you were in their employment. Without sounding too ungrateful, I felt that I generated quite a sizable revenue for the company. As I weighed well over two hundred pounds this gave a great endorse-ment to the strength of the components for active amputee users.

Toward the end of 1986, I had already decided to apply to medical schools both in Ireland and England. I had been accepted in one of the medical schools in England, but I was holding out for my interview at Trinity College in Dublin. To be honest, I couldn't wait for the inter-view to arrive, for I was very keen to get back home. I also decided that I had reached the end of my days with Hanger. Thinking back, I'm sure it had something to do with my annoyance over the photograph and the advertising campaign.

I flew over to Ireland for the interview. I wasn't sure how many candidates were vying for the coveted two places. All I knew was that I wanted a place like nothing else in the world. When I walked into the massive Victorian room, there were eight professors facing me on the interviewing panel. I was astonished to say the least, and was very nervous. I introduced myself to the panel from Professor Maire O'Brien of Anatomy, whom I knew from sports assessments prior to the Olympics, to Professor Bonner of Ob/Gyn. Professor O'Brien treated me wonderfully and gave a glowing account of my sports achievements to the panel.

I can still hear Professor Bonner saying, "When chronologically did you decide to study medicine?" I was a little surprised at the question. For the first time I found myself really having to think about exactly when I had made my mind up; my whole life flashed before me, as I thought from my childhood dreams about being a doctor. Finally, I hastened to Dr. Childer's lecture and realized that it was that exact time that I had the strongest conviction about medicine. So, I responded to Professor Bonner, "1986." To which he replied, "As recent as that?" I felt obliged to say, "That was when I felt mature enough to make the decision." There were many other questions on different areas relating to work, academic record, and experience looking after the sick. I handled these questions well but what I can remember was that my shirt was stuck to my back with perspiration. The interview lasted nearly forty minutes and I was really relieved when it was over. I had done the best I could. I had no idea what they thought of me and at that particular moment, I didn't much care. Something inside gave me the feeling I had been successful.

On the fifth of August I received a letter from the Admissions Department of Trinity saying I had been accepted for the following semester. My first task was to inform Hanger that I was leaving. Chris was disappointed. He appeared quite skeptical and wasn't sure if I was going to study medicine or work for their competitor Ottobock. I told him not to have any concerns regarding that issue. I had no intention of working for any other prosthetic company.

The next person I phoned was Fiona. She was shell-shocked, but that was nothing to how Dad reacted when I told him. I explained to him that I needed to get out of London, as the job was giving me no fulfillment. Dad viewed it differently. He felt I had attained independence and security with this job and that I was throwing it all away to follow a dream. Then he finally blurted out, "You're not an academic. You'll never stick with all the study." This was the first time Dad had ever openly said that he felt that I couldn't achieve something. I knew it was said out of concern. Mam on the other hand was delighted and felt that the job in London was leading nowhere for me. Dad wasn't so happy about her reasoning but they both unconditionally supported my decision.

* CHAPTER 14 *

When I think back on those two years I really was very fortunate for I had seen nearly every country in Europe and made some fantastic friends.

One of my fondest memories was working in Copenhagen that summer as an export area manager for Hanger. On July 26 Fiona was back in Ireland in the throes of labor. When I finished my meetings, I went to have a meal by the river with my colleagues. It was a beautiful summer evening, but all I was thinking about was Fiona. At about 10 P.M. my brother-in-law Pat phoned me with the news that I was now an uncle. Fiona and my new niece Shonagh were both doing well. We toasted both mother and daughter till the early hours. I could hardly speak the next day.

On the fifth of October I sold my house in England and made a good profit on the sale. I had worked out that I had enough money to put myself through college for four years without having to worry. I got myself a flat on South Circular Road in Dublin. As I had to sell my car, Dad brought me up to Dublin with a bicycle in the trunk of the car for my transport. We had a great discussion on our way to Dublin. He told me he was glad I was back home and hoped that he would see me come out the other end of these six years as a doctor. He said he'd bow down. We both laughed. When we finally moved everything into the apartment, we drove down to see Trinity College. I knew he was very proud of me despite his concern. He looked around and said, "What a wonderful seat of learning we have in this country." On leaving for home, he gave me two hundred pounds and said, "I know it's nowhere near enough, but it will help contribute to some book payments." "Every little bit helps," I said. I told him I was set for four years and after that I'd come knocking on the door for help, but I really had no intention of asking him because he had done so much for me in the past.

The following morning I got up at seven. I was like a first-year student starting all over again, a second bite of the apple so to speak. As I made my way through the traffic on my bicycle, I began to daydream what it would be like after my first year, my second year . . . I never got beyond the second year as I was quickly brought back to reality when I was blasted off the road by a taxi driver. After that frightful start, I entered through the great archway with pride, making a silent prayer to God that I not leave Trinity College until I had six years completed. Just at that moment a small, burly chap wearing a multicolored sweater and walking on the edge of his shoes strolled past. I smiled to myself and hoped that for some odd reason he would be studying medicine. I watched carefully where he was going, as he seemed to be heading in the direction of the science block. He went out of sight, so I paid no heed, as I was too preoccupied in getting to the induction course for medicine. When I arrived into the lecture theater, there was the same chap larger than life sitting in the front row of the lecture. I sat down beside him and asked if he was doing medicine. He replied that he was. As quick as lightning, he also said, "You're a little older than us." I laughed and said, "You'll get no marks for that observation." We both laughed and introduced ourselves. His name was Keith Synott and from that moment on Keith and I became the best of friends. By the end of the first week, both of us had teamed up with four or five others like ourselves: Liam from Cork, Mick from Mullingar, Alan from Mayo, Dave from Galway, and a few others. We went to the Pavilion Bar and had more than a couple of pints.

Two months into the course, Liam and I got a flat together. It worked out really well. He lived in the bottom section and I lived in the top. By Christmas of my first year, I knew I had made the right decision. I was never happier. I was working very hard and attending every lecture. Professor Brown was our chemistry lecturer. He used to constantly remind me to go to the Legion of Mary to meet girls of my age, as this was how he met his darling wife. He would refer to me as "Man Mountain," to the amusement of the class.

There were seventy-two students in the class, but we knew not all of us would make it through the first year. This scared the living daylights out of me. But like everything else I had done up to then, I was determined not to fail. The first year's exams commenced in May. They were extremely tough and I was a little nervous waiting for the results. Then I received a call from Bengt Rangstrom in Sweden, asking me to come to the ISPO (International Symposium of Prosthetics and Orthotics) conference in Oslo for three days. I accepted and the results of my exams came out on the second day of my trip. I had arranged with Keith's mother to get my results. At 7 P.M. I rang, and she held me in suspense for five minutes talking about my trip to Oslo and other insignificant things. I just had to stop her and beg her to tell me the outcome. "Oh yes," she said, "the results. All your buddies passed . . . as did you. They're planning a major celebration on your return." Unaccustomed as I was to celebrating, I decided to have a rehearsal.

The final term of first year was taken up with Anatomy. This is where I met Professor Maire O'Brien for the first time since my interview. She asked me how my exams had gone. I was delighted to be able to tell her I had been successful. She responded with a smile. "You're on the way, but remember the tougher areas have yet to be faced." I realized this, but I still decided to have a little fun, as I was sure there wouldn't be too many opportunities later in the course.

As the third term progressed I became more of a social animal. It was during this period that I met a really nice girl who was studying pharmacy. We met in the Berkley Library. It started off with a simple coffee break and from there we went into a raging romance. I have to say I was walking on air. We went everywhere together and had a fabulous time doing so. However, there was a fly in the ointment of this relationship: her father. He was extremely protective of her, as I'm sure all dads are of their daughters. I had already gotten a job in the U.K. for the summer. I was leaving on the first of June. She decided that she also wanted to work in London, so she could be with me. This move did not please her father. Eventually he decided to visit us, even though we were living in separate accommodations, quite a distance apart from each other. But he seemed overly concerned about us. I reassured him that we were fine and would keep our heads. That was enough to keep him content, but unfortunately our romance didn't survive the summer.

One of my first stops on my return to London was the Swan Pub in Twickenham. Everything about the pub was still the same, and more important, my favorite buxom barmaid was still serving. Naturally when she saw me she gave me a big kiss, which annoyed my girlfriend to no end. But I had to explain to her that that was the type of woman she was, full of affection and loving to express herself physically. During that summer, I was training for the Olympics in Korea, and once again returned to the gym in Scoops in Ealing. I also returned to Strawberry Hill for training in track and field.

I realized that it was going to be quite expensive to travel to Korea despite the fact that the IWA was paying for the tickets. I also needed a new pair of limbs at least six weeks before the competition. I had made good friends with an American prosthetist named Jim McInneny at the World Championships in Sweden. He was also an athlete. Jim offered me a set of limbs back then if I could manage to get to his home in Nashville. He was working with this new Flex Foot and claimed it was the way forward in prosthetics particularly for those people interested in sports. It had major potential as it was made of carbon fiber. This material is known for its capacity to store energy. The more demands made on it, the greater it enhances the performance of the athlete.

I wrote to Virgin Airways for an airline ticket and Shell for sponsorship for the trip expenses. I was successful on both counts. I planned my trip for August so I could also put in some training with Jim while I was there. Everything worked out according to plan. I stayed three weeks in total with Jim and returned to Ireland in late September with a new pair of limbs built to conquer the sports world. Within three days I flew to Seoul, South Korea, with the Irish Paralympic team. The trip took nearly twenty-three hours in total and we were all exhausted after the journey. We all desperately needed a much-earned rest.

The opening ceremony was two days after our arrival. We were dressed in the Irish uniforms that were issued to us, the lads in beige trousers and green jackets with a white cotton shirt and green tie, the ladies in green suits with a beige scarf.

The ceremony was the most spectacular of all the games I had ever seen. It was held late in the evening, which meant that all the dancers carried torches while they danced in a dragonlike style. The whole event was full of mystique and intrigue, culminating in a massive fireworks display that must have lasted over an hour.

I had about four days before I was to compete. One morning while I was out training with the javelin, I decided to work on my planting technique. Unfortunately, the spike of my shoe got caught in the ground. My foot stayed in one position and my knee rotated. I fell down like a sack of spuds, roaring in pain. Luckily for me, some of the American athletes were training at the same time. One of their physiotherapists came over immediately to help me. I felt that it was a ligament tear and he agreed. I was brought immediately to the physio department that had been set up in the Olympic campus and the American worked on me for a good two hours with a combination of ultrasound and heat and ice therapy.

My first competition was the shot put. The physio strapped my knee up so that I was unable to bend or rotate it. Throughout the entire competition I was only able to perform standing throws. I was beaten by 0.10 cm in distance with the last throw, losing the gold medal to the German. It was the first time in six years that I didn't win the gold in the shot put. I was disappointed but at the same time very happy with the result considering what I had to work with.

Every night there was entertainment in the Olympic Village. After the shot put, I had a week off before my next competition. I decided to go out with some of the wilder members of the team. One notable character, Jerry Dunn, was from Dublin, and was a swimmer on our team. We arrived at the hospitality tent, where there was a brass band playing a lot of Gershwin music. I had been known by the Irish team to sing "Summertime" from *Porgy and Bess*. Unknown to me, Jerry had approached the bandleader and asked if they would let me sing. As I was sitting down and enjoying a drink, I heard my name being called out. I went up and asked if they could play "Summertime." The key suited perfectly and I launched into the song. Before long, the whole tent stopped talking and became very attentive. I was given rapturous applause and they screamed for me to sing more. To my amazement, the band knew "Danny Boy" and played it beautifully. I could have sung all night, but at that time my repertoire was very limited. When I returned to my seat, I was on a high. Somewhere deep in my heart I felt a major pull toward performing and the immense satisfaction that one attains from it.

Jerry swam in the one-hundred-meter freestyle and the two-hundred-meter backstroke and even though he made both finals, he didn't place. By this time, Jerry and I had become superb friends.

As the twenty athletes from all parts of the world entered the great hallowed walls of the powerful Seoul Olympic Stadium in Korea my heart was pounding with excitement and the adrenaline was surging around my body like lightning. I had been having extensive physical therapy for the torn ligament in my right knee, but now my moment had arrived. The knee was well on the road to being fully workable. The discus final beckoned, my last opportunity to win an Olympic gold medal.

My mind was focused. At 8 o'clock on that beautiful warm evening, the lights of the stadium were resplendent, plowing out their rays of light all over the massive field. Every corner and crevice were highlighted. I was so engrossed in my surroundings that I became completely oblivious to the tumultuous applause of the crowd. When I came back to the reality of the situation, I was being introduced: "Tynan, Ronan, Ireland."

The Irish contingent, though small in number, had confined themselves to the right corner of the athletic stadium at the back of the discus-throwing area. They made a whale of a noise when they heard my name. Anyone would have thought I had paid them, such was the power and enthusiasm of their support. I was the fifth to throw. I had watched all the competitors in the warm-up area prepare. Even though

I was quietly confident, I was only too well aware that no matter how well I felt, with one imbalance it would be gone.

I put on my well-worn red discus shoes and tied the white laces tightly as I had done so many times before. I was quite nervous and just at that moment I placed my hands on my head and asked God and my twin, Edmond, to help me perform to the best of my ability.

When my turn came I walked slowly into the discus area. It was surrounded by a half-moon rope net to protect the spectators, just in case some athlete had the misfortune to release the discus prematurely. I stood in the circle and gazed out at the field and the white lines that marked out the distances beyond forty meters. I never felt so focused in all my life. I could feel every muscle in my body prepare for the demands I was about to make on them.

As I turned and took my position at the back of the circle, I could hear Bernie, my old coach, saying, "Keep your center of gravity low and drive slowly through the initial stage of the turn. Keep your arm back and drive forward with your hips—wait, wait, wait."

I felt like poetry in slow motion. When I finally released the discus it flew like a dream; its angle of trajectory was spot on. I gave a loud roar after I released the discus, expending every last bit of emotional energy that was inside of me. It all seemed so easy. Eight years of training poured into thirty seconds of glory. My eyes followed the flying saucer's flight. I knew even before it had left my hand it was the business. It came down beyond the forty-meter mark. The crowd roared with elation. At that moment I was stunned into silence, just awestruck. On that glorious night on my very first throw I broke my world record, which I had previously set at the World Championships in Gothenburg, Sweden. By the end of the six throws I had broken that record five more times and beaten my nearest rival by nearly fifteen meters.

I turned to the crowd and thanked them. Not only the Irish but all the spectators cheered and applauded. I was overcome with emotion and tried very hard to conceal my tears of joy and elation. It was overwhelming to realize in such a short period of time that all the work I had done over the years had paid off.

I was immediately escorted to the drug-checking area to give a sample of my urine. I had nothing to fear, but the officials were adamant that I couldn't have excelled to such a level without the help of an anabolic steroid. The tests positively proved that I had won on nothing but my own hard work and determination. At 10 o'clock in the twilight of the evening, the medal ceremony took place amid the splendid colors of the world's flags.

The three athletes from China, Germany, and, of course, Ireland walked to the victory podium. I was positioned in the middle of the two. The bronze medal went to China and the silver medallist was my old friend Hubert from West Germany.

When I stepped onto the podium, the gold medal was placed around my neck. I was thrilled. It was the answer to my prayers, all the birthdays rolled into one. As I watched the Irish flag being raised and heard the National Anthem played, I felt a tremendous sense of pride at being an Irishman. I wished more than anything that Dad were here to see the whole spectacle. I recalled how Dad used to say, "To see the Irish flag flying high is such a great honor." Although I had won many medals in the past, this one meant so much more than any of the others. I knew everything was right. Everyone I had called upon to help had turned trumps. This gold medal was not just for me. It was for everyone who had willed me to succeed.

I tried to hold back my tears of joy but I couldn't. I cried like a child but it didn't matter for this day I would remember for the rest of my life.

That night Jerry and I did some serious celebrating and were no better for wear the next morning. My final competition was the javelin. This had never been my best event but having had such success in the discus I was on a high and managed to eventually take the bronze medal.

I returned to college at the start of November having missed the first month. As I entered the lecture theater the class gave me a standing ovation. Then Keith got up to speak, which of course surprised me. His praise of my achievements embarrassed me and then to my astonishment he presented me with a silver tankard that all the class had contributed to. I was overwhelmed at their wonderful gesture.

As it was a Friday, at least fifty of the class went to the Pavilion Bar to celebrate and more important to drink out of the silver mug! We drank into the late hours by which time I had given several renditions of rugby songs that were certainly not for sensitive ears!

By now I had a serious reputation in the Pavilion Bar for singing and the more frequently I visited the bar the greater was the demand for me to sing. I now like to think that I went to the Pavilion primarily to work on my singing and that the pints were simply a by-product of my fledgling act. It's a good story and I'm going to stick to it. Trinity College also gave me a crystal bowl with three bands of gold, silver, and bronze and bestowed on me the honor of my Pinks, which is an award given to students who have excelled in sport. The president of the Sports Association, Trevor West, organized this.

There was also an elite sports fraternity for men in college called the Knights of the Campanile. This is the oldest fraternity in Trinity. To become a member one had to distinguish themselves in sport and also be known as a social character. I obviously fulfilled the criteria and was made a knight in November 1988. I realized that Trinity was very proud of me and this highlighted even more how little Thomond College thought of my achievements in 1984.

Keith and other members of the class brought me up to date on the lectures I had missed. By Christmas I was up to speed. Thankfully all my exams went well, which made my trip to Korea all the more sweet. At this time I was living in rooms in Trinity, which was really very convenient as it saved me a huge amount of traveling through the city. I went home to see Ralph and Theresa and we had a ball that Christmas. Theresa was very proud of me because I had passed my exams, thus proving that I was capable of the discipline needed to study. I returned to college on January 8, 1989, fully committed to the job at hand. Theresa wrote to me quite a lot while I was in college. As it was the lambing season, her descriptive accounts of ewes lying on their backs unable to turn over because of their size were wonderful. She wrote,

"They lie on their backs invoking the gods with their four legs, thrashing furiously, begging to be relieved." I often said to her that she should write a book as she had a wonderful ability with the English language. She always was concerned for my health and worried that I wasn't eating properly. There was never a worry of that!

I would normally get one letter a week from her giving me all the gossip but on the week commencing January 19 I never received one. I was a little surprised, but thought no more of it at the time. On Saturday morning at 2 o'clock, Mike O'Sullivan, the head porter, came to my room. He had to knock frantically on my door to wake me up. I was immediately concerned as no one calls at that hour. Mike told me that someone belonging to me was seriously ill in Beaumont Hospital. My first thought was that it was Tom but when I got to the phone it was Ralph crying, "I'm losing her." I immediately got in a taxi and went out to Beaumont.

Theresa was in Intensive Care in the Neurological Ward. As I arrived I was met by Ralph, who relayed the whole story to me in detail. Theresa had become ill on the Friday of the previous week with a severe headache and intermittent vomiting. Ralph took her to the local county hospital in Kilkenny. They diagnosed a subarachnoid hemorrhage, but unfortunately they weren't equipped to deal with such an emergency. Ralph decided not to ring me so as I wouldn't worry about her. The saddest part of all was Theresa never regained consciousness and I didn't get the chance to say good-bye to my dearest friend.

The funeral was held in Muckalee in her home parish. There was a huge turnout as all the parents and children were present. I managed to sing "Abide with Me" but inside I felt my world had fallen apart. I had lost a person I really loved. Dad understood only too well how much Theresa had meant to me and was very sad for me. He said that it was important for me to grieve and that only time would help ease the pain I was feeling. Theresa was very fond of Dad and often told me that she felt he was a special person.

When Ralph and I returned to the house it seemed so empty. My heart went out to him as I knew he was confronting the harsh reality that he would never have Theresa to come home to again.

Time went by and before I knew it, I was in the middle of my exams. Then came the start of my third year and I was on my way to my clinical years. I was really looking forward to this, as it would be my first opportunity to meet and examine patients.

At the start of my clinical year I was made president of the Knights of the Campanile. Keith was made secretary and we decided that we would really try to improve the status and reputation of the knights. We arranged the annual cocktail party, but made it a formal occasion and charged ten pounds for admission. It was a great success. For the first time in years we put the account into the black and had fun doing it. I became much more active socially that year and also became class representative. This position gave me the responsibility to represent the student body of the class if there were any problems with courses or with the professors themselves.

Prior to entering the clinics all the class had to select where we wanted to train. All of our group decided to go to the Meath Hospital, mainly because it was relatively small. More important, as a group we got on extremely well.

I also became great friends with two other girls in the class, Debbie and Deirdre McNamara. While they both had the same surname, they were not related. I really admired Deb as she used to work in restaurants to pay for her school expenses but was still able to keep her position among the top five in the class. Deirdre was similar to Debbie both academically and socially. I attribute my return to riding to Dee, as we used to go horseback riding every Saturday. Our rides were followed by a quick trip to the pub for a few pints and a chat about life.

I had only one worry starting my clinical years: Would my limbs stand up to the rigors of walking around the wards and the late nights without resting? I made up my mind that I would cross that bridge when I got to it.

CHAPTER 15

I had now started studying social and forensic medicine. This finally gave me some time free to look into other matters, so I set about finding out where I could have singing lessons. I decided to visit all of the music academies in Dublin, which at that time consisted of two: the Royal Irish Academy, and the College of Music in Adelaide Road. My first port of call was the Royal Academy. I didn't get past the reception desk, for I was told, "To apply to this academy for the academic year, you must have made your application a year in advance, then be called for an interview. Subsequently, a place will be offered if you have satisfied the board." I explained that I needed to start straightaway. The receptionist looked at me with disdain. "I'm sorry, you're too late, and possibly too old!" Never one to be told I can't do something, I retorted, "Get used to seeing this face. You'll be paying to see me perform as I'll make it in music some day." Quickly putting that rejection behind me, I headed off to the College of Music in Adelaide Road. As I got out of my car, I could hear a young girl singing scales from the second-floor window. Something told me that this was it. Once again, I went to the reception desk and asked for an application form for the upcoming year. Once again, I was told, "We're sorry, all applications have been closed for the current academic year. Please put in your application next year."

I knew that if I could get to the second floor and meet the singing teacher, I might have some chance of putting forward my case. There were a lot of people milling about in the foyer. While no one was looking, I sneaked into the elevator and went up to the second floor. The doors opened across from the room where the girl was singing. From this proximity, the sound was far from pleasing and I could only assume that she was a beginner. As brazen as one could be, I knocked on the door. Quite quickly the singing stopped and I was greeted by a very splendiferous lady. She asked quite calmly, "Are you here for an audition, lovey?" For the first time in my life, my brain kicked in before I opened my mouth. I answered in the affirmative. She then inquired as to where I was from. I told her that I hailed from Kilkenny. She turned and said to the young lady, who also happened to be auditioning, "Would you mind, darling, leaving the room while I audition this young man, as he has come a long distance, and has to catch a train." She had made this last part up and I was delighted at her creativity.

She then proceeded to bring me over to the grand piano and asked me what I would like to sing. I had no music with me. All I knew were Irish ballads, and bits and pieces of songs that I had learned from Mario Lanza tapes. She said, "Never mind, darling, we will do some scales." She started at middle "C" and just kept playing up the scale waiting for me to hit my top limit. To her amazement, I was able to reach a top "C" and then some. She paused. "I have one place left and I will give it to you, darling. Now tell me," she said, "what level of musicianship have you?" I thought that this would be a stumbling block, so I answered that I had covered some grades. She looked at me straight in the eye. "Now, darling, at what level are you, really?" I held my head down and recalled what my father used to say, "Tell the truth, and you'll never be caught out." I responded, "When I was small, I took some piano lessons, but as far as theory of music goes, there is a major vacuum." She gave a great laugh. "We'll put you into prison. You must enroll in the theory class that is run in the college every Tuesday night." I responded with delight, "I surely will!"

She then said, "By the way, lovey, what age are you?" "I'm thirty-two. I suppose I'm too old?" I replied. "Not at all! A good tenor only matures when he's forty. At least all the ones that I've sung with. What have you worked at up to now?" she then asked. I told her that I was in my fifth year of medical school. She smiled and said that I wasn't her first medical student. She also had a fifth-year medical student from the College of Surgeons who was a very fine bass. "You will have two lessons every week, starting at eight o'clock in the morning." I thought this was fantastic. It added a purpose to getting up early in the morning, and I used to love going in to see her and doing all of the vocalizing from "Lilly, lally" to "Sadie" to "Me-ma-me-ma-mo."

This wonderful lady, under whom I had the great fortune to study, was Dr. Veronica Dunn. She was a renowned operatic soprano who had sung all over the world. She had a tremendous reputation both as an opera singer and a teacher.

In the meantime, I hadn't been neglecting my medicine. Having to divide the precious time I had carefully between medicine and singing focused my mind and brought a discipline to my life that I hadn't really needed before.

I returned home three weeks later for a weekend. I told Dad of my great fortune. Amazingly, he had heard of Dr. Dunn and said that I was very fortunate to have such a great woman take an interest in me. "There must be something to this voice—well, there is no doubt in my mind where you got this talent from," he said. When we discussed Veronica's career he amazed me with how much he knew about her. He then told me that years ago, when he was very young, he had sung for a German man called Herr Hoos, a master singer from Munich. He was visiting Ireland at the time giving master classes and also looking at the Irish educational system for teaching music. Herr Hoos knew the celebrated Irish tenor Count John McCormack and acclaimed him as one of the greatest tenors in the world.

When Dad sang for Herr Hoos, the verdict was amazing. He wanted to take Dad to Germany to study with him at one of the conservatories on full scholarship. Hoos even approached my grandfather to ask for permission. Unfortunately for my father the request was denied. Dad was needed to work on the farm. Singing was certainly not considered a viable profession by the farming community in Kilkenny when I started and it was less valued in my father's day. I sensed a tone of melancholy as Dad reminisced about this lost opportunity, but he had never been one to cause trouble or go against the will of his father. I got the feeling that Dad was going to relive some of his singing aspirations through me.

In November 1991, I went in for my usual lesson on a Monday

morning. Veronica, known affectionately to her students as Ronnie, showed me the curriculum for the national singing festival, known as *Feis Ceoil*. The Tenor section required the singer to present two songs. The first was a prescribed piece "Now Sleeps the Crimson Petal" by Quilter. The second was your own choice of Irish song. She chose "Moya My Girl" by Vaughan. She told me, "Lovey, I don't think that you will be totally ready for this, but it would be a good experience for you to sing in public for a more distinguished, critical audience." I responded confidently, "I'll win the Tenor section of this competition! Wait till you see." She laughed. "There's no holding you back." "That's right," I said. I learned the "Crimson Petal" within a week. For several lessons, Ronnie hammered the melody on the piano while I equally bashed out until she felt I had a handle not only on the notes but on the interpretation as well. I knew that "Moya My Girl" was a good song for me as soon as we started to work on it. It gave me a full range to go through. It also showed the expressive quality of my voice.

The competition is always held during the month of March, just prior to the Easter break. Hundreds of singers from all parts of Ireland enter this competition. All of Ronnie's students took part. There was no doubt in my mind that Ronnie had some fantastic singers studying with her. Quite quickly we all knew each other. She also set up a little opera studio where we were given different roles, singing and staging various opera excerpts for different corporate functions.

I became great friends with Miriam, who was a phenomenal young mezzo-soprano from Kerry; Marie Hagerty from Roscommon; Cora Newman, a beautiful contralto from Dublin; Aran Maree, the bass who was a fifth-year medical student like myself; a young soprano from Wexford called Deirdre Masterson, who had amazing potential at the tender age of sixteen; and a baritone called Nial Wolf, who had the most wonderful timbre in his voice. There was no apparent rivalry among us. Each of us respected and encouraged the other's talent.

Meanwhile, I had completed my social medicine rotation by December and subsequently did my three weeks' clinical practice in January 1992 in a little village in County Meath. I really enjoyed this time, as it showed me the full experience of being a general practitioner in a community setting. I started my pediatric rotation in February at the Children's Hospital on Harcourt Street. This was a two-month residency, which also brought me great satisfaction. I enjoyed playing with the children as much as Patch Adams. On several occasions, I was found acting the clown with them.

During that time, I did a lot of work with children who had cystic fibrosis. This disease mainly affects the lungs, but also has detrimental effects on the entire system. It often leads to a child requiring lung and heart transplant surgery. I learned so much from the children with their wonderful, positive nature. I was also impressed by the tremendous strength with which their parents supported them, irrespective of the outcome. I grew to respect and admire both the parents and children. I vowed then that I would always maintain sensitivity toward any individual who needed help. As a result of my experiences with very sick and terminally ill patients, I learned how fortunate I was, despite being physically challenged. I realized that I could lead a perfectly normal life, whereas most of the people that I encountered here would never be able to survive for any substantial period without full-time medical assistance. This also helped to form the emotional subtext of my song interpretations, for I believe that only one who has seen such hardship and sorrow can bring it to his art.

Prior to the main *Feis Ceoil* in Dublin, I decided to enter one of the smaller singing competitions in Arklow, County Wicklow. I entered the Tenor section, the Moore's Melody section, and the Light Opera section in order to get as much experience singing in front of a jury as possible. I drove down with one of my friends from class, Catherine Harden, who lived in Wicklow at the time. I brought her down for moral support. She was not only a beautiful woman but also a lovely person. Her ear was unparalleled and I could count on her opinion, which I knew wouldn't spare me but wouldn't be uncharitable.

My first competition was the tenor solo. Coincidentally, the same piece of music was required as for the *Feis Ceoil*: "Now Sleeps the Crimson Petal." As I had already battered this song around several times a day for the last four months, I couldn't have been better prepared. Yet, when I was asked to perform it, I was as nervous as I had ever been. Luckily, after the first phrase of the song, my voice opened up. The truth was revealed to all: raw talent at its best, trying to be refined. The judge loved my performance, and after I had finished, came up to me and shook my hand, saying, "What a beautiful young voice!" I was delighted with myself and left on cloud nine full of confidence and determination to really let loose in the Light Opera section. I won the Tenor section. Two hours later, I came back to sing "You Are My Heart's Delight" from *The Land of Smiles* by Franz Lehár, in the Light Opera section. I also won in this category. Finally, I had to sing in the Moore's Melody section. The Moore's Melody is a competition in which all the songs are settings of Thomas Moore's poetry. I chose "She Is Far from the Land." The challenge here for me was stylistic more than anything. I had to bring down the power element and develop a parlor type of setting. Unfortunately I didn't execute this too well. Nevertheless, I was given second prize. All in all, it was a fantastic experience and I couldn't wait to tell Ronnie.

The following Monday, I returned triumphant and felt that I was Luciano Pavarotti. Ronnie was delighted for me but warned that the competition would be a lot keener in the *Feis Ceoil* and not to pin my hopes too high. I was a little taken aback by that. But determined as ever, I persevered. That Friday, at two o'clock, in one of the smaller rooms in the Royal Dublin Society, the Tenor section commenced. There were twenty-five tenors. The poor judge had to hear all of us sing the same song.

Two nights prior to the competition I went to hear another singing competition, which was being adjudicated by the same judge. The winner whom he chose had a fine, big voice that was still developing. He spoke, after he announced the winner, about her style and remarked, "If a singer has a big voice and is required to sing softly, they should start the selected piece at a slightly stronger dynamic, so that they can highlight the *piano* element of their voice when required without ever singing off the voice, or singing falsetto in a male." I kept this in mind, as I knew that this advice particularly applied to me.

Interestingly enough, this bore out in the competition. Several tenors started too softly and then had nowhere softer to go when the music required it, and sang falsetto. This did not appeal to the judge and they didn't make the final cut. When my turn came, I started at a fairly strong dynamic, which amazed a lot of the singers, as they felt that I was too strong. However, this allowed my *piano* to really shine through. I thought of Ronnie as I went to sing a particular phrase, ". . . slip into my bosom . . ." She always said, "Make the audience feel that you want them to slip into your bosom! Then you will have achieved the sentiment that Quilter wanted to convey." I'm not so sure about that, but one thing I do know: I made sure they felt the sincerity of my plea.

The judge announced the four finalists within ten minutes after the first round was completed. I was one of them. I knew that once I had gotten through to this stage, no one would be able to touch my interpretation of "Moya My Girl." I was last to sing and, boy, did I let it flow, enjoying every minute of it. Even the porters and the usherettes came in to hear it. I won the silver platter given as first prize, which automatically qualified me for the final of the John McCormack Cup, which would take place on the final day of the *Feis*. When I returned to the hospital the next day I told the lads how I had done. Rather than keep it quiet, John Caird announced my success to all in the lecture theater. He encouraged anyone who could to attend the final of the John McCormack Cup on the Friday of that week. I rang Dad, who said he would try to make it for the final but as he had cows calving it might be difficult. Fiona would definitely attend.

Ronnie wanted me to have at least two lessons before the competition, but I was nervous that I might just do too much and take the freshness out of my voice, so I stayed working in the clinic till five that evening. I then went over to the concert hall about an hour before the start to warm up.

The competition was to commence at 6:30 P.M. Having warmed up for about an hour, I decided to see if Fiona had arrived. When I went around to the side entrance of the concert hall, I could see her sitting down with about twenty of my classmates. I tried to sneak up behind so as not to cause any major disturbance in the concert hall. This competition is attended by many older people, who go purely for the enjoyment of the quality of music that's performed. I sat down beside Fiona. She grabbed my hand and said, "Are you not supposed to be backstage?" "No, there are two finals before the John McCormack final," I said. On hearing my voice, my friend Keith turned and said, "Hey, Ronie!" I told him to keep quiet, but I was too late, for all the boys started to chant, "Hey, Ronie!!!" On hearing this uproar, the judge turned around quite annoyed and asked us to quiet down. I tried to disappear under the seat out of embarrassment, and Fiona said, "There's your chance blown." After that episode, I left them straightaway.

I returned backstage to meet the other five competitors who were all warming up and very composed. I thought this calmness showed their far greater experience. At exactly six-thirty, the John McCormack final commenced. The basses sang first, followed by the baritones, and then finally the tenors. As I had been the winner of the tenor competition, I was the last to sing. It was customary to wear suitable attire for such a prestigious competition, and as they say, I wore my Sunday best. I was really nervous walking out onto the stage. As soon as I was in view of the public, the lads started chanting, "Hey, Ronie! Way to go, Ronie!" I smiled at them nervously. The judge stood up, turned around to face my rabble, and gave them a furious look. "It is extremely unprofessional to cause such a racket at this event. Could you please refrain from doing so until the competitor has finished his recital," he said. At that moment, I despaired quietly inside thinking that the judge knew that this crowd was with me and would judge me accordingly.

I had to sing the same two songs as in the tenor competition. I felt that during the "Crimson Petal," my voice wasn't as free as it had been. However, when I started singing "Moya My Girl," my voice opened up completely. I could be heard in the road outside the hall in

Ballsbridge. On completion, all the audience clapped furiously. I graciously bowed. After ten minutes' deliberation, the judge got up to talk about this particular competition. His comments were as follows: "This competition is not just for the polished singer, or for the singer with the best technique, or even for the singer with the best interpretation. It encompasses many facets of vocal ability. It is also about seeing which singer has the greatest potential, irrespective of whether they are polished, or whether they still need a lot of work. We have heard six fine singers this evening. All of them are at different levels of their training. But tonight, we have heard one singer with great heart, and a lot of potential. The winner of the John McCormack Cup for 1993 is Ronan Tynan. I can only assume from the uproar that I've heard throughout this competition that this gentleman will be a very popular winner with the audience." After his announcement the place went into a big uproar. I am sure that the Royal Dublin Society Concert Hall had never witnessed such an outburst in the past, nor will they see anything like it again anytime soon.

I was presented with the John McCormack Cup, and all twenty-five of us, including Fiona, went to the Ballsbridge Inn. We drank to John McCormack and each other. I rang Dad at about nine o'clock that night and told him the great news. As per usual, Dad was overcome and said that he was very proud.

I met Ronnie later that night and gave her a big hug. She was surprised that I had won, but pleased. She said, "Darling, you have a lot more work to do." I accepted her point, but for the moment, I felt as if I were king of the castle.

The following Monday, I received a phone call from the College of Music. The great Italian tenor Hugo Binelli was holding master classes in Ireland with a view to selecting some singers to study in Genoa with him at his summer school. I was asked to attend the class. He asked me to sing an aria, and I chose "Una Furtiva Lagrima" from Donizetti's *L'Elisir d'Amore*.

When I had completed singing, he asked me to sing it again. This time, he started to correct me. He kept me singing for nearly an hour, and I was exhausted at the end of it. I had never had such an intense session on one particular piece. He concentrated on two basic elements: first, maintaining a basic line throughout the whole song; second, working the cadenza so that it began with each note clearly articulated and culminated in a very pure open sound at the climax. He wouldn't let me sit down until I had got this completely right. The time and attention he showed me didn't go over well with some of the other singers! At the end of my audition with him, he said, "Tomorrow night I put on a concert in the House of Lords, in the Bank of Ireland. I have selected six singers among you to sing one operatic aria." He announced the first five singers straight off and then said, "The final singer is a unique singer. He has a lot of talent but not a lot of technical knowhow: *Il dottore* [the doctor] I have chosen for this reason. He will show you tomorrow night how beautifully he can sing a cadenza." A lot of the people sitting in on the master class were very pleased for me, but some of the other singers had some serious reservations.

On that fateful night Dad and Mam came in support. Dad was dressed in his grey flannel suit, with the red tie that I bought him. This was unusual for him because he was always a man who wore tweed sport jackets and khaki trousers, with brown leather shoes that had to be custom-made for him, as he had terribly shaped feet.

The concert started at eight and was packed to capacity. There was no doubt about it; I heard some of the finest singing ever from young Irish singers. One notable memory was the magnificent mezzo-soprano Miriam Murphy from Kerry. She sang Delilah's aria from Massenet's *Samson and Delilah*. It was phenomenal! Then came my turn with "Una Furtiva Lagrima." It went quite well and Binelli hailed me as king of the cadenza.

At the end of the concert he announced that he would like to have some Irish students attend a two-week workshop in Genoa that July. Ronnie thought that this would be of great benefit for anyone who was invited. Thankfully, I was one of the chosen few.

During the month of April, it transpired that one of my rugby-playing friends had suddenly taken ill. No one was aware at that time what the problem was. Soon a neurologist from one of the hospitals communicated that Brian had a brain tumor. All of us were devastated. Brian's parents took him to the best consultants that they could find. One of the places they went was Harley Street in London. It was thought that the type of tumor that he had was of an operable nature, but the operation would be very costly. The Knights of the Campanile and the Rugby Club decided to organize a benefit. We weren't quite sure what to do, when someone got a great idea and said, "Why doesn't Ronie sing? We'll charge people to come and hear him." This was the bicentenary year of Trinity College, and many major events were planned for Trinity Week. The culminating event was the big Trinity Ball. We all decided that the best time to run this event would be during Trinity Week.

Each of us had a job to do. The Rugby Club organized tickets and posters, another group embarked on asking Trinity whether we could put this concert on at the start of Trinity Week. Owing to the reasons behind such an altruistic event, the authorities supported us 100 percent. We rented a huge tent, which we erected in the rugby field. My job was to organize the music and the singers for the program, bearing in mind that I was supposed to be the major attraction. I contacted five of my friends: a bass, a baritone, a soprano, a contralto, and Alison, the pianist who was married to the baritone. All of the artists agreed with me that we would make it a mixed evening of opera, West End, and Broadway material. We had three weeks in which to publicize the entire event.

On the night of the performance it poured rain. In spite of this, we filled the tent to capacity. Over fifteen hundred people came to see the performance, each contributing between £15 and £20. We raised over £30,000. After expenses we were able to give Brian well over £10,000 to use at his discretion. Brian died within the following year. Sad to say, I was away for the funeral, but I will never forget the great nature and willingness of a group of men and women to help out a fellow colleague unconditionally.

I completed my Pediatric rotation by the end of April and commenced my Obstetrics and Gynecology two-month rotation in May and June. While I enjoyed this rotation, it was one area in which I didn't plan to make a career.

At the end of June, I had successfully completed all of my medical requirements for that year with the final phase to commence in September 1993.

I went to Genoa on the sixth of July with five other Irish singers. We stayed in small, cheap hotels. This was not a good move. When I returned to my room on my second night, I discovered that my bed was a mass of ants. I had inadvertently left one piece of fruit on the bed that morning and millions of devastating ants descended on my bed and attacked the fruit with a vengeance. I quickly relocated to an insect-free zone.

The weather, as usual in Italy, was superb. On the culinary front, I just couldn't eat enough gnocchi and the delicious dessert called tiramisu.

After the first few days, Hugo had decided to select different arias for us. This time I was asked to learn "M'appari tutt'amor" from *Martha* by Flotow. I had never heard this aria before. That evening I bought a CD of the legendary tenor Gigli singing this song and spent the evening listening to it and learning the words. The next day I returned to the course, whereupon Hugo said to me, "Well, Pavarotino [little Pavarotti], have you looked at the aria?" As proud as can be, I said, "I know it!" In a surprised tone he countered, "Let's hear it!" Well, I launched into it with my usual gusto. He was delighted, but said, "Your Italian is incomprehensible. We must sort this out." So he had me work with a repetiteur for a few days to straighten out my Italian diction, as well as some minor musical problems. By the end of the second week, he indicated that he would now put on two concerts in different parts of Genoa. He selected me to participate in both.

The concerts went really well and I was extremely well received by the Italian public. Then, one afternoon before I went home to Ireland,

Hugo invited me out to his house. It was there that he said to me, "Why don't you forget about medicine and concentrate on becoming an opera singer? You can work with me for two years, and after this you will be ready to sing in the concert halls of the world." I was very, very flattered, but told him that I had put too much into becoming a doctor, and I couldn't let all this work go for naught, especially as I only had one year of medical school left.

He understood, but reaffirmed that I was a late starter in this profession, and it would be a lot more difficult to succeed as a singer without his expert tutelage. We parted very amicably and kept in touch for a short time after that.

I returned to Ireland and commenced my Geriatric elective. This was compulsory. I carried this out in Blanchetstown Hospital. It was during this elective that I realized how fragile human nature can become and how we as young people can forget that someday we too will become old and need a kind hand to hold and face to talk to. It's an invaluable lesson to learn.

CHAPTER 16

*O*n completion of my Geriatric elective, I started my final year. It was September 1993. I realized that my commitment to music couldn't be foremost in my mind, as it was essential that I commit myself completely to medicine. While this was the plan in my head, my heart had other ideas. Offers to perform for private functions were coming in. Many came from medical consultants for whom I had worked. It became very difficult for me to refuse. On top of this, I really enjoyed these musical diversions.

My first set of finals was Pediatrics. This consisted of a three-hour written paper, followed by a major case examination of a child with a problem that I had to diagnose. After this, one had to examine three minor cases. This often included a newborn examination. I loved my two-month Pediatric rotation, so I didn't fear this part of the exam at all. In actual fact, I looked forward to it. However, Medicine and Surgery were a different story. Those examinations were like walking through a minefield. You had no idea what you would encounter in this part of the examination.

The Pediatric finals went extremely well. As we finished the exam toward the end of the year, people relaxed for a few weeks before preparing for the long, final four months. During that Christmas break, I performed a holiday concert for Professor Thomkin at the Royal College of Physicians. This was attended by many of the consultants from all the different hospitals that I had been attending. After the concert, one of the professors of Gastroenterology from St. James's Hospital approached and congratulated me on my performance. However, there was a little sting in his remark "Everybody knows that you enjoy singing. But be very careful, you still have your finals in medicine to complete. Don't draw attention to yourself. People might think that you're more interested in singing than in medicine. I'm sure this is not the case." But to make certain, he invited me to attend his unit on a Friday evening for tutoring in the Clinical Medicine examination. I accepted gratefully. This turned out to be a good decision on my part. I realized quite quickly, having attended my first tutorial with him, that he was a superb teacher. He was extremely knowledgeable and I learned a great deal. Rather than simply show me how smart he was, he pressed me for my diagnosis and demanded that I explain how I reached my conclusions.

The finals were held in April. Each day leading up to these exams consisted of examining as many patients as I could see. After seeing patients, I would attend various lectures and tutorials given by the consultants. Our days never seemed to end. I often wondered when I would actually get a chance to study, as most of the time I was exhausted by the end of the day. The time spent with patients and in lecture halls, followed by the sheer exhaustion, took a heavy toll on most of the students' personal lives. Both men and women suffered as their other halves learned the hard reality of being involved with people about to become doctors. Some relationships ended altogether; the stronger ones were battered, but survived. New relationships never got off the ground.

We started our written finals in the second week of April. We had two exams in Medicine, which lasted for nearly six hours. Surgery consisted of one exam lasting three hours. Psychiatry required another three-hour exam, as did Obstetrics and Gynecology. This whole process took an entire week to complete. After that, we were given a week off to lick our wounds, massage our overtaxed brains, and prepare for our clinical exams.

You are required to attend your clinical exams in suitable attire. For a man, this meant a conservative-looking suit. So, I decided to buy a blue suit with a pale blue shirt and a fairly calm tie. I thought I looked great!

My first clinic was in Medicine, and I was sent to St. James's Hospital. I arrived with Keith and Liam at 8 A.M. to be greeted by Professor

Webb of Psychiatry. He asked me how I was feeling, to which I responded, "Quite nervous, thank you, sir." At that moment, my stethoscope fell to the floor. I bent down to pick it up, naturally enough, but lo and behold, the backside of my new trousers ripped from the crotch to the belt. Now this was the second time that the seat of my pants gave way just after I met an important person and needed desperately to make a good impression. Unfortunately, this time I didn't have an overcoat to wear around for the day. As soon as I felt the tear and the sudden freedom I jumped up. I must have looked as if I had seen a ghost, for Professor Webb said, "Are you feeling okay?" I responded in total shock. "Sir, it's like this: I went out yesterday to buy a new suit for my finals, and today, just two seconds ago, my trousers have split." He wasn't able to look at me because he found it so amusing. Within seconds I was ushered into my first set of minor medical cases.

The hospital was warm and I was nervous. I was walking around with the crotch of my pants split open and I was about to learn a lesson about wearing a colored shirt on a warm day. As I moved around the hospital the sweat started to drip from my neck onto my new pale blue shirt. This started an attractive two-tone motif with a sort of water-color look as the moisture wicked through the material. Dr. Gerrighty, who was a cardiologist, greeted me. He was ever so friendly, as he recognized me from attending all his lectures. I appeared quite agitated to him. I'm sure he felt that this was just nervousness, for he reassured me that everything would go like clockwork.

The external examiner, whom I didn't know, was more aloof. He brought me to see my first minor case, asking me to examine this patient's abdomen. This examination required me to kneel down at the bedside in order to examine the abdomen properly. Normally this is a straightforward job for anybody. In my case, it was a little difficult because I haven't a great kneeling capacity. However, with my crotch split open I did have enormous capacity to show off my underwear. When I split my pants open in London, the personnel director suggested I wear dark underwear in the future, to make the incident less obvious. I half followed his advice. I didn't wear white underwear that day. Unfortunately, the red underwear that I had on that day didn't seem to make matters any better. I tried to conceal this sartorial split, but Dr. Gerrighty piped up, "What's the problem, Ronan?" I responded, as I had earlier to Professor Webb, "My trousers have split, sir." At that moment, the external examiner just glanced down at me and then about-turned and faced the window. From his shaking, I knew that he found this quite amusing. Professor Gerrighty smiled and advised me not to wear red underwear in future, as it was like waving a red rag to a bull. This broke the tension in the room, and I plowed on, making a mental note: no white and no red. The rest of the exam went superbly. As I was leaving, both men wished me well.

I was then brought to my major case, which was a sixty-two-year-old lady with a past history of multiple myeloma. This is a malignant proliferation of B cells in the blood. I was surprised by being presented with this patient, as I had only once seen a case like this and that was a year and a half ago. However, the woman was extremely helpful, and I recalled quite an amount of material related to this disease. My external examiner was the Professor of Medicine at Oxford University. My second examiner was Professor of Hematology at St. James's Hospital, Professor McCann, under whom I had studied. I excelled in this exam, whereupon the external examiner proceeded to give me an oral exam, which meant that I was doing well. My final question was: "What would be the immediate side effects of using the treatment of steroids in this woman for the disease?" I thought long and hard and out of nowhere piped up, "Psychosis." He responded, "Correct." My mouth then engaged and I said, "Wasn't that a stroke of luck!" He looked at me with slight disdain and said, "Thank you." Professor McCann grabbed my arm after the external examiner had left the room and said that I had done remarkably well, but my big mouth and my blatant honesty might have lost me Honors in Medicine. I genuinely didn't care, as I was thrilled that I had done the best I could. I knew deep down that I had passed.

The results of Medicine came out that afternoon, and it was as I expected. The following morning, I attended the Adelaide Hospital for my Obstetrics and Gynecology exam. This time, I was evaluated by one of the consultants from the Rotunda Hospital, with Professor Crowley accompanying him. Professor Crowley was a great fan of opera and appreciated the fact that I sang. But I also knew that she was very fair and wouldn't play favorites with me. Thankfully, we had no resurgence of the trousers episode, as I had the forethought to go back to the suit shop after my medical exam and create an uproar over their loose stitching and my red underwear being exposed. They were very apologetic and as a token of their good will, they gave me a new shirt to wear for my Obstetrics exam. Once again, this exam went without a hiccup. The following afternoon the good results were posted.

The custom for receiving Obstetrics and Gynecology results is that all the candidates are assembled in a room. Then the names of candidates who are heading for honors are read out, as are those who will be required to sit an oral exam to help them get through. Those whose names aren't called out are already deemed skillful in that particular area. The names are always called out in alphabetical order, which meant that I had to wait till nearly the end, as there were only two Welshes and a Wall after me. When they skipped my name, I let out a little cheer, to which Professor Crowley responded, "Yes, Dr. Tynan, you are nearly there."

The final medical exam was Surgery. I had always been very interested in this area, particularly in Orthopedics and Ear, Nose, and Throat. The chances of getting an ear, nose, and throat patient were very slim, but there was a good chance of getting an orthopedic patient. However, I was given a general surgery patient who was confused about her history. This made matters that much more difficult, as it appeared that her history didn't tally with her ailment. The only way I could make sense out of it all was to carry out a detailed physical examination and then present my case. I presented her to the Professor of Surgery, Professor Hennessy. In the process she began to interfere with my presentation, by contradicting what I was saying. This caused the sweat to come right through me, but I implored God and His Blessed Mother to come to my aid! Thankfully, she was one of Professor Hennessy's patients, and he was aware of her nature. We went straight into the physical exam, and it was at this point that I demonstrated my ability to find gross surgical signs that were evident. He was satisfied with my ability to isolate signs and took me to my minor cases, where we met the Professor of Accident and Emergency (A and E). These two cases presented some problems and a bit of controversy between one of the examiners and myself. Without going into too much detail, I stood firm with regard to the position of the patient and was supported by Professor Hennessy. His word was enough.

The results came out that afternoon. Once again, I was successful. That evening, at six o'clock, the final list was posted. I read the results. The final verdict: *qualify!* After six wonderful, long years, I had achieved one of my biggest ambitions: to become a medical doctor. The only sadness that entered my mind was that my aunt Theresa wasn't alive to see this day. I rang Dad with the news, as I had not kept him apprised of my progress until I was sure of the results. He was over the moon! "My son a doctor! Fantastic! God bless you, son. You've really shown people what you can do."

That night all the young doctors, freshly qualified and full of the joys of the world, took off around Dublin City to celebrate until the early hours of the morning. Keith and I had decided that we would go off on a holiday, a last-minute one, so that we could get the best deal possible. We flew to London the next morning, and the first travel agent we visited had a holiday for two weeks in the Caribbean, flying out that evening. As they say, "Have bags, will travel." The two of us took off.

We arrived in Costa Rica after a ten-hour flight and were completely exhausted. If this was going to be the start of the holiday, I wondered how it would finish. However, we soon got into the swing of things and became the life and soul of the party. We met up with loads of people and were having a great time. But no holiday with me is without its incidents. One day we decided to visit a waterfall. At the bottom was a beautiful lagoon. We were told to be very careful swimming, as there was a strong undercurrent. Always ready for a challenge, I jumped in and started to swim around the corners of the alcove. Quite soon, I realized that the warnings we had received were indeed accurate as the current was overpowering. As I didn't have the leg propulsion to drive me forward, I had to rely totally on my arm strength.

A lifeguard, who was also on holiday there, advised me, from land, to try and dive underneath the falls. In this way, he reassured, from land, I would avoid the drag of the current. I don't know where he got this theory, but I wished he wasn't on holiday and would jump in and pull me out. As that wasn't happening, I duly dived under, but I was still caught. Bad advice from the dry vacationing lifeguard. The current started to rotate me. I didn't seem to be going in any direction except down. My eyes were wide open; I looked around me and thought that I was going to drown. It was as if my life flashed before my eyes, and all I could think was, "Sacred Heart of God, I'm going to drown in Costa Rica!" Just as I was about to curse the lifeguard with the aversion to water, I was catapulted out of the vortex and ended up about fifty yards downstream, sitting in the shallow water like a Buddha. I don't know what saved me, but I guess it wasn't my time to meet my maker.

Keith approached me with a little bit of concern and said, "You were under for quite some time. People started to worry when all they saw come up was one of your artificial legs." Then he started to laugh hilariously and said that he could see that I was all right. I started to shout at him, "I could have drowned!!! And you couldn't have cared less . . ." Then he really started to roll around the place laughing. I eventually got up and started to make my way back up the mountain. Three quarters of the way up, I met a priest selling towels for some charity. I gave him a hundred dollars and asked for his blessing. He was quite enthusiastic in giving it to me! Keith thought that I was mad in making such a large donation. What the hell did I care? I was alive to tell the tale.

That was our first mishap. Toward the end of the trip, we hired a Jeep and driver to see some of the island. We were quite late returning home and visibility was poor. Whether the driver's night vision was not up to scratch, or his mind was wandering, all of a sudden we collided with something quite large on the road. The animal hurled up through the windshield and its rear leg hit me in the arm. Once again, I was the subject of a close call. I required stitches in my left arm and for several years after that, I had glass in my arm making its way out. When we returned to the site the next morning, we found that the animal we had hit was a pony. Of course, no one laid claim to the pony, so no one was accountable. Between Keith and me, we had to pay over two thousand pounds in damages for the Jeep before we were allowed to leave the country. Even with those two near misses, we still had a good time. Actually, I think Keith had the better time as both near misses were near me and he had a good laugh watching my artificial leg float out of the lagoon.

We returned home in the middle of June and prepared for our graduation ceremony, which was to be held a week later. It was compulsory to wear black tie with robes at this ceremony. Mam, Dad, and Fiona arrived for the day. I have to say that this was one of the happiest days of my life.

CHAPTER 17

I started my internship in the Meath Hospital on the first of July in the Emergency Room, and I was there for three months. This was a real eye-opener, as quite soon I was in the thick of it, dealing with every aspect of acute illness, as well as with individuals who had drug overdoses and other frightening problems. After the first week, I was sitting in the lounge watching a bit of television to relax, when an advertisement came on inviting people to enter a talent competition called *Go for It*. The competition was a joint venture between RTE and the BBC television networks. I remember thinking that I would like to enter, if for no other reason than to find out what people thought of my voice. What better way to confront reality?

I duly submitted an application form and within a week was asked to attend the preliminary round in one of the RTE television studios. I told no one that I had entered, and luckily for me the first round was on a Saturday. The following Monday, a message was left on my answering machine that I was successful and could I make myself available in two weeks' time for the second round. There was no question about attending!

The second round was a bit more difficult in terms of getting time off. Luckily, one of the house officers at the hospital told me that he would cover me for the hour I needed. I had told him that I had to go to the Medical Council to sort out my forms. I still didn't want anyone to know until they had to. When I arrived at the studio for the second audition, there were three people on the panel. One was the director from RTE, one was the BBC director, and the other was Marion Dwan, a lady with whom I later became great friends. Once again, I was successful and advanced to the semifinals, which would take place in Belfast at the BBC studios. These proceedings, unlike the first two rounds, would be televised. The semifinals were to be held in December. I decided to sing an operatic piece by Cilea called "E la Solita Storia del Pastore." I was still studying under Ronnie Dunn, who had moved from the College of Music in Adelaide Road to the Leinster School of Music. It was time for me to inform her that I had entered the competition and had made it to the semifinals. She wasn't convinced that this was the right thing for me to do. This seemed to cause a small ripple in our relationship. However, we persevered together. Occasionally she would make a little remark to somebody who entered the room, "This character has just entered into a talent show for pop singers! I ask you: What is he thinking of?"

By this time on the medical side of my life, I had moved from A and E to my residency in General Surgery and ENT (Ear, Nose, and Throat). I planned my voice lessons with Ronnie on my lunch breaks, always bringing my beeper with me in case of an emergency. I would ride over to the Leinster School of Music and climb the four flights of stairs to Ronnie's room. At the top, I would always be out of breath. I would thunder in and quietly ask the other individual to leave as time was precious and I had none to waste. Ronnie was quite amused with me, as I would appear in a white coat and stethoscope. Occasionally she would say, "Lovey, would you ever listen to my chest? I don't feel well." We would laugh and then get on with the job at hand. On one of these occasions, I came in on top of Anthony Kearns finishing his lesson. Ronnie said to me, "Listen to this fellow sing." I duly did, and did I hear a voice! It was a very, very fine instrument with a lot of youth on its side. I took note of this fine voice and thought that he would go a long way.

I found the Surgery residency extremely tough on my legs. Particularly difficult was being on call all night, or all through a weekend. While the spirit was willing, my legs hurt from all the standing and running up and down the stairs. I would often go to a shower and leave my stumps under the cold running water to cool down. They were quite raw from the friction with the prosthesis. It was at this time that I would ask some of the other interns to help me with my night calls. While it appeared to some of them that I was trying to escape my workload, I never alluded to the fact that I was having problems with my limbs. I needed to complete my residency without drawing too much attention to my disposition.

Ronnie at this time had also set up the Leinster Opera Studio, to which I belonged. In this studio, I sang excerpts from *La Bohème, Don Giovanni,* and many other operas. Most of the studio's work was done for corporate functions. These in turn would fund the studio. As the semifinals of *Go for It* were approaching, I was unable to commit myself very much to the studio. I thought this also displeased Ronnie, but there was nothing I could do. I had to prepare myself for the competition. There was no way around that. Sadly, Ronnie and I were beginning to drift apart, and there was very little either of us could do about it.

The semifinals took place on the seventeenth of December. There were eight contestants in my group, which was one of ten groups. This left eighty contestants, out of a field of three thousand entrants. The BBC assigned a classical accompanist for me named Elizabeth Bicker. She was wonderful and was very stylistic in her approach. She also gave me some great tips on the performance of the operatic piece. I listened to the rehearsals and realized that the competition was very stiff. They were all singers of different styles—mainly pop and country western— and I stood out among them because I was the only classical artist. There was one girl from Kerry that I can particularly remember. Boy, could she deliver a song! She sang a jazz piece and it had tremendous clout. My piece was extremely well received by the jury panel, which consisted of three people: Bill Hughes, who was an independent TV producer, a singer named Rosemarie, and a guest juror. I scored top marks and was deemed the winner of the semifinals. I was now going to sing on St. Patrick's night in the concert hall in Limerick at the finals of *Go for It*. This gave me three months to prepare.

I returned to the Adelaide Hospital, where I was now working for Professor Thomkin, an endocrinologist. I had just commenced working for him that day, and the planned ward round was for three o'clock that afternoon. While we went around meeting patients, most rooms had televisions, which were turned on. As we entered a female patient's room, I overheard the jingle for *Go for It,* announcing semifinalist number four. My heart went crossways, as I knew that I was about to be broadcast. I tried to position myself between the patient and the television, but to no avail. When my turn came to sing, Professor Thomkin looked up at the television monitor and straightaway knew that it was me. He exclaimed with amusement, "Ronan! How can you be on television and be here at the same time?" So, I explained that I sang in this competition the previous Saturday and that the repeat program went out today. "How did you do?" he asked. I replied, "I won." Upon hearing this, the patient started clapping and Professor Thomkin asked me to sing at a Diabetic conference that he was planning in April. I couldn't believe his positive reaction and how much approval I was getting. By the end of the day, consultants, nurses, and other staff were all congratulating me and wishing me well. But my singing and my success drew a negative reaction from some who questioned my commitment to medicine. In my mind, there was never a conflict.

One Saturday morning in February I got a phone call from Ronnie to inform me that Gegam Gregorian, the great Armenian tenor from the Kirov Opera, had become ill. Ronnie had been asked if she had a tenor in her stable who could sing on short notice in the concert hall. She recommended me and said that this was my big break. The tenor for that evening had to sing at least eight arias: four in the first half, and four in the second. This was possibly the total number of arias that I knew! Once again, Ronnie had decided that I should have a lesson with her before singing, and I had the fear that if I went to Ronnie she would go through all my arias and tear them to pieces. The offer was pointless in any event. We couldn't avail ourselves of that opportunity, as the promoter, Barra O'Tuama, wanted to hear me at a rehearsal at two that afternoon to see if I was suitable. Once he heard me sing the first aria, "Una Furtiva Lagrima," he was very pleased and hired me.

The concert was to commence at 8 P.M. I opened my debut with Puccini's "Recondita Armonia" from *Tosca*. When I soared to the top B flat at the end, the crowd gave me a standing ovation. I was overjoyed! There was now no turning back; I was euphoric. For the first time, I felt the pull of the opera world.

The Sunday paper came out the next day. The headline ran, IS THERE A DOCTOR IN THE HOUSE? The review was wonderful, using phrases such as "tremendous potential," "ease of facility," etc. Ronnie was very pleased, but told me to get off my high horse and concentrate on doing some serious technical work. Looking back on it now, I'm sure that she was right.

The following Monday, I returned to the hospital. Once again, I was greeted with kind words from my colleagues. That afternoon, I received a phone call from Marion Dwan of RTE, who asked me to attend an audition they were holding. This audition was for the chief conductor of the National Concert Orchestra, Pronnsias O'Duinn. I arrived at the audition at four o'clock, having asked Keith to cover me for two hours at the hospital. I sang "E Lucevan le Stelle" from *Tosca*. O'Duinn obviously liked what he heard, for he asked Marion to hold me back until the end of the auditions so that he could work with me. Pronnsias had to be one of the most gracious people I have ever met. He has an unbelievable knowledge of the singing voice, and he commands a wonderful style of interpretation. We worked for nearly three hours, at the end of which I asked him if he would help me prepare for the final of p

He agreed, and for the next three weeks, I had two sessions per week with him. These sessions were invaluable, as they helped me to achieve the appropriate style.

During my final session with him he asked me what I planned to do with my future. He said that he could hear an Italianate sound in my voice, which made it very appealing and also very commercial. He advised that if I was considering a career in singing that I should go to an opera school in order to learn my craft. He felt that this was the only way that I could develop the necessary skills correctly. The seeds of opera were firmly planted in my brain, but I had to avoid letting any-one else know of my thoughts so that my medical colleagues wouldn't feel that I was neglecting my commitment to medicine.

On the fifteenth of March, which was Fiona's birthday, I drove down to Limerick. On the sixteenth we had rehearsals for the *Go for It* finals. I was a little nervous, but the voice seemed to be in good form. There was one other classically trained competitor, Neil Everett, who was playing the piano, although he was playing a jazz piece. The news-papers were tipping me to win this competition. YOUNG DOCTOR WILL SHINE ON PADDY'S NIGHT, said one headline.

At two in the afternoon of March 17, all ten finalists were dressed in their performance clothes, ready to go through the final rehearsal of the talent competition, which was within hours now of drawing to a close.

Dad and Fiona had come to the rehearsals to give their support and also to give a critique of my performance. I was the seventh competi-tor and the only classical singer in the competition. I was very nervous and this was only the warm-up. When I walked onto the stage I had no idea where to stand. The small orchestra was situated in the right-hand corner of the Limerick University Concert Hall stage, so I thought I should stand next to them. As I made my way over to that area, the stage manager gave a loud shout "Where do you think you're going?" "Well," I responded, "I thought I was . . ." and before I could utter another word he said, "The audience and the judges would like to see your big mug, so get back to center stage." We both laughed and that really helped relieve some of my nervousness. I started to sing, and pretty soon I was getting into the song but felt a bit uncomfortable with the orchestra, as it was my first time performing with them. Fur-thermore, the conductor wasn't standing in front of me, thus I had to keep a sharp ear to hear where they were in order not to be behind or ahead of the music. All these small things were having an effect on my performance.

Dad said to me afterward, in as kind a way as possible, "You'll have to do better than that if you are going to be in the shake-up tonight."

I knew he was right. The only thing I could do was pray to God that on this night it would all fall into place for me. I stopped at a church on the way to the hall that night and asked all my friends up there to give me the strength and wisdom to do the best job I could. The rest was in the hands of the jury.

I arrived at the University Concert Hall at about six-thirty in the evening. By seven I was removing the pins from my new dress shirt, trying to keep focused as well as calm. Every so often one of those blessed pins would somehow make its way through the skin of my fingers and draw an infinitesimal amount of blood. When it happened the third time, I cleaned up with a rag and in the process smeared my new shirt with a nice tincture of my blood.

I was devastated. I immediately went to the wardrobe lady and asked her for assistance. She greeted me with a smile. "Don't worry, Ronan. I'll sort all this out for you. Relax and get ready to give the performance of your life. My money's on you to win." After that she gave me a hug. This had an extremely calming effect upon me. It was like a weight had been lifted off my shoulders.

The concert hall was packed for Ireland and Northern Ireland's nationally televised talent search. There was hardly room to swing a cat. The place was thronged to capacity with supporters and television cameras.

I had accrued about forty supporters, as all the contestants were asked to bring family and friends to support them. Besides Dad, Mam, and Fiona, there were also two of my medical colleagues, Debbie and Deirdre McNamara, and some of their relatives.

While I knew my voice was strong, I didn't think I stood a chance of winning, given the amount of talent I was up against. The four judges sat close to the contestants, but I couldn't worry too much about them. I had plenty else to worry about. My voice in rehearsals had felt tight and nothing had been coming together for me. But more than that, it was the first time I'd ever sung live on television, the first time I'd ever really declared myself a singer so publicly. The thought of all those invisible viewers out there watching had me rattled.

At eight forty-five that night I walked onto the concert hall stage dressed in tails, looking like a classic tenor, and ready to deliver "Return to Sorrento," a mournful love song sung in Italian and made popular by Mario Lanza. It was one of my dad's favorites, and as I stepped onto the stage, I caught sight of Mam and him in the audience, both brimming with excitement, rooting for me. I could feel the quiet sensation of suspense coming off Dad and the words of the song he would be singing silently with me. I knew I had at least one man truly in my camp. As the pianist began, I took all the emotion I'd been feeling in the weeks leading up to the competition, all the nervousness and fear of failure, and prepared to pack it into the song. With the prelude vibrating in my chest, I relaxed and my voice left my mouth as if I were releasing a burden.

But what a lovely burden. The Italian lyrics speak of the beauty of the sea, the music of the water, and the wilting of the flowers in the garden where a lover waits. My voice was bright as a button for it. Like so many of the best songs, this one found love and the torment of separation reflected in all of nature. As I sang, I reached out to the audience with both hands as if pleading. I became both the departing lover and the one left behind. As I traveled closer and closer toward the high note, praying I would reach it, I closed my eyes and took that last step up, the one that feels as if I'm jumping from an airplane. The high note comes on the word "I" in the phrase "Then say not goodbye, else I must die." And I hit it. That top B rang out through the entire hall. My eyes widened as I sang it, and when I came down to finish the song off, there was a tremendous ovation from the audience. I knew from that moment this was really what God wanted me to do.

Once the final competitor had completed his performance, all the artists were sent to a room while the adjudication got under way. The tension was incredible. All of us were on edge, fully aware that whoever won this night would have their lives changed forever. Before the voting commenced, the winner of the competition from the previous year gave a rendition of his winning song. All of us were stunned by how professional he had become after just one year.

Finally the voting commenced. There were four people on the jury from different areas of the entertainment industry: television, radio, music, and film. Each contestant was scored out of twenty possible points, so the maximum score one could receive was eighty. I had no idea how the judging would go. All I knew was that I had given the best performance of my short singing career. Each judge scored individually, without consulting the others. After waiting what seemed an eternity, the results were announced. I received a perfect score of twenty from each one of the four judges. Eighty points in all. I was shocked and thrilled that I had won at all, and even more so that I had received perfect scores from each judge. When I was brought down to receive the Waterford crystal vase, I passed by Dad and Mam. Both of them reached out to congratulate me. Dad was visibly overcome with delight—his eyes were welled up. I knew both of them were very proud; it was truly a great moment for all of us. We celebrated till the late hours. Needless to say this was the turning point in my life.

Reality struck me in the face when I returned to the hospital for ward rounds at seven-thirty the following Monday morning. It was as if it had never happened. There I was, two nights ago, in the limelight on national television having won the contest of my dreams, bathing in the accolades and general euphoria of success. On Monday morning the crowds were gone, the applause a distant memory, and I was looking at blood results and interpreting data. But this didn't faze me too much, as I realized that I could have my moment of glory and return down to earth within minutes. But I was still grateful for the opportunity. What I didn't realize was that, subconsciously, the seeds of performing and singing to the public had taken root. There would be very little that I could do to alter this line of destiny, much as I would try.

By May, all the interns were applying for their house officer jobs in different aspects of Medicine and Surgery. I had a very keen interest in Rehabilitation and Sports Injuries and I set about doing a two-year rotation in this field. I also applied for the lecture post in Anatomy at Trinity College, working under my good friend and mentor, Professor Maire O'Brien. Keith had applied for this post as well, and we hoped that we would fill two of the four positions. As it turned out, our wishes were fulfilled, but neither of us took the post, for very different reasons, which I will come back to later. At the time I put in my application, I was working for the Orthopedic Consultants, a group of four. I was responsible for looking after a total of thirty-four patients, who all resided on the top floor of the Adelaide Hospital. Climbing up and down the stairs really wore me out, as did standing in the operating theater assisting different procedures that were being carried out.

By this time, all of the consultants that I had been working for were well aware that I loved to sing. On one occasion, Professor McEllwain brought me into his rooms prior to seeing patients. I had no idea what he was about to say to me. I could only assume that I had done something wrong, as his manner was quite stern. He seated me and asked me what my plans were for next year. I told him what my thoughts were in relation to Rehabilitation and Sports Injuries, and that the possibility of doing a master's in Sports Injuries was available to me through taking the lecture post in Anatomy. He said to me, "In life people are given talents. Other people have the ability to put themselves into a position in which they enjoy doing their work. You can always come back to medicine. It will always be there, but if you don't give your singing career a chance to bloom, you will never be content." I was stunned at these words and really respected his opinion. He also told me that this wasn't just his view. Many of the consultants from different areas of surgery felt the same, that I should follow my dreams. This was not to say that he didn't think that I would make a good doctor—he said I was already that. Then he said, "If you ever need time while on my rotation to pursue your music training, do so. And on that note, let's get to work and save some lives." I thanked him and realized that he was right, but I was too scared at that time to make such a significant decision.

I subsequently returned to Pronnsias and asked for his opinion. He advised that if I was serious about my singing career, I should apply immediately to the English colleges to gain entry for the coming October. His advice threw me into a lot of confusion. Pronnsias said to me, "I will help you as much as I can, and should you require a fund-raiser to go to one of these colleges, I will give you my services free." This was the kind of gentleman I was dealing with and I held him in great respect.

My next plan of action was to apply to the Royal Northern College of Music in Manchester for their post-graduate course. I realized that I might have been too late in applying, but like everything that I have pursued in life, I left no stone unturned to see if it was possible to gain entry that year. As luck would have it, auditions for the Belvedere International Singing Competition in Vienna were being held in May in Ireland, and I was invited to attend on the following Saturday. Contestants were required to sing two contrasting arias. I chose, once again, "Una Furtiva Lagrima" from *L'Elisir d'Amore,* and "La Donna è Mobile" from *Rigoletto.* On the panel of judges was the current director of the English National Opera, Guus Mostart. After I completed my audition Mr. Mostart asked who my teacher was. At that time, I was between teachers. He said, "May I make a suggestion? You should try and gain entry to the Royal Northern College of Music in Manchester." What a coincidence! He also suggested that I look to study under a Mr. Robert Alderson, who had quite a reputation for producing singers with solid technique. I wasted no time. I rang the RNCM the following Monday and asked for an application. It so happened that I was just under the deadline. After that, I requested to speak with Mr. Alderson. He invited me over the following weekend to have a singing lesson with him. I was over the moon, as everything seemed to be falling into position. I returned to Pronnsias and told him of my progress. He was very pleased, and admired the intensity and speed at which I had moved on the matter.

The next problem was finding funds. This wasn't going to be that easy. As the consultants were all aware that I had a major interest in singing, particularly opera, I decided I would approach them for some monetary assistance. Naturally enough I started with the man who suggested that I look very carefully at the talent God had given me to see if he would put his money where his mouth was. I was anxious about approaching Professor McEllwain, but I couldn't turn back. I explained everything, including my recent travels to Manchester to have singing lessons. Without as much as a blink of an eye, he said, "I'll give you a thousand pounds. Make sure you knock on some of the other doors, as you will be well received. Of that I am certain." I next approached Mr. Feeley, of vascular surgery fame. He was delighted. Mr. Beasley was the same and gave me £2,000. Dr. Crowley, from my days in the Coombe Hospital, who had a great love for opera, gave me the same amount. Mr. Dowling and Professor Thomkin also donated with the greatest of pleasure, and wished me well on my choice. In total, they gave me £8,000 to pursue my dream. I was, and still am, eternally grateful.

My next difficult task was to go down to Professor O'Brien in the Anatomy Department and tell her that I had decided to go to the RNCM to pursue a post-graduate course in opera. This did not please her, and she piped out, "Your legs will never cope with the pressure." To which I responded, "If I have been able to get through my internship and come out the other end standing, I will survive any course." She sighed and said, "I was so much looking forward to having you on the team. But if this is your wish, so be it and the very best of luck." I gave her a big hug and thanked her for being so understanding. Then she said, "Please don't tell me that Keith isn't taking the job!" I put my head down and said, "You'll have to ask him yourself." Then she said, "Don't tell me he has taken up singing as well?" I laughed and said good-bye. Once I had completed this task, I was free of all of my commitments.

* CHAPTER 18 *

As a result of winning *Go for It*, I was offered my first solo concert recital with the BBC Ulster Orchestra. The program was "A Night at the Opera," conducted by Adrian Leaper. It was my first time standing in front of a sixty-piece orchestra. The enormity of the task left me in awe. I was tremendously excited and yet terrified at the prospect of performing. The concert was to take place in May 1994 in the prestigious Ulster Hall in Belfast. This was a magnificent architectural structure, with a wonderful acoustic design. There would be no need for a microphone in this venue, as the voice, properly projected, would hit off the back wall. My program that night was a mixed bag of opera, Viennese operetta, and Neapolitan songs. I was asked to sing all the old favorites, from Lehár's "You Are My Heart's Delight" to Bizet's "La fleur que tu m'avais jetée," finishing with that good old Neapolitan song, "O Sole Mio." The audience stamped their feet in approval. It was another great night to remember.

I finished my internship at the hospital at the end of June. As was customary, all new medical posts commenced on the first of July of each year. For me, I was embarking on a major change of career. I had decided to go to Munich to the Bayerische Staadt Opera, to study for three weeks with an American, James King, and an Australian tenor, Ken Neath. On my way, I had to first stop in Manchester to complete my audition for the post-graduate course. This consisted of singing three songs and then sight-reading an unknown piece. This was a nightmare for me, as my sight-reading skills were nowhere near what they should have been. But if raw talent had anything to do with gaining entry, I was sure I would make it. This must have been the case, for they gave me a place in the course. I rang Pronnsias O'Duinn and told him of my acceptance. His response was, "You've now taken the appropriate steps to embark on this career. It's full steam ahead from here on, and by the way, I have asked for you to be one of the soloists in Haydn's *Mass of St. Cecilia*. I was really honored, but he warned me, "Get working on it now, for it's not so straightforward." I assured him that I would.

My next stop was Munich. I arrived two days late. This wasn't a major problem, but it meant that I missed the introductory lectures. When I arrived at Mr. King's class, he asked me immediately to sing an operatic aria of my choice. I sang "E la Solita Storia del Pastore" from *L'Arlesiana* by Cilea. He was impressed but felt that I should have a much deeper, stronger sound. I was taken aback by this comment, as I always looked at myself as being a light, lyric tenor. He was trying to turn me into a heroic tenor. Two days later, as I was warming up in a rehearsal room, a small man entered. In broken English he asked me under whom I was studying. I responded Herr King and added that I didn't feel he was very happy with me, as in his view my voice wasn't developed. This man, Soto Papulcas, was Herr Matternich's assistant. He asked me to sing, so I sang "En fermant les yeux" from *Manon*. It delighted him. "This is a beautiful lyric voice. You do not need to sound like a heroic tenor. You have a very beautiful voice, suited so well for Massenet, Donizetti, and early Verdi. I would love to work with you in the evenings, if you like." I was thrilled and immediately asked him, "When can we start?" "Right now if you want," he answered. I had daily lessons with Soto until the course ended. It was an invaluable experience.

I returned home from Germany in August. For a long time I wanted to buy a place of my own, so that I would have a base from which to work. In addition, I wanted my independence more than anything. Dad and I went to see some houses in the area of Laois, where his family came from. We found an old rectory, which was in a beautiful setting by the river. I turned to Dad and said, "I'll never be able to afford this place!" He said, "You don't know until you ask." It was situated on six acres of land. When I inquired as to the price, I was right; I couldn't afford it. This disappointed Dad a bit, but he realized that it wasn't a good idea to be stretched, having no definite income at this stage of my career. Subsequently, we drove around the Kilkenny area. On returning home, we decided to go by Tullaroan just to see if there was anything that might suit me. Lo and behold, I came upon a nice little country house, which had a hay barn, stables, and an outdoor riding ring. I immediately fell in love with it and knew that it was the place for me. Dad wasn't as convinced, but then Dad wasn't going to be living there, which I jokingly informed him. We inquired as to the price. This place was a lot more reasonable and within my means. I bought the house by the end of August and moved in immediately.

I left for Manchester on the fifth of September. My car was packed to capacity with bedclothes, clothing, and personal effects. I arrived the night before the college was to open and moved into a house with four female singers. Maybe this wasn't such a good idea, but at the time I didn't complain as I had a place to stay. The following morning, I parked my car in the teacher's parking lot, as I had been given a special dispensation owing to my disability. I greatly appreciated this. The first person I met while registering was a chap from Mexico called Rafael Rojas. He was a wonderful tenor. As it turned out, he was just putting in his time in England in order to develop his career in Europe. The next guy I met, who became a very great friend, was Damian Whiteley, a bass from Australia. Damian had the added bonus of being a very fine pianist, which, as you can imagine in a school with lots of singers, was invaluable. Quite soon, Damian started to teach me my pieces and we suddenly teamed up to perform concerts. At this stage, I had received numerous invitations throughout Ireland to perform recitals. My partner in crime for most of the year was a chap named Kevin Mathews, a tenor from Blackpool and a real character. He was also a very good pianist. There were some wonderful female singers in our class who were lovely people, as well—Zoë and Emma, to name but two.

We were all expected to be part of the major gala concert, which was to be held after four weeks. I found this very entertaining, as Kevin and I used to sit beside each other. We spent the whole time laughing or trying to out-sing each other. We were usually pretty parched when chorus was over, so we tried very hard to keep a regime of regular visits to the pub to quench our thirsts. As we both found comfort in routine, we discovered that closing time was a good time to call it a night. Not a great start to my professional singing career! We attended several different classes, from dance to stage management to proper recital etiquette. The recital etiquette class was taught by Elaine Bevis. I remember on one particular occasion she remarked that my feet were too small for the size of my body and that I should really consider getting bigger feet made. I was dumbfounded by the thought of just getting bigger feet and found the comment quite amusing. However, other members of the class didn't take it so lightheartedly. I'm certain that she was trying to be helpful with her comments.

One thing this class did teach me: Never sing in a foreign language unless you understand every single word. This is paramount in any aspect of interpretation. I recall one incident, singing a very sad song, "Chanson de l'Adieu," written by Tosti. I smiled at a particularly sad part of the song and was pulled up straightaway and asked to explain in detail what I had just sung in French. I had no idea what I had sung. My face turned red as a rose and I got all tongue-tied. From then on, anytime I was asked to perform a song in a foreign language, I was asked to translate it first. Should it be an aria from an opera, I had to explain in detail where it fit into the story and also give a synopsis of the opera. As you can imagine, I became very careful at choosing my pieces.

Work seemed to be flowing in from Ireland, which meant that I often flew home for a weekend. In October of that year I performed the *Mass of St. Cecilia,* which was my first oratorio. Pronnsias was wonderful as the conductor. To me he was like a traffic cop, for I was so terrified, I literally needed someone to guide me through it. We had three performances, and by the third one it was reasonable. He must have been relatively happy with my performance, for he offered me the Verdi *Requiem* in April of the following year.

Upon my return to Manchester I decided to use Damian, the Australian bass singer, as my accompanist, for we were able to work together in Manchester and be well rehearsed prior to the performances. He came to know my strengths as well as my weaknesses, for which he compensated admirably.

After six weeks on the course in Manchester, the Webster Booth Competition was advertised on the notice board. It was open to all the singing students in the college, and everybody in the whole college auditioned. This was also a very prestigious competition, and the prize money was exceptional. The singers had to provide their own pianists. The college staff were quickly booked by other singers, so I decided to stick with Damian. The names of the six finalists were posted at the end of the week and I was thrilled to be on the list. I was ecstatic and told Damian that it must have been his playing. The finals were to be held the following May, which was a long way away, as we were still only in the middle of October.

My lessons with Mr. Alderson hadn't been going that well due to a clash of our personalities. So both of us decided that it might be better if I changed to another teacher. I was then put with Anthony Roden, a lovable sort of man, who had been singing tenor all his life and had had quite a wonderful career. Tony and I got on superbly well, and soon I was singing very naturally once again, with no effort whatsoever. Unfortunately, in early December, Tony broke his leg. This was a disaster, as I was once again without a singing teacher. Left to my own devices, Damian and I worked together using the vocal exercises that Tony had given me.

By Christmas I had performed fifteen concerts with Damian and the National Concert Orchestra. I was benefiting from studying in Manchester. However, I was made aware that I wouldn't be given a major role in any of the opera productions put on by the school. I was told by a friend, in confidence, "I don't see you ever getting a role on the opera stage owing to your disposition." I was upset by his comment and said that I'd prove him wrong. He replied honestly, "I have no doubt that you will, but it won't be in this school." That made my mind up that I wasn't going to return the following year.

I met another singer, a bass originally from Israel named Guidon Sachs. We became great friends. Guidon's advice was invaluable. Like me, he had also taken time to find the right singing teacher, but you would never think that he needed one after listening to him. He had the most wonderful voice, with endless shades portraying the emotions of the songs that he sang. He told me that I would have no problem performing an operatic role and that if a director chose me to perform a role, he would work within the limitations that I presented. "If they want you, Ronan, they want you!" I confided in Guidon with regard to all matters relating to the school, and he was always helpful. But his career took off and he was available less and less as that year progressed.

I returned after Christmas to set about learning the Verdi *Requiem* in earnest for April. I wanted to be very polished so that Pronnsias wouldn't have to play traffic cop with me throughout the entire piece. He had chosen top-class soloists, all of whom had distinguished themselves both in opera and in oratorio. I was a little overwhelmed by such esteemed company, but everyone was very gracious and willing to help a new colleague. I spent two days every week working on the *Requiem* with different opera coaches or repetiteurs. I always presented a section of it in Oratorio class. This sometimes annoyed the other students, as they wanted to look at different pieces. Irrespective of their wishes, I always performed a different section of the Verdi *Requiem*. I got Damian, Emma, and Zoë to do the quartets and duets with me. Singing this masterpiece gave me a tremendous feeling of fulfillment.

I returned to perform the *Requiem* on April 23, 1995, to a capacity audience. The review was very, very pleasing—unlike the one I had received for the *St. Cecilia Mass*. They acclaimed me for my interpretation of the "Ingemisco" and the "Hostias." On completion of the full evening piece, I was physically exhausted to the point that I didn't even recognize people coming into the dressing room. Pronnsias was very pleased with the work I had done and subsequently offered me the oratorio *Messiah* by Handel for November of that year.

I returned to college triumphant, but nothing had changed except that

Tony's leg had healed and he was back to teaching. I was delighted, as the Webster Booth Competition was drawing near. This required me to sing three types of pieces: oratorio, operetta, and opera. For the oratorio I chose "Ye People Rend Your Hearts" from Mendelssohn's *Elijah*. Operetta was represented by a duet "Love, What Has Given You This Magic Power" from Lehár's *Land of Smiles*. Finally, I trotted out my opera warhorse, "Una Furtiva Lagrima."

On that famous night, I was tired vocally as well as physically, owing to constant rehearsing for three to four hours each day before the competition. "Why is there so much rehearsal needed for just three songs?" I asked. The question was greeted with great disdain, so I desisted from asking any other questions.

I was the final singer in the Webster Booth Competition and had to make my entrance from the top of a staircase and walk down without the assistance of a banister. For most people, walking downstairs would not present a problem. But for me I felt as if I was on show. Not being particularly graceful at climbing or descending stairs, even those with banisters, I could feel the tension building in my body. I tried my best to walk without assistance. When I reached the bottom of the stairs, I was soaked in sweat and singing was the farthest thing from my mind. I felt as if I had just given the performance and I wanted to walk off to get a drink of water. But, funny enough, the audience wanted more from me.

I opened with the oratorio, which went really well. Then followed the aria, and finally the pièce de résistance, the duet. At this stage of the competition I was in trouble, for I had to make my wobbly walk down the stairs again, this time accompanying my beautiful soprano. By the time we reached the end of the stairs, I could hardly sing a note. With God's help we got through. I didn't win the competition, but I did get highly commended, which I thought was very fair. The college authorities were very pleased with my performance, which I suppose was good in itself.

I resumed classes the following Monday and noticed an advertisement on the college notice board announcing the International

Pavarotti Competition. I decided to enter. The preliminary rounds were located in various cities throughout Europe. I had missed the U.K. location. The next nearest one was in the Bastille Opera House in Paris. I flew to Paris the morning of the competition, which wasn't very clever, for I had no idea what effect flying would have on my voice. I soon learned. It was very dry on the plane, and I tried to drink as much water as I could. Then the train leaving the airport was late, which left me with little or no time to warm up prior to my audition. They actually called me to the stage as I was putting on my trousers. I thought, "What the hell. Here goes nothing!" All the singers up to this point had been asked to sing one song. So, as usual, I rolled out "Una Furtiva Lagrima." The judging panel included the director of the Pittsburgh Opera, Tito Capobianco, and one of the directors from the Bastille.

Having finished singing my first aria, I was about to go, when I was asked, "When did you get in?" "About five minutes ago," I answered. The woman on the panel then said, "So that explains your appearance." I was shocked and quickly looked at myself. Indeed, half my shirt was hanging out of my trousers. I quickly stuffed it back in, to the giggles of the two jurors. Then Mr. Capobianco asked me, "Do you have a second aria prepared?" I responded, "Yes." "We would like to hear 'La fleur que tu m'avais jetée.' " I sighed quietly to myself, because this was a very difficult aria and I still wasn't well warmed up. Nonetheless, I persevered. After completing it, Mr. Capobianco informed me, "You must always give yourself plenty of time to rest before you sing in a competition. This often means arriving at least one day before." I thanked him for his advice and told him that I would always make sure in the future to be well prepared and have adequate rest.

Two days later, I got a phone call from America informing me that I had been successful and was asked to attend the finals in Modena. This really surprised me, as I was aware of only three candidates getting through. The thing that pleased me the most was that it showed the people in Manchester that opera people in the rest of the world appreciated my talents and maybe saw some possibility.

June 12 was the date of the final. The requirement was to have five arias, in contrasting styles, prepared. There were at least a hundred competitors from all over the world; I was the only one representing Ireland. I listened to the other singers for hours and heard some of the most amazing voices from such young people. It became quite apparent to me that I still wasn't ready technically for such a prestigious event. But all I could do was my best. Luciano Pavarotti and Tito Capobianco were the jury. I approached the stage, and Signore Pavarotti said, "Tynan, *cosa canterai per noi?*" I responded very nervously in a shaken voice, "Canteró, 'Una Furtiva Lagrima.' " He said, "*Scusi?* I cannot hear you!" So, I changed my mind and said, " 'Oh! Fede Negar Potessi' " from Verdi's *Luisa Miller.* "*Avanti,*" he said. As this piece has quite a dramatic opening recitative, it gave me a chance to settle down and use the nervousness in my voice to create drama until I got to the lyricism of the aria proper.

After I had completed the aria, I was in a state of shock, having sung for the great maestro. He said, "Thank you, thank you. Next!" Well, I thought that was some experience, and all he said was "Thank you." I was hoping for more, but more wasn't coming. About an hour later I was walking behind the theater when by chance I bumped into Signore Pavarotti himself. I said, "Hello." He responded, "Yes, the Irishman. You have a very nice voice. Very pure, but for such a big man, the voice should be bigger." It was now my turn to say, "Thank you," and I did. I felt honored that he liked my voice, whatever size it was.

That evening I was sitting outside the theater with a couple of the other singers, when Tito Capobianco approached me and said, "You sang really well. Much better than the time I heard you in Paris. Keep working. I'm sure that we'll be hearing more from you."

I returned to Manchester for the final month and decided that I wasn't going to return the following year. I still planned to continue working with my teacher, Tony, whenever possible.

At the Pavarotti event I met a baritone from Venezuela and we discussed singing competitions. He advised me to enter the international French competition in Marmand, Toulouse. This is the biggest international competition in France, and there were sixteen jurors, all from the different regional opera houses in France. The jurors included M. Pierre Medecin from the Opéra Comique in Paris. The competition was to be held in August. Luckily for me, the baritone had a spare entry form. I sent off the entry straightaway and made the deadline by two days. For this occasion I had to prepare quite an amount of material, fifteen songs in all, which encompassed oratorio, opera, operetta, Italian and French songs. There were several different subdivisions within the competition, and once again, I had decided to restrict myself to singing only in the Opera section.

I flew out two days before the event, bearing in mind what had been said to me by Tito Capobianco about resting prior to singing. On this occasion, there were 428 competitors and the competition lasted over a week. My first aria was by Cilea. As I walked out onto the stage, I wasn't as intimidated as I had been in the past. My delivery of the aria was very strong from the onset. Each competitor sang only one aria in the first round. After the first two days, the number of singers was halved, and I was among the half that got to stay.

On the Wednesday, I was asked to sing two pieces. On this occasion I sang the aria from *Luisa Miller* and an Italian song. I had deliberately avoided singing French, as I knew that my diction wasn't good enough and that all the jury were French. Once again, I advanced to the next round. As I was preparing for it, I couldn't help but notice that all of the other competitors were dressing formally; my wardrobe consisted exclusively of casual trousers and short-sleeved shirts.

In the third round, there were twenty singers left. At this point, I sang "Questa o Quella" from *Rigoletto*. That evening the finalists were posted, and as I was viewing the list, I got a little tap on the shoulder from someone behind. It was Pierre Jourdan from Théâtre Impérial de Compiègne. "Monsieur Tynan? I hope that it is your intention to sing a French piece in the next round, as you realize that this is a French international competition and you have not yet graced us with a French piece. I also hope that you have a tuxedo, as the final requires you to wear black tie." I was quite taken aback by the request for the

French piece—the formal wear I had figured out by looking at the other competitors. I said to him, "I have two French pieces. One, the aria from *Carmen*, the other, the aria from *Manon*." "May I suggest that you sing the *Carmen*?" said he.

The finals were to be held at eight o'clock the following evening. I needed first to get a pianist, as the pianist that I had used for the previous rounds was not comfortable playing the next piece. Also, I had to find a tuxedo. The latter was the more difficult problem, and as of a half hour prior to the performance, I still hadn't found one. One of the French singers staying at the same hotel was trying to help me out. Eventually, we located a hotel bouncer who was about my size. I offered to hire his dress suit from him for the duration of the competition. This tuxedo was about a size and a half too big, which made me look slimmer, and had a vague smell of tobacco and old drinks, but beggars can't be choosers. In some respects I was setting a new fashion trend with loose-fitting garments.

While waiting to sing, all the contestants were assembled backstage. What was very noticeable was the degree of competitiveness, which to me appeared quite unfriendly. However, there was one girl from Korea who, in broken English, was quite warm and charming. It also happened that she had one of the better voices. We wished each other luck. We were the second to last and the last to sing. I sang first and, of course, in my rented French bouncer's tuxedo, I picked a French aria. It was very well received by the audience. The jury also clapped. The Korean girl followed and she sang Delilah's aria from *Samson and Delilah*. It was wonderful and I knew that she couldn't be beaten. The jury took over a half an hour to deliberate. While they were out, all the members of the audience were given a slip of paper to write the name of the singer who they felt gave the most crowd-pleasing performance, technique aside.

Prior to the main announcement by the jury, they announced, in order of three, the public's favorite. I was number two and a Spanish baritone was number one, having sung a Zarzuela song. The order of the official competition was as follows: best male, best female, and overall best singer. The best female was the Korean girl, the best male was given to me, and the winner of the Victor Laudorum was the Korean girl. I was told afterward by Pierre Jourdan that it was a split decision between her and myself, but that the casting vote was made by the chairman of the jurors. I was ecstatic and I was very happy for her. I received 10,000 French francs for my troubles.

At the post-competition reception, Pierre Medecin of the Opéra Comique approached me and said that I had a God-given voice. Pierre Jourdan of the Théâtre Impérial de Compiègne offered me the role of Henri Smith in the opera *La Jolie Fille de Perth*. The following morning I met Jourdan at the airport. He offered to buy me a ticket to Paris and to have me spend a day with him in the Compiègne. I went and I have to say that it was one of the most beautiful theaters that I have ever seen. It had amazing acoustics. You could literally hear a pin drop.

I returned to Compiègne for several coaching sessions and several times I vowed that I would never return. The French phonetics were so difficult and frustrating that I wanted to throw in the towel after each session. However, I bore with it. I made so many blunders with the language, often thinking that I had said one thing when, in reality, unintentionally, I had said something quite crude. A fine example of my French/Irish style of speaking came to the fore when I sang to the soprano in a love duet. I should have said, "With my heart and on my honor I'll be there for you," but my French let me down. I apparently told my love that I would be there for her, but it wasn't with my heart and on my honor. The nice thing about not having any idea of what you've said is that you're only partially embarrassed at the time. You know something's wrong by people's faces. The rest of your embarrassment has to wait for translation. After my crude slip, my progress in the French opera came to a sudden halt.

This was a wonderful experience overall and gave me a great grounding in the French language and repertoire. I worked with some wonderful people, in particular, a lady named Irene Etoff, who was a superb coach. The plan was to sing the fully staged opera of *La Jolie*

Fille de Perth, but due to financial difficulties, this project had to be postponed.

By September 1995, I was asked to sing in the Voices of the World gala concert. This was held in Landsdowne Road Rugby Stadium in front of a crowd of twenty-six thousand people. I was accompanied that night by the Irish Symphony Orchestra, conducted by Garoid Grant. Besides myself, there were a tenor from Italy and a wonderful Russian tenor. Susanne Murphy, a leading Irish soprano, was also on the bill. This company also went to Cape Town, South Africa. It was my first visit there and a tremendous experience.

When I returned home in October, I started preparing for my first *Messiah,* conducted by Pronnsias. I had worked quite hard at this and felt very secure. However, minutes before the first performance, I got a panic attack and had to delay the start by twenty minutes until I composed myself. This was the only time I have had such an attack, and I hope never to experience another. The program went extremely well and the following two nights were equally successful. By December 1995, I had sung in nearly every major city in Ireland—a total of forty concerts that year.

My final concert of 1995 was in Belfast. Once again, the BBC offered me an operatic evening. Because of my lifelong admiration for Mario Lanza, I asked if we could make this night a tribute to the legendary tenor. The producers were in favor, and so a complete program of Mario Lanza favorites from "Be My Love" to the serenade from *Student Prince* was performed. All the old favorites were sung and some well-known operatic pieces associated with him were thrown in for good measure. In addition to singing Lanza, I was thrilled that Pronnsias was invited to conduct, as I felt very secure under his baton. That night went wonderfully well, and I was brought back onstage to sing four encores.

I had traveled home from the concert with Pronnsias. He told me that he had plans to do Mendelssohn's *Elijah* for Easter 1996 and asked if I would like the tenor solo. The answer was a firm yes, as I particularly liked the work of this great early Romantic composer. We got back to Dublin late in the evening, and I cannot recall whether I locked the door before I went to sleep. But in the early hours of the morning I woke suddenly to see a dark figure entering my room. I roared my best tenor roar, "Who's there?" and picked up one of my legs and hurled it at the door. At this point I heard an unbelievable clatter as the man ran down the stairs. It was a burglar. I leapt out of the bed, picked up my other leg, and ran on my knees after him. I threw the other leg down the stairs at him. As soon as my second leg left my hand I realized that I was pretty defenseless. Thank God the man wasn't bright or observant, or else he would have realized after seeing space-age limbs fly at him that there was a very short man with a high voice at the top of the stairs. Not exactly intimidating stuff.

At my next port of call, I decided to enter the Francesca Vinnas competition in Barcelona. I departed for Spain in late January 1996. As with the previous competitions that I had entered, there were quite a few contestants. The requirements for this competition were similar to those set out in the French competition, fifteen assorted pieces. I met two Dutch people, Frank van Achen and Eva Westbroch, when I arrived at the hotel. We became superb friends and supported each other throughout the rounds.

All three of us made it to the semifinals. However, the night before the semifinals we went out for a meal and, unfortunately, had one or two too many bottles of wine. Frank and I started to sing. We sang for all we were worth and kept it up for hours. Funny enough, this work-out didn't help our voices the next day. That morning we awoke sounding like basses. We didn't have much success in the semifinal round, but we really enjoyed our impromptu restaurant gig the night before.

During the month of March, my sister Fiona took a call from some people in Waterford, asking me to sing with the Barrack's Street Band. They were celebrating their 125th anniversary and wanted me to be their soloist for the occasion. I was honored and agreed, but I had never heard them so I didn't know what to expect. When I arrived at the rehearsal, I was greeted very warmly and introduced to the forty-five band members. The rehearsal went really well and the band members played their hearts out. I grew very fond of all the members and of Captain Liam Daley, their conductor. Pascal Cody was the treasurer of the band, and he and I formed a friendship that has lasted to this day. I performed several more concerts with the Barrack's Street Band, and each was well received. I am proud to say that I am only the second person to have been granted an honorary membership in the band.

In April 1996, I performed Mendelssohn's *Elijah*, with Pronnsias conducting. The review read as follows: "Tenor Ronan Tynan sang with directness and ease, and appropriately without most of the Italianate mannerisms which have been such a feature of his beautiful style in the past."

When I was preparing for *Elijah*, I had also been working on a semi-staged concert version of the opera *Madama Butterfly* by Puccini, for the gala concerts to be held that July. This was going to be my first major operatic debut. I was really looking forward to it. As usual, Pronnsias was conducting, so I felt very secure. Much to the amazement of the producer, director, and the audience in general, I moved quite well on the stage. I enjoyed the interaction of all the different cast members with me. However, at the very end of the opera, when Butterfly lies dead, having committed suicide, the tenor usually races in and cries, "Butterfly, Butterfly!" For this last scene I was to run onto the stage through a door. As I entered, I tripped over the doorsill. The next thing I knew I was on top of the soprano, a tiny Japanese lass who weighed maybe 120 pounds. I came down on her tiny, frail body like a ton of bricks. She grunted as I landed on her, and I overheard the producer saying, "If her committing hari-kari didn't kill her, Tynan just made sure of it!" Even the audience gasped.

The curtain went down and I got up off her as soon as I could. I wasn't greeted with a cheery smile and there wasn't much communication between us that night at the reception, but I felt that I had achieved a milestone in my life. Having been given the opportunity and the belief that I could do it, I succeeded. Interestingly enough, the reviews mercifully made no reference to my stagecraft and were quite complimentary to my execution of the role. However, they did feel that my voice would need to be a little bigger to sing Puccini.

RTE, the National Television Company of Ireland, had decided to give me a night in the National Concert Hall on my own, doing my second tribute to Mario Lanza. This was to be held in September 1996. Having completed *Butterfly*, I took some time out to enjoy myself and do some horseback riding. On one particular day, I had the misfortune to have a fall, and I fractured the ethmoidal bone in my face. Within a couple of days I was having serious problems with my sinuses. After a few weeks, I could tolerate it no more. I asked a good friend and ear, nose, and throat specialist to perform a CT scan on my face. It showed a narrowing in my sinuses, as well as the fracture. The narrowing restricted proper drainage, which meant that I suffered from a postnasal drip.

I underwent surgery to relieve this problem and was told to stay away from the horses and any other dusty environment, as the last thing that I needed was an infection. I obeyed the orders for three weeks but was becoming so bored that I had to do something. I thought that as long as I didn't clean out a stable or brush down a horse, I would be okay. I was wrong. I got a fungal infection in the area, which caused tremendous problems and delayed my recovery. My biggest fear was that I had a major performance coming up in the Concert Hall. I had jeopardized my second tribute to Mario Lanza, which had been set with a full orchestra. However, I had over two months to recover, so I felt reasonably hopeful that everything would be fine. As the time drew nearer, I still hadn't improved much, and because I hadn't been singing, I had lost my stamina. To take on the arduous program that had been suggested was suicide. But I had no way out. I had to fulfill my obligations.

The concert was on a Friday evening at seven-thirty. The hall was packed to capacity: a sellout. From the very first song, which was "Be My Love," I was in trouble. The fear of God was in me and yet I was imploring God to help me get through the night. By the end of the first half, I had sung eight pieces. My final piece of the first half was

"I'll Walk with God," and when I went to finish the song, the top note wasn't there. I was struck with fear and bowed with the orchestral postlude. I went into the changing room, put my head between my hands, and cried. Pronnsias, who was conducting, said to me, "Dig deep, Ronan, you'll get through it." I went out for the second half, which consisted mainly of opera pieces and opened with "La Donna è Mobile." Amazingly, I held the top B without effort. It reinforced my belief that when one implores God for help, He doesn't ignore it. I got through the concert but was unable to give a second encore. The crowd applauded, but I'm sure that they were aware that something was amiss. This was the start of the end, I thought.

Keith, my friend from medical school, went to the concert. I asked him to be very candid with me and tell me what he thought of the performance that night. He genuinely thought that it was good but had heard me sing better. However, he was sure that the audience was pleased and got their money's worth.

After that night, I asked Fiona to start canceling engagements. I began to consider how I was going to earn a living without singing. It was at this point that I decided to set up my own medical clinic in Johnstown. I took some sports medicine courses in England and Germany. On completion, I opened up the clinic beside my brother-in-law's veterinary practice. Dad was very supportive and would often say, "Weren't you the lucky man that you persisted with the medicine. Where would you be now if you hadn't completed your degree?" My brother Tom and I hadn't been very close for some time but he was also very supportive. His support put an end to any ill feelings that existed between us. We became great friends and he respected the way I dealt with the situation. As I said to him, "There was no other way."

On the day I opened the clinic, I received six phone calls and four patients. Dad came down and sat in the waiting room with the patients who were waiting for treatment. At the time I wasn't too clear why he was there. He later informed me that he sat in the waiting room for support. He figured if it appeared to the other patients that I was busy, it would instill confidence in them. We often laughed about that incident, but he said that when things are going badly, put your best side forward. Within three weeks, word of mouth had spread that I had set up a clinic, and my roster of patients had improved significantly. There were also rumors that I was finished as a singer and would never sing again. I didn't in any way fuel this, but as you can appreciate, scandalmongering is rampant in the artistic profession.

I quickly got back to the routine of working in a full practice again and started to really enjoy my work. I enjoyed the work so much and was so busy that twelve-hour days were common.

* CHAPTER 19 *

*B*y Christmas 1996, I had decided to return to horse riding and I bought a wonderful bay mare called Ballybeg Queen. She had a similar history to mine. She got hurt while jumping and fragmented a bone in her foot that required six months' rest. Even then, there was no guarantee that she would be right. Two of the three vets who saw her X rays told me that the mare was fit only for the slaughterhouse. One vet, Jeremiah, a friend from college, told me that he thought she would fully recover, but that she would need careful rest and attention and would have to be brought slowly back to work. My plan was to go on the amateur show jumping circuit with her. Amateur show jumpers are usually people who work for a living but are passionate about their horses and love to compete on their days off. It was a perfect fit for me.

It was around January 1997 that I noticed Dad's health was beginning to deteriorate. As it was always one of Dad's dreams to go racing, I decided that we would invest in a racehorse. I had bought a Thoroughbred brood mare back in 1994, and at that time she had her foal with her. Three years later, this filly was in training. We had no idea whether she was any good, but that didn't really matter. What was important for both of us was the enjoyment we both got going racing together and watching her run. We named her Siog, which means "fairy" in Irish. Prior to her first race, we took her to a well-known trainer's track to try her out against one of his three-year-olds who had performed well on the track. Siog ran marvelously and showed super potential. This heightened our hopes.

Her first race was in Gowran Park Race Course. She was in a mile and two. She led for three quarters of a mile and it was great. But then her lack of experience kicked in and she ended up placing sixth, out of a field of sixteen. Nonetheless we were delighted with her first performance and waited with bated breath for her next day out, which was to be in Clonmel three weeks later. Dad and I went together to the races in Clonmel. We were excited when the trainer said that he thought Siog could possibly get placed in this race, as she was racing at a shorter distance. Two furlongs from home she was challenging the lead, when suddenly she slipped coming around a bend. Our hearts stopped. There was no injury evident, but after that race she never performed anywhere near her ability. Dad and I were both disappointed, as it curtailed our visits to the horses' enclosure.

By mid-March, the clinic was booming, but Dad's health was still deteriorating. I sent him to Dublin to have a checkup. While his medical condition appeared reasonable for his age, they noted that he had become quite congested in his lungs and had developed mild heart failure. Also, there was a query about his prostate. Dad was a very private man. To get him to have medical attention or to take medication was extremely difficult. The prostate was another matter altogether. His attitude was "I'll be fine! What are you worried about?" I was worried and also recognized that he was losing weight. Fiona and Tom were aware of his problems but felt that I, as the doctor, should handle Dad's medical issues. I continuously sent him to his general practitioner for renewed prescriptions and blood pressure checks. He also started taking heart medication and low-dose steroids to keep his chest open and allow him to breathe easier.

For about six months he was stable. Unfortunately, at this time Mam was diagnosed with Alzheimer's disease. This made matters worse for Dad, as she became very active during the night, constantly looking for things. Dad wasn't getting the sleep he needed. Several times Dad asked me in desperation if I could do something for her, but unfortunately Alzheimer's is a disease for which very little can be done once it takes hold. Mam's and Dad's illnesses had them going in different directions. Mam's physical disposition was very good but her mental state was deteriorating. Dad's physical condition was quickly declining, but mentally he was sound.

I started to compete on the amateur horse jumping circuit in March

1997 with Ballybeg Queen. Our first outing was at the equestrian center in Cavan. The Clark family, who are super people and very supportive amateur riders, run this center. The camaraderie among the amateur competition is extraordinary. Each rider encourages the other to do as well as he can, and if someone is unfortunate enough to fall, everybody shows concern. It's a wonderful, close group of people who usually arrive at these events on a Friday night. But you have to be careful, as bouncing around on a horse on Saturday can be difficult on the constitution if you've visited the pubs with the other competitors on Friday night. This has been well proven by many of us. What happens is a major lapse of concentration, often resulting in a fall or confusion as to where the next fence is located.

I purchased a horse truck with sleeping quarters and I brought Dad to some of the one-day shows. The truck was a tremendous advantage when going on long journeys. You always had a place to rest and a stock of water on board for the horses. Dad reminded me that it was a far cry from the old Commer truck that we used to have. I can vividly remember going to the Piltown Show in County Waterford and having the brakes fail in the old Commer. Dad had looked at me and told me to hold on to the side ring of the door in case we crashed.

Dad loved anything to do with the horses. On these trips it was all about horses and nothing else. Then one day as I was driving down to Cork to the Millstreet Show Dad asked, "How is your voice?" It had been over eight months since I had last sung, and word was out among the music lovers that I was off the circuit and more than likely would never sing again. I said to him that I felt I was healing and didn't want to try anything for a good period of time. Dad understood and didn't pursue it any further. But it set me thinking. Even though I was very happy practicing medicine and my clinic was going well, I did miss singing and the wonderful enjoyment that I got out of it.

It was at this time that I had a phone call from an old friend of mine who was a renowned composer, producer, and documentary filmmaker. Seamus Healy was also a lovely person with a very soft heart. Seamus was direct. "Where the hell are you? Have you disappeared off the face of the earth? I have an idea and I hope that you'll be interested in it. I want to do a documentary on your life." I laughed and said to Shay, "Jesus, they only do those kind of things about people who are dead or are about to die." "Not at all!" said he. "Your life is full of trial and tribulation and is a story worth telling the world. This way others can benefit from your experiences." Knowing Seamus as I do, I couldn't say no, and he knew it before he called. But I said quite seriously, "I don't want my life to be sensationalized, and if there is any element of this in the documentary, we're both history." He promised me that everything he would do would have integrity and good taste. He thus set about putting the wheels in motion.

I told the family of Shay's plan. They were delighted, particularly Dad. I guess that he was so fond and proud of me that he wanted the whole world to see what his son had achieved at this point in his life. Every so often, he would come down to the clinic and wait until I finished and ask whether Shay had been in contact. I said to him, "All in good time, Dad, I promise you. And you will have a major part to play." Dad was very fond of Shay. He respected the work he had done in the past in documentaries and was also impressed by Shay's ability to write songs.

Shay came down to commence filming the documentary in May 1997. There was great excitement and he was a true professional. He interviewed Dad and Mam separately. It was amazing to hear both of them talking about me independently of the other. I always knew that I had a special spot in Dad's heart, and it became very apparent when he spoke of me to Shay. He said that when I was born, he was saddened by the fact that I had a deformity. But being a farmer he knew that nature does these things, and he likened it to the deformities he had seen in calves. His view may have been simplistic, but it was very down-to-earth. He followed this by saying, "We never killed the deformed calves. We did the best we could for them. I was going to do the best I could for Ronan and let God do the rest." Shay asked him about how he felt when I won the Olympic medals. He replied with tears in his eyes, "They were some of the happiest memories of my life." He recalled the phone call from New York after the games in 1984, when I told him that I had watched the flag go up for Ireland. This made him very proud of me, even though he wasn't there to share the glory. Dad was, without doubt, a true Irishman, very proud of his country and its people.

Mam was interviewed in the dining room of Fiona's house. She asked that they not film any of the documentary in the family home. I have no idea why she made that demand, but I can only assume that she somehow realized that the house wasn't looking its finest. She didn't want to let the side down. It wouldn't have mattered to me, but I didn't want to upset her. Dad said to me, "Anything for peace, Ronan." Naturally, I wouldn't go against his wishes. Amazingly, on this occasion, Mam was very coherent and had a vivid recollection of my youth and, more to the point, her goals for me as a child.

As part of the interview, Mam and I browsed over a photo album, which contained several pictures of me growing up. She recalled the events in the photographs as if they'd happened yesterday. She then commented that I was much fitter at the time of the photographs compared with the day of the interview. "Thank you, Mam," I said. We both laughed. Sometimes one gets very confused looking from the outside at someone suffering from mental illness and the way that it manifests itself. At the time of the interview, talking to my mother, you would never have known that she was afflicted with Alzheimer's.

Shay then interviewed Fiona, who needed no help whatsoever to start recalling my past. In the course of the interview, she made reference to my getting married and said, "Whoever will marry Ronan will have to be very special. She cannot in any way tie him down. Ronan is a free spirit and will always remain that way. Whoever she is, she will have to fit in with his life such as it is, full of new adventure." I think that was Fiona's way of saying that I'm a handful.

Having completed all the interviews, Shay decided to hold a party for all my friends in my house at Tullaroan. I invited some friends from college, as well as those I'd met through fox hunting and old friends from childhood. Wine and song flowed all night long, with intermittent eating. It was a hell of a night and a hell of a party. Everybody enjoyed it, and I really was delighted so many people turned up. I knew then that Shay would do a super job on the documentary.

But he still hadn't interviewed me. Shay scheduled my interview for the morning after the party. I think he was hoping that I'd be easier to handle after a good night of celebration. Shay was well rehearsed in what he was about to ask and very selective in approaching delicate issues. We discussed all aspects of my life, including romantic liaisons. I told him that I didn't think I was ever going to get married. I admitted that I would be very difficult to live with and had difficulty staying in one place for too long. I doubted that any sane woman would be able to put up with me. The woman I married would be as daft as I was, or I'd stay single.

A week after Shay's departure, I got Ballybeg Queen ready to go to the Mallow Show in County Cork. This event was the last qualifier before the Dublin Horse Show. It was one of my dreams that someday I would get a chance to ride in the Dublin Horse Show. On that great day in Mallow, I was thrilled to qualify with Ballybeg, finishing in eighth position. Only the top nine qualified for the Dublin Horse Show. I drove my lorry home that evening and planned the next day to go to another show in Limerick with a horse called Cavaradossi. This horse was high-spirited and often took a while to settle down. I decided to exercise him when I returned from Mallow, so that he wouldn't be too fresh the next day at the show.

I went out to the arena at about eight o'clock. It was a beautiful evening, and I started doing some groundwork with him. After about twenty minutes of straight riding I thought he was settled enough to begin jumping. Everything went fine until we reached the double fence. After Cavaradossi landed the first part he gave a ferocious buck. This unbalanced me and my feet came out of the stirrups. As the horse sensed my imbalance, he gave another buck, more powerful than the first. I was thrown into the air. I landed on my back on the hard ground. I couldn't move.

I had felt a sudden tear at some point in my back, but I couldn't ascertain exactly where. I immediately ran my hands down my thighs to see if I could still feel my legs. Thankfully, I had lost no sensory perception, but within seconds I developed the most horrific pain in my pelvis and lower back. The pain was so intense that it was almost unbearable. I began screaming at the top of my lungs for help. I realized no one was coming and tried to get up. The pain was so intense that I passed out in the process. When I came to, I dragged myself the sixty meters from the arena into the house. I crawled on my hands and knees, but mostly used my arms to maneuver myself along the stones. Thankfully, I had left the house door open.

I eventually pulled the phone down and called for an ambulance and then called Fiona. After that my next recollection was of a number of people around me. I was brought by ambulance to Kilkenny County Hospital, where I was immediately taken for X rays. I was given a painkiller that, thank God, lessened the pain considerably. The consultant on duty, Mr. Farrell, showed me my X rays. It showed an open book fracture of the pelvis, as well as four transverse fractures of the facets of lumbar vertebras L1–4. I had broken my pelvis and my back. I cringed as I saw my opportunity to ride in Dublin slip away.

The following morning, I was sent by ambulance to the Meath Hospital in Dublin for surgery. I felt every bump on that road and cursed the County Council for not maintaining the roads properly. When I arrived at Meath, I recognized many of the old familiar faces. I had worked with many of the nurses during my stay at the hospital. I was put under the care of Mr. John McEllwain. What a turn for the books! This was the same man I had worked for three years previously. He asked me, "What have you done to yourself?" I replied, "I think the pelvis is gone, and there are some cracks here and there in the lower part of the back."

He turned to me and said, "We'll have to externally fixate your pelvis to correct the fracture." I looked at him in shock and said, "Surely you can put in a plate. If you externally fixate me, I'll be completely immobile for at least three months. I can't afford that; I have a clinic to run and horses to ride." Upon hearing this McEllwain got a little angry and said, "Listen, friend, you're in a bad way, and I'm responsible to correct the problem that you have just presented me with. If I feel that we can plate you satisfactorily, then I will do it. Otherwise, I will use my expertise to correct the problem." He turned away, and I said, "Please don't externally fixate me. It would make my life very difficult."

The next morning, I was sent to the operating theater to have surgery. The whole process lasted about two hours. When I awoke from the anesthetic, the first thing I did was to look down at my pelvis, and I gave a sigh of relief when I saw no external fixators. I was heaped full of painkillers to relieve some of the throbbing pain.

That evening, Mr. McEllwain appeared for his ward rounds. As he approached me, he said, "Well, Ronan, how do you feel?" I told him that I was as sore as a boil, but that I was very grateful that he hadn't used external fixators to mend my pelvis. McEllwain is a big man, standing six foot four with an imposing presence. But at that moment he was as gentle as a lamb and very tender. I said to him, "I always knew you had a soft side. You just don't like to show it to your subordinates." He said, "That's right, Doctor!" He laughed and walked off saying, "See you tomorrow. Sleep well." "Sure," I said.

All of my friends in the amateurs came to visit me. After ten days, having pursued rigorous physiotherapy, I decided to check myself out of the hospital. This did not amuse Mr. McEllwain. When we met in the corridor, there were words. The final quote from me was "It's my life. I'll be held accountable for it. I have a practice to run, and a mortgage to be paid. So just let me get on with it." "You're as stubborn as a mule," he snapped, "and a thick one at that!" I just hobbled on. Then he shouted, "Make sure you turn up in my outpatient clinic in two weeks, so I see how you are progressing. Mind yourself." "I will," I said, "and thanks for everything."

I was collected from the hospital by Brian and Steve Mullins, who are amateur riding friends of mine. They brought me up to Old Castle in County Meath for the weekend. I returned home on the Sunday night. I was washed out completely. The following Monday morning I went to the clinic and started to work. The sweat poured out of me because of the pain I felt as I struggled to make every movement. The nights were not much better, and I took to biting the pillow every time I had to turn onto my side.

I became much stronger as the weeks passed by. It was only sudden movements that would give me a dart of pain. After four weeks, I felt that I could try to ride the horse again. I returned to see Mr. McEll-wain after a month. He greeted me like a son. I was quite taken aback, as I thought that he was going to lambaste me for not turning up sooner. He was amazed at how much I had improved. I informed him that I was one of God's own and He just wanted to get me back on the road as soon as possible. This way we could see how much more damage I could possibly do to myself.

The Dublin Horse Show was on within two weeks. I had asked my good friend Ger Smith to keep Ballybeg Queen fit for me. I decided the Saturday before Dublin to go ride in a little show so as to restore my confidence. The show went really well, but my pelvis ached like hell once I got off the horse. I knew that would be the case because I hadn't been riding in such a long time.

I drove up to Dublin the night before the competition and parked my truck on the grounds of the Royal Dublin Society. I slept there all night in quite a bit of pain, which worried me. I took two anti-inflammatories in the morning and the relief was almost instantaneous. The competition was to start at eight that morning. As luck would have it, I was the first competitor. This was not what I wanted, because I wanted to see others perform, to see if the course had any hidden dog legs, etc.

Shay Healy also wanted to tape this part of my life, but he was unaware that I was first up. He arrived as I was just starting and sent the cameraman flying down to the arena to get as much on film as possible. Ballybeg was in super form that morning, maybe a little too fresh. She stood off a little too far from fence number six and touched the pole, which rolled off. Naturally I was disappointed, but that subsided very quickly. I had achieved my dream. Against the odds and in spite of the excruciating pain, I rode in Dublin. More to the point, I was the first double amputee to qualify and compete in the Dublin Horse Show.

When I left the arena and came out into the passageway, whom did I spot? Mr. McEllwain was there walking with his son. He didn't recognize me immediately until I shouted, "Hi, John!" He looked up. "My God," he said, "only six weeks ago you were on the flat of your back. Have you any sense at all?!" I responded, "Yes, I have of course. I must pack as much as possible into this life before it's taken." We laughed. "Any success?" he asked. "Four faults, unfortunately."

My brother, Tom, and his wife were there. It was at this point that Shay interviewed Tom. Tom's famous quote: "Ronan has no reverse gear. It's only forward. But I'm happy that he now has a proper profession." I often joke with him about this comment. He defends himself by saying, "You knew what I meant when I said this." Yes, I did.

CHAPTER 20

By mid-November of 1997, Dad's health had deteriorated quite badly. Shay had suggested that I should record an album, which was one of Dad's dreams for me. Dad repeatedly brought up the project, making it clear that he thought it would be good for my career. I realized that time was running short for Dad, so I agreed to do it. As I hadn't been singing for some time, my biggest fear was the condition of my voice. Shay had negotiated a deal with Sony records in Ireland to finance the album.

The choice of songs was left up to me, so I decided to let Dad help me pick the music. He felt that it was very important that we choose popular favorites that would be easily enjoyed and would stick in the memory of the general public.

We selected sixteen songs between us. Many of them had been sung by Mario Lanza. However, each of us had choices we wanted to include. Dad loved a song called "The Roses of Picardy." From *Carousel,* he selected two songs, "If I Loved You" and "You'll Never Walk Alone." I, on the other hand, love the music of Ivor Novello. So, we decided that I would have two of my favorites and that he would have two of his. We would have to mutually agree on the balance of the material. Dad also suggested that I not record any opera arias on this album. He felt that the bigger portion of the Irish public enjoys popular songs. I couldn't argue with that point. The project seemed to give his step an added spring. From that day on, he used to ask me constantly, "Any progress on our album?"

Sony had decided to use Frank McNamara as arranger and producer of the album. This pleased both Dad and me, as I knew Frank from my childhood when we were in primary school together. I knew that Frank would be amenable to my needs. The recording was planned for

January 1998, with the idea of releasing the album in April or May. Everything seemed to be fitting into place. I started to slowly get back into singing by vocalizing on my own. Once I felt that I was ready, I decided to go back to Tony Roden for singing lessons. This was all to happen in the early part of 1998. On December 19, 1997, Dad suffered a stroke and was rushed to the hospital. Something inside me at that time told me that was the start of the real end for him. While my voice became stronger with every passing day, I would have given up singing forever just to have Dad here with me. Unfortunately, God doesn't allow those privileges.

Dad was moved to a private hospital around December 23. He had suffered a left midbrain infarct, which left him with aphasia, a great difficulty in speaking. As he was also unable to swallow, a PEG feeding tube was inserted directly into his stomach. When I went in to see him, he wrote down on a piece of paper, "What is wrong with me?"

I'm not much good at telling lies, so I told him the truth. He had suffered a brain hemorrhage. He then wrote, "Will I recover?" I told him that there was a good possibility that things would return to normal. But I was only too well aware that he was already in cardiac and respiratory failure. It was only a matter of time before his kidneys would fail. In spite of what I knew as a doctor, as a son I convinced myself that he would recover from the stroke.

I had arranged to go away for four days to Belgium. Someone had fallen ill, and I was asked to be part of a concert performance. Fiona thought that it might be a good idea for me to get away so, reluctantly, I went. On my second day there, the phone rang just as I was picking it up to call Fiona. It was Fiona on the other end of the line. She informed me that she felt Dad had deteriorated quite badly over the last twenty-four hours and feared the worst. I came home immediately and went straight to the hospital to see him. To my astonishment, he was sitting up in his bed, eating biscuits! "Wow," he said, "I bet I had you worried!" I gave him a hug and said affectionately, "You old tramp!" We laughed, and it appeared that he was coming around and that there was a good chance he would make a recovery. The family was all relieved and there was a glimmer of hope among us all.

Christmas came and went. It was quite different without him at the table. We decided to celebrate the day at my house in Tullaroan. Fiona did the cooking. Although all the external trappings were there, the mood was somber and reflective. Mam was holding her own. Occasionally, she would become a little confused, but in general she was good.

The album's first recording with the orchestra was planned for the eighth of January. The day before, I went in to see Dad and told him that our project was just about to start. He was really pleased. "Make sure and let me hear the first unedited version." I said, "Dad, that could be terrible." He said, "It could also be the best of the day!" Both our spirits were good.

I recorded three songs on the eighth. One of them was Dad's favorite, "The Roses of Picardy." I still felt that he wasn't out of the woods and God forbid that I would be right. I wanted him to hear as much of the album as was possible. I returned that evening and went into the hospital. He was fine. I had a cassette of that day's recording session. Unfortunately, the tape I had didn't have the vocal part. We listened to the arrangements and Dad thought that they were really beautiful. "Shame that they didn't get the voice with it," he said. "But not to worry, it will be great, and you're finally leaving something worthwhile behind."

I returned to see him again on the afternoon of the ninth. This time, there was a notable change. Dad and I had discussed taking him home for a day for a visit. He was really looking forward to this, but when I broached the question of coming home with me, he declined the offer. Dad said, "I would hate to think that I would get a cold at this stage, having gone through all the rest of the problems." I was a little sad, as I was really looking forward to his visit, but I understood his concern.

The change that I had noticed that day was in his demeanor. He just seemed to be down, almost faded. A week later all of us were in visiting him and he asked me how the album was going. I said that it was going fine and that Frank had decided to put down all the instrumental tracks first and then add the vocal line when we could get a couple of days together. No sooner had I told him this than he got a biscuit into his hand and started shoving it into his mouth without beginning to chew it.

I knew straightaway that he was going downhill faster than I had expected. He talked very little to us after that. I told Fiona and Tom that the end was much nearer than we realized. It would be better for all of us, when we found him coherent on future visits, to say our good-byes, as we might not get another chance. His mind would likely be elsewhere. Within a couple of days, he was extremely agitated and unresponsive. Mam had no idea how bad he was but became frustrated with all the drips and lines that had been inserted in him. She herself had to be supervised whenever she was with him.

By late February, all of us were visiting him daily in shifts. I often took the night shift, as it was the quietest time and I was able to assist in suctioning out his congested chest. Every time the phone rang at home I would fear the worst. It was usually the hospital keeping me up-to-date on the status of his health. By the end of February, his breathing had become very labored. He was unaware that anyone was visiting him. From that point on, it was just a matter of when the Lord above would decide to take him. In spite of all that was going on, I had not given his death a great deal of thought. More to the point, I didn't know how I would deal with it when it did occur.

Fiona was teaching in Kilkenny and would visit Dad at every free moment. On the fifth of March, she went in to see him at lunchtime and brought him my recording of "You'll Never Walk Alone." She said that she saw a tear in his eye when she played it for him. At the end of the song, the sound engineer had left a question I had asked: "How's that?" Fiona said that Dad responded, "Fine."

At twenty past three, on March 5, 1998, my dear father, Edmond, died. I was in the clinic at the time, and Margaret, my brother-in-law's secretary, knocked on the door and asked me to come into the office. She told me the news and I immediately went into Kilkenny. I met

Fiona and Mam, and looked at Dad. It was the most peaceful I had seen him since this illness had started.

We had to make a decision. First of all, were we going to give him a wake at home? Fiona wanted this to be done in her house. We decided to send his body to the funeral home to be embalmed. The next day, we would bring him home for the wake.

The funeral home was situated in the Butts, in Kilkenny. This was an area that Dad was very fond of. He often referred to the people who lived there as the backbone of Kilkenny. I couldn't sleep all that night while he was in the funeral home. I felt that I had done the wrong thing by sending him there, as he had no one around him. Fiona reassured me that he would be happy there.

We brought him home the following evening and waked him all that night. The next evening we said the rosary in the house before he was moved to the church. My heart wept as they went to put the lid on his coffin. I couldn't cope with the fact that it was the final good-bye. I stopped them from closing the coffin. I wasn't ready. Eventually, the lid was put down and we brought him to the church.

So many people turned out for the funeral. I had decided for the church the next day that I would give him his own private concert as a send-away gift. I rang both Damian and Frank to see if I could get either of them to play the organ. Both of them obliged. Damian came from France and Frank from Dublin. I also asked Deirdre Masterson to sing at the funeral, which she did. On that morning, I was up at five o'clock, as I couldn't sleep. Mam was in the kitchen having a cup of tea. I was getting my music together, preparing for the ceremony. I could hardly speak. She asked me what I was doing. I told her I was getting music for the funeral mass.

"Whose funeral?" she asked. I nearly died. I started to explain to her that Dad had passed away. It was like it had never happened. I called Fiona and for two hours we talked to Mam, until we had got her mind back to the situation.

The funeral Mass began at eleven o'clock and the church was packed.

It looked to me as though the whole town had closed down and everyone came to pay their respects. Frank McNamara, the man who produced my first solo album, and Damian Whiteley, my pianist and colleague from the opera school in Manchester, came to play the organ for my father.

As the last song my father had heard me singing was "You'll Never Walk Alone," we decided to start the proceedings by playing my recording of that song. I then sang "Be Still My Soul" and the Mass began. I struggled with "Be Still, My Soul," feeling very out of sorts both in mind and body.

I sang four more songs that morning but moved over to the head of the coffin and kept my hands in a final instinctive embrace of my father. While I knew that there were hundreds of people in the church, it was just me and Dad one last time. I sang for all I was worth, but I was singing only for him. My final farewell to him was "Danny Boy," a song Dad loved. He had always instructed me to sing the last line ". . . and I shall sleep in peace until you come to me" softly, fading away at the end. I managed to finish, as he would have wanted, but was soon overcome.

The funeral was hard on me and equally hard on my Fiona, who read a poem entitled "Dad." She struggled at times but stood up to the trial and did a great job. But the most difficult task that morning rested on my brother Tom's shoulders. We called on him to deliver the eulogy. He gave a wonderful account of Dad that was both humorous and moving, and I remember it to this day.

Dad was buried in the family grave in the church grounds. Within three hours, the whole ceremony was over. By the following Tuesday I was back to the clinic and it was business as usual. But there were no more visits from Dad to make up the numbers. No phone calls to Tom with Dad on the other end of the phone telling Tom how many patients I had seen that day. It was a lonely time.

Shay's documentary, *Dr. Courageous* premiered on April 7, one month after Dad died. It was a beautiful piece, and we were very lucky to have been able to view Dad before his sickness really took hold. The documentary received great reviews and has given hope to many physically challenged people. This was a wonderful reward for such an undertaking.

I completed the album by May. *My Life Belongs to You* was dedicated to Dad. The album was released in August 1998. It jumped straight onto the charts at number five. It went gold after five weeks, and platinum after three months.

CHAPTER 21

In July 1998, I rode into the massive show jumping arena at Arnheim, Germany, and was met by a magnificent burst of colors. From horseback, I surveyed the course that appeared decorated with spectacular rainbows. To me it looked like the sun was penetrating through a blanket of mist several miles in the distance.

The extremely powerful bright lights allowed no shadow, and every fence sparkled. Great pots and displays of green shrubbery and beautiful floral arrangements marked the center of each jump. On this occasion, I was representing Northern Ireland at the International Championships. There was no doubt in my mind that this was truly the pinnacle of my career as a horseman.

My horse, Uptown Lady, was a beautiful chestnut mare standing about 16.2 hands high, with a central blaze down her forehead and a flaxen mane and tail. She became the talk of the place, not only because she was so beautiful but also because of her genuine and loyal nature.

Uptown Lady was at her peak, and over that championship weekend I received many unsolicited offers to sell her. But she wasn't for sale at any price. No money could replace the love and fun she had given to me over that past year. She had placed in several competitions around Ireland prior to being selected to compete for the international event.

The first time I saw Uptown Lady was at the Millstreet Horse Show in August 1997. I was with Dad that day when all of a sudden I saw the rump of this fine chestnut mare. Dad and I looked at each other and commented about her build. I had decided I was going to buy her no matter what. We watched her perform and she was pure class. She seemed to really enjoy what she was doing. When Dad went off to meet Mam, I went off to meet Uptown. I asked the rider if he was the owner. He told me no but said, "The owner is very near at hand and I believe she wants to sell her." That was music to my ears. Uptown hailed from Claremorris, County Mayo. She was American-bred. I talked to the owner for a while, and we finally came to the price she had in mind. Uptown's name was well deserved, as she was clearly on the expensive side. But I was willing to stretch that far considering what a fine animal I was getting. We made the deal that day in Cork.

On the following Tuesday I took off to Claremorris to pick her up. The trip took nearly five hours and I got there about five in the evening. On the return we had to drive through the town of Knock, where there is a famous religious site dedicated to the Blessed Virgin Mary. I parked the horse truck just outside the basilica and went in to pay my respects. While I was praying, I sensed that someone was with me. This wasn't unusual for me when I was deep in prayer. But that day the feeling was stronger than ever. As I looked up I saw Uptown looking in a large window at me with her ears pricked. From that moment I knew she would be with me for the rest of her days.

On the day of the International Championships her mane was tightly platted, over twenty plaits closed over by white rubber bands. Her tail was free-flowing and her hooves glistened in the light dew. She looked radiant—just like a supermodel ready to walk down the catwalk. Like a finely tuned athlete her musculature was so well defined that any veterinary student would have been thrilled to have her as a surface anatomy specimen. She was powerful enough to carry my weight effortlessly with most of her power coming from her hindquarter. She was the classic show-jumping model—built like a tank but graceful as a gazelle. Like me, she reveled in the anticipation of the competition.

I knew from the very moment we arrived in Arnheim we were in sync. Our first competition that weekend was the speed round. As we entered the decorative arena, Uptown decided to stop at the massive mirror that was mounted on the right wall. I didn't interrupt her few seconds of vanity as she checked herself out, pricking her ears and giving her usual nod as if to tell me, "Right, Ronie, I am the babe in this arena; let's show them how a real lady performs."

She looked a million dollars and I wasn't too far behind her with my brand-new jacket and brilliant white jodhpurs, not forgetting my black boots, which I had spit-shined for nearly two hours the night before. Uptown sniffed the air, thick with sawdust and that unmistakable smell of horses that only horse people love. She proceeded to get into her elegant and gathered canter and we started. Both of us were full of confidence, and I gently directed Uptown to do what she did best, clear obstacles.

She jumped like a stag, not putting a foot wrong. Our time in that competition got us sixth place. I was beside myself with delight. As for Uptown, she just gloated in the attention. Every time we finished a round of jumping she always got her customary Polo Mints, which she loved crunching, a small reward for such a great performance.

The Grand Prix, the main event of the championships, was held on the second day. Sixty competitors from ten European countries were entered. Thirteen fences stood four feet high before us. I knew this would be a serious challenge but not beyond our capabilities. All was going according to plan until we came to the final vertical fence, five black-and-white poles standing in line with three or four inches between them, approximately four foot three in height. Rounding the corner going away from the entrance pocket, Uptown slipped on the brown loosely bound clay, going down on one knee. The crowd let out an audible gasp. My stomach churned as I was thrown onto her neck. My feet were no longer in the stirrups. It seemed a no-win situation, but Uptown quickly regained her stride and, pushing me back into the saddle, balanced us. With just three strides to the fence she vaulted up cleanly over. It was as if she had wings. This rescue showed great heart and I loved her for it. The normally sedate crowd went wild. I gave her the biggest hug after I dismounted. I was full to the brim with love for her and I didn't care who saw me.

After the final, Uptown and I were rewarded with a yellow sixth-place rosette, which was pinned on her bridle. Three other Irishmen took first, second, and third. Standing with them I took pride that I'd performed to the peak of my ability. Much more important, I had gotten there on my own merit, competing against able-bodied men and women from all over Europe. Seated proudly on that magnificent horse I watched through my tears as the green, white, and gold Irish flag was raised above the stadium.

That evening I celebrated in typical Ronan style with all the other competitors, drinking into the late hours and belting out, as hard as I could, some of the old Irish classics. Boy, was that a night to remember after a morning filled with intangible solemnity.

They say that a foal takes its traits from its mother. I've often wondered whether God coded Mrs. Tynan with a special gene for obstinacy and motivation when she conceived me. I think of myself as an ordinary, God-fearing man who has done extraordinary things only because the people closest to me have had such a strong belief in me and willed me to succeed. Most important of all, the Man Upstairs has wanted me to.

I've persevered through pain and failure after failure, knowing that to succeed at anything you not only have to practice, you have to have the inherent will to succeed.

The harder I've worked the more luck I've had and the more I've been able to enjoy my successes. In preparation for the International Championships at Arnheim, Uptown Lady and I had worked so hard that the competition itself was the beautiful white icing on the cake. As an unorthodox horseman, I have certainly had to struggle to find the technique that was right for the horse and me. Still unable to bear my heels down on a horse as most do, I have to keep my backside firmly anchored into the saddle. Rather than using external prods I must will the horse to turn, riding more by rhythm than touch.

✷ CHAPTER 22 ✷

*B*ack in February 1998, I received a phone call from Bill Hughes. He was head of Radius Television in Dublin. I had known Bill since my time on *Go for It,* where he was one of the judges. I got on very well with him. On this occasion, he asked me whether I would be interested in becoming a member of an Irish Tenors group. I told him that I would. He told me that this group he was putting together would mainly be singing Irish material. I was delighted and said, "Count me in." He then asked me whether I knew of any other good tenors who would be interested in such a project. A name came straight to mind: Anthony Kearns. I had heard Anthony sing in the *Feis* only once, but I was very impressed with the voice. He told me that Finbar Wright had been asked, but due to contractual difficulties was unable to become part of the group. I wondered whether he had asked Frank Patterson. He replied in the affirmative, but said that Frank had indicated that it was too late in his career to embark on any new endeavors. His solo diary was full. He said, "Ronan, at the moment, this is just a thought. But should it become a viable proposition, can I rely on you?" "No problem," I replied.

In late June, I received another call from Bill telling me that the project was moving forward. They had teamed up with TV Matters and Faust Productions, who brought John McDermott to the table. John was from Canada, of Irish heritage. PBS was planning to do an Irish Tenors special with John. When Bill Hughes, Daniel Hart, and Pat Faust met they decided to combine forces and produce an Irish Tenors special in Ireland. This would take place on the thirteenth of October, at the Royal Dublin Society Concert Hall, in the Ballsbridge section of Dublin.

On August 15, John flew in from Canada. Bill Cosell was selected to be the director of the show, having previously directed The Three

Tenors in Los Angeles. A couple of weeks prior to this meeting Bill Hughes had asked me who I thought would be a good musical arranger for such material. I suggested Frank McNamara, remembering the wonderful job that he had done on my album. Not being familiar with arrangers and musical directors, I had no idea other than Frank. Bill contacted him and he came on board as well.

More than a hundred and fifty songs were to be played through on this weekend. By the third day the list had narrowed down to thirty. By the fourth day, the program was selected. We each had four solos. I had sung "The Town I Loved So Well," written by Phil Coulter. I particularly liked this song and felt that I could do justice to it. There was a unanimous decision made that I would sing this song. All in all, there were twenty tracks: twelve solos and eight trios. The music then had to be arranged and harmonies had to be put together for the three of us.

This didn't prove too difficult. John, most of the time, sang the melody, while Anthony and I sang the harmony. Frank presented us with the music six weeks before the program. I was extremely nervous, as I only knew one or two of these songs in full. My work was cut out for me. It was different for Anthony and John, as both of them knew most of the material that had been selected. I decided to bring Damian over from England to work with me for three weeks prior to the concert, so that I would be secure musically.

Five days before the show, we were all booked into the Herbert Court Hotel in Ballsbridge. This was within walking distance of the concert hall. Rehearsals started in earnest. Frank would arrive at the Radius building and we would have piano rehearsals from ten in the morning until three in the afternoon. Two days prior to the show, we had our first orchestral rehearsal. When we heard the wonderful arrangements, it brought the whole show up to a different level, and our adrenaline started to pump. We rehearsed the night before the show until midnight. We were exhausted and I feared that we had blown the performance by overrehearsing. Thankfully, the next morning I got up feeling great, having had a really good night's sleep, and was really excited.

The show was to start at 8 P.M., and as this was a recording for television, the audience was asked to refrain from clapping or singing along. We walked out onstage to tremendous applause. At that moment, I knew that this show was going to be a great success, not just in Ireland but all over the world. It would follow in the footsteps of *Riverdance*.

We opened with a medley of songs, starting with "Minstrel Boy." "Believe Me If All Those Endearing," sung by John, followed. Then I sang "I'll Take You Home Again, Kathleen." Then Anthony sang "Mountains of Mourne." The audience showed wonderful appreciation. This had a great effect on the three of us, and we all started to sing wonderfully. For me, the three songs that I felt moved the audience the most were John's interpretation of "The Old Man," Anthony's rendition of "Boolavogue," and my emotional performance of "The Town I Loved So Well." The crowd seemed to be overcome with the euphoria of the whole show and the nostalgia and sentiments of the songs being performed.

By the end of the show, we were all exhausted, but it had been one of the most memorable events of my life. I really wished that Dad could have been present. He would have surely loved every minute of it. But I knew, deep inside, he wasn't too far away during that show.

My singing career had once again taken off, with even greater impetus than the first time. Bookings were coming in from all over. Once again, I had to turn down work, not because I was sick, but because I wasn't able to be in two places at once.

I was invited to Limerick to perform in the New Year's Gala concert in 1999. This was quite a prestigious event, and it went really well. I realized that I had come back much stronger vocally than I had been prior to the accident. Every time I would sing, I asked Dad to intercede for me, so that my performances would be as good as I could give. That's all I asked. As yet, he has not let me down.

PBS had planned their fund-raising drives during the March period. As they were using the *Irish Tenors Show* as one of the major draws of the campaign, they requested The Irish Tenors to be on the set, live, when they were asking for pledges. We started in Boston and then went to Hartford, Philadelphia, Long Island, and finally New York. This was great fun, but exhausting. As a result of this drive we realized the impact the show had on the American audience. Between the great reception for our show and the recognition that there are forty million people of Irish descent living in America, it dawned on us that we might have something here.

In July of that year we began an American tour in the Northeast and continued to the West. Our first show was in the Fleet Center in Boston. The Royal Philharmonic Orchestra from London traveled with us, and Frank McNamara conducted. We brought the rich tradition of Irish song to all those people who joyously celebrated Ireland's spirit with us. I will never forget walking out on the stage for the first time in Boston. There was such a tremendous uproar—it was an emotional high, and we reveled in it. I didn't think that that could be topped, until I walked out to sing my first song in Madison Square Garden in New York. There were fifteen thousand people there and they bellowed their approval. We were likened to David who conquered Goliath. We sang triumphantly, full of emotion and heart. We had similar experiences at all the other venues. Our fan base, which wasn't limited to only the Irish, seemed to be increasing in number every day.

The first leg of the tour was an outstanding success. By the completion of the West Coast leg, album sales were over one million copies. We were number three on the *Billboard* charts for a period of twenty-six weeks. It was like living the American Dream.

When we returned from this first leg, we recorded our Christmas album, called *Home for Christmas*. It was released in November 1999. This album also sold quite well, considering that during the Christmas period the market is saturated with this type of music. Nevertheless, The Irish Tenors' fans made sure that we would not remain on the shelf. They wanted us for Christmas, and that was it. Thank God for the fans!

During the month of September 1999, I received a call from one of the directors of the show *20/20* on ABC. He asked me if I would allow them to do a documentary on my life. I was quite amused, as this was the second group of people in the space of two years who were interested in what an Irishman got up to during his life. I was flattered and honored that the American public would find my life story worthy of attention. I agreed to the project. Within three weeks, a TV crew plus a producer and a director flew over to start the five-day filming.

They followed me everywhere and interviewed many of my close friends as well as my family. They attended one of my concerts and watched with great interest how I prepared for my solo performances. The documentary was executed very elegantly. There was no hidden agenda, and questions were put in a very dignified and tactful manner. It aired with an introduction by Barbara Walters. She was apparently very moved by my life story and was very generous in her praise. As a result of this documentary being shown in America, I no longer had the anonymity that would be afforded most artists. My life was now an open book.

I had no idea what it was going to be like as a singer to be suddenly thrust into the limelight. In many respects I felt exposed and insecure. Soon I had an offer to appear at Feinstein's in the prestigious Regency Hotel on Park Avenue in New York. They wanted me for three weeks in December. I was absolutely thrilled, but I needed to find a pianist to accompany me. Up to that time, I had always worked with Damian, but now that he was studying in Switzerland I needed to find an able replacement. This I found in a charming man called Patrick Healy, with whom I immediately established a great rapport and friendship. We were sent a program by Michael Feinstein's manager outlining what he wanted me to sing. Patrick worked with me for a few weeks to get the program up and running. It consisted of Irish songs, Christmas favorites, wartime songs, Broadway hits, and some opera. Patrick and I flew over four days prior to opening night and rehearsed in a mid-Manhattan studio.

The day before we opened we had to let Alan, Michael Feinstein's manager, hear the program in its entirety. He was delighted with what he heard, and Patrick and I gave a great sigh of relief. This was the first time I had not had any input into the songs selected. The afternoon of the show we rehearsed at Feinstein's and it was there that I met two wonderful people, Sherry Laveroni, general manager of all the Loew's Hotels, and her husband, Jerry, a larger-than-life figure whom I adopted as an older brother. Sherry was enormously supportive no matter what I sang. She became very emotional when I sang "Danny Boy" and "The Impossible Dream." I knew then that I could be a success in an intimate setting.

The show was planned for eight o'clock. It was sold out and there were a number of people representing the press. This definitely set the heart crossways in me, but there was no going back. The show lasted an hour and ten minutes, and I had a meet and greet afterward. Fiona had flown over for my opening night, which was a great support to me, as did Bill Hughes, Daniel Hart, and some of the lovely people I had met while on tour with the tenors. The critics from *The New York Times* and the *Post* were also there. Occasionally, I could see them write down little notes about the songs they were hearing. I wasn't fazed by them, but I knew that within the next week their reviews would play a role in the numbers attending the show. I had the great pleasure of meeting Michael Feinstein, Rosemary Clooney, and Phil Coulter, to name but a few. I was particularly excited when I received a big bottle of bourbon from Rosemary, wishing me the best of luck on opening night. She is truly a wonderful lady.

The owners of the hotel, the Tisch family, also attended the opening night. John Tisch and his parents were very pleased with my performance and had great words of encouragement, which all combined to make this a very enjoyable and memorable evening. Over the next three weeks I performed twenty shows. The staff at the Regency cared for me very well, as if I were one of their own family. It was such a delight to have a home away from home at the hotel. I met some wonderful people, many of whom have become great friends.

While I was performing at Feinstein's, I used to wake up early in the morning and go straight to the review page in the newspaper. At the start of the second week, the review from the *Times* came out. The headline read: SINCERITY AND STANDARDS FROM AN IRISH TENOR. It was very complimentary: "Tynan has a beautiful voice, but what makes him an endearing performer is his utter lack of peacock strutting showmanship . . . his respect for his material and his mixture of innocence and fervor are keys to rediscovering the simple emotional truths in the most tired warhorses. In its peeling away of decades of encrusted sentimentality, Mr. Tynan is an exercise in purification." I was thrilled to bits and rang anybody and everybody I knew to tell them. I knew then that the show was a success.

I left for home on the twenty-second of December a very tired but very happy man. My singing career had started in earnest. The plans for the new millennium were already taking shape. The Irish Tenors were going to record another live album. This time it would be in Belfast.

CHAPTER 23

Having reflected on my life thus far and all the events that have occurred up to now, it started me thinking. Where did that spirit really come from that has allowed me to reach heights far beyond what a boy with physical challenges could ever dream of? How have I been able to put so much into my life in such a short space of time?

I believe it has come from two major motivating factors. First is the belief of others in me and the continued encouragement and reinforcement of that belief. Second, my belief in knowing I would succeed irrespective of the challenges I might face. This belief, love, and encouragement from my family and friends has instilled in me positive attitudes that can't be shaken. Growing out of all this has come the opportunity to live life to the very fullest. More important, I've learned that to succeed in whatever we do, we have to turn to others for support, for help, for reinforcement. Going it alone doesn't work.

It is very obvious from what I have written that I am very close to Fiona and, as I've already mentioned, have become good friends with Tom. My parents, in particular my father, were always there for me. All of them were supportive and willed me to go forward. Fiona was always concerned about how people treated me. You see, she was my shield and my first line of defense. Being Irish, she has the great quality of taking on my problems and making them her concerns. That's the nature of the girl and she will never change, thank God.

I would be lying to you if I said the teasing and the narrow-mindedness of some people's comments didn't get to me. But they didn't stay with me because of the love of many and most particularly the words of my father, who kept saying to me, "You're great." Early on in my life I had transcribed that message into my brain. As I grew older I would look in the mirror and say, "You're great." If you do this often, you really believe it. You see in yourself what others have seen in you—a strength waiting to be harnessed. I was able to focus on what I have instead of what I want. If you focus too much on what you want, you can end up dissatisfied much of the time.

My relationship with Mam has always been somewhat difficult. While there was often friction between us, on reflection, I have come to suspect that some of that friction existed because, in ways large and small, we are very much alike. Seeing yourself in someone who is driving you mad isn't easy, and it is much more difficult when you're a young man coming of age.

But the truth of the matter is that I inherited my drive and my ambition from my mother. She was the one with the fire that is so much a part of my life today. It's probably natural that I was closer to my dad, for he was the one who was, well, easier. Everything I did was great in his eyes. As I said before, my dad always accepted me for what I was.

Mam, on the other hand, always saw what I could become and planted that vision firmly in her mind. There were times when I felt that her acceptance of me was viewed against where she thought I should be and what she thought I should be doing. One thing is for certain, without her and without the conflict, I would not be who I am today.

As a result of my life not being a solo flight, my focus is always on the endless possibilities that I have discovered are there for me. Think about it. I might not have been fast enough with two perfectly good limbs to compete and win the 100-meter sprint, but with the assistance of modern technology, I became a world champion at this event for double amputees. I revel in the fact that my physical challenges have made me take risks far beyond what I normally would have even dreamed of.

Today I truly believe my life is being steered from on high, with a little help now from Dad, Theresa, my twin brother, Edmond, and all the other great souls that try to guide me.

That famous group of doctors who not only guided me in my medical progress but supported me in my musical ambitions have given me two career options. Today I wear two hats, although I must say my medical hat has become a small cap and my musical hat is now the top hat and tails. I now have the great pleasure to be able to sing to audiences around the world.

Finally one of my favorite quotes, which I feel epitomizes my faith and belief: "Faith is the bird that feels the light and sings when the dawn is still dark." My hope for you is that you will feel this light and truly sing your song of success before the dawn of another day.

When I wrote this book I decided that the only part of my life with
The Irish Tenors that I would share with you was that wonderful day
in Madison Square Garden in 1999. That period was too new in my
life, and I always found that the passage of time allowed me time to
reflect on events and put things in better perspective. But for this brief
ending, I feel compelled to skip ahead to June 2001.

On Father's Day, 2001, three New York City firemen, all of them
fathers themselves, were tragically taken from their families in a fire
in the borough of Queens. After I sang at my father's funeral on
March 8, 1998, I made a promise to myself that I would never sing at
another funeral again. On that sad day I sang for the man I truly loved
most in this world, and I didn't feel I would ever be able to do it again
and deal with the heartbreak and terrible loss that I felt that day. But
on Wednesday afternoon, June 20, I was sitting in a restaurant with my
good friend Dennis Mullins, who is also my attorney. We read in one
of the local newspapers that one of the firemen, Brian Fahey, had been
listening to The Irish Tenors before he went on that final call. I knew
that I had to reach out to the family in the only way I knew how. I had
no sooner said this than Dennis flew into action.

Dennis is a larger-than-life man with a countenance that is as open
as the day is long. We met by accident in Rosie O'Grady's, a well-
known restaurant and bar on Forty-seventh and Seventh in Manhattan. As I was on my own, he approached me and shook my hand and
told me how much he loved my music. I was a little tired, and as I
looked up at him, I was greeted with a great smile and I immediately
thought, "My God, I have just met my twin." Needless to say, I didn't
say that to Dennis. We have since become great friends. You know,
God does things like that to me and I am really ever so grateful.

We both returned to his office, and Dennis proceeded to make calls to the New York City Fire Department, which put us in touch with Lieutenant Kevin Dowdell of Rescue Company 4, the unit that had lost two men in the fire. Lieutenant Dowdell approached the family of Brian Fahey and told them of my offer to sing. Word came back that the Fahey family would accept my offer. Lieutenant Dowdell, who stressed the appreciation of the fire department, then said, "You know, we're burying two of our men tomorrow. Is there any chance that we could make the same offer to the family of Harry Ford?" I was only too willing to oblige as it was my honor to sing at both funerals, if that is what the families wanted me to do.

I then thought, "How can I sing at two funerals and not at that of John Downing, the third fireman who tragically lost his life that day?" One of my deepest regrets is that John Downing's funeral was on Friday morning, June 22, and conflicted with a flight that I had to take in order to make a performance with the Tenors in Boston.

I stayed out on Long Island with Dennis's family the night before so I would be nearer the location of the funerals. The next morning was dull and overcast. It seemed justly appropriate on such a sad occasion that the heavens would weep. I rose at six forty-five and commenced kicking my voice into action by seven-thirty. Dennis and his wife, Kathleen, were a great fortress of strength for me on that day. Dennis made sure everything would run as smoothly as possible. They even went out and bought me a blazer the night before, as I didn't have one. Such is the nature of these great people.

I had been told that there was nothing as impressive and moving as a funeral for a New York City fireman or police officer who died in the line of duty. But nothing I had been told prepared me for what I saw and felt that day. The first Mass of the day was for Harry Ford. It was held in St. Ignatius Martyr Catholic Church in Long Beach, New York. The small streets of the town were overflowing in every direction from the church, as some ten thousand firemen from New York and beyond came to pay their respects. It was a kaleidoscope of navy blue, demonstrating the intense strength of this community. My mouth was open in awe and my heart took refuge in their power of unity.

In the sweltering choir loft of St. Ignatius I prepared myself to sing two songs, the "Ave Maria" and "Panis Angelicus." While the church was small, there was no microphone and I had to push myself to ensure the songs were delivered with the power that the Mass deserved. The church was packed with Harry Ford's family and friends and dignitaries. And, of course, there were the firemen in their navy blue uniforms. Many of the older ones looked weary, and it seemed to me that they had done this too often before. While I was singing the birds were singing in accompaniment, and I immediately recalled what Pappy, my grandfather, had said: "If the birds sing in the church as the funeral Mass is continuing, they are rejoicing for the arrival of a new angel."

Once I had completed the two songs, Dennis, who was also visibly moved by the occasion, escorted me out before the huge crowd would gather to honor Harry. I was told that it was important that I get out of the town before the traffic from the funeral made the roads all but impassible. As I was walking from the church, firemen who recognized me thanked me for coming out that morning and singing. I told them that it was my honor to be there.

Dennis then decided that I needed food to keep my energy up. So he duly drove me to a restaurant where we were met by Kathleen and their daughter, Caitlin. Kathleen had brought me a change of shirt, as I was sweating ferociously. I was ever so grateful.

We then made our way from Long Beach to East Rockaway and St. Raymond's Church for the funeral Mass of Brian Fahey. Again, the sea of firemen in their uniforms was remarkable and their sheer number seemed to engulf the small town. Again, I went up to the choir loft and rehearsed the same two songs that I had sung that morning. Before the service began, one of the firemen asked if I would sing "Danny Boy," as it was one of Brian Fahey's favorite songs. I said of course I would but wanted to make certain that the parish priest wouldn't object, as some people don't think it an appropriate song for church.

The priest agreed, and it was decided I would sing that selection right after the people had come into the church.

The afternoon's funeral, which was supposed to start at one o'clock, was late by a little over one hour. It was no surprise to me that the Mass would be late, considering the sheer number of people that had to be moved from location to location. Then, at shortly after two o'clock, the massive crowds outside grew quiet and I heard the bagpipes in the distance.

There was no window in the choir loft at St. Raymond's, so I stood at the rail overlooking the church as the priests moved down the aisle to meet the coffin. The people crowded in below and some came into the loft for seats, and I was given the cue to begin "Danny Boy." As you might imagine, I have sung "Danny Boy" literally thousands of times. The last verse of the song should really be sung more softly than most people realize, and it's always a challenge for me to hold back just the right amount but still be heard. That afternoon in St. Raymond's was about as good as I ever remember singing that song, and I couldn't think of anywhere else that I wanted so much for it to be right.

After singing "Ave Maria" and "Panis Angelicus," I was taken back into Manhattan, courtesy of the New York City Fire Department. I had just enough time at my hotel to grab a quick shower and get my clothes together before I needed to be at Radio City Music Hall for a rehearsal for that evening's performance with The Irish Tenors.

I have always believed that my voice was a gift from God. I try to use my singing and indeed the example of my life and the obstacles that I've overcome to help inspire others and to make people feel good about themselves. When I heard the tragic tale of those brave firemen, I thought that my singing might somehow help ease just a small amount of the pain that was being felt.

I also wanted to attend as an acknowledgment of an act of kindness that was shown to me back in 1984 when I was in New York for the Paralympics. That summer a New York City fireman who was at the games was kind enough to take me on a tour of the city that I have still not forgotten. We went all over the city, stopping at various firehouses along the way. The people I met that day were extraordinarily kind and welcoming. The fire department treated me wonderfully back in 1984, and I saw in the Father's Day tragedy a chance for me to give a little back.

As I mentioned before, I had not sung at a funeral since my dad died. While I would have it no other way, singing on that day prevented me from doing what I should have been doing, grieving for the loss of the man who loved me fully and unconditionally in whatever state I was in. As I stood in the choir loft of St. Raymond's, I looked down on the young children left behind by Brian Fahey and a tear ran down my face. How sad that they should lose their father at such a young age. I then also realized how lucky I was to have had my father for as long as I did. I feel that I moved a long way that day in my continuing process of grieving for my own father. As I was leaving the church someone told me how grateful they were that I had come to sing. I replied that it was I who was grateful for being there.

Back at Radio City, the sold-out crowd had been seated and we were about to walk out onstage. I said a prayer that night, as I always do, asking God to help me through another performance. But this time I knew that my voice and my body were in trouble. I looked up and prayed silently to three firemen, "Come on, boys, I need all the help I can get." In the middle of the show we dedicated a song to the firemen, and I asked the audience for a moment of silence. I closed my eyes and all I could hear was the soft hum coming from the air conditioning system. It was as if I were in the great hall alone. But after two standing ovations at the end of the show, I knew that wasn't the case. Harry, Brian, and John had made one more rescue in New York.

Acknowledgments

There are so many people throughout my life who have helped shape me and who have guided me to where I am today. To all of you wonderful people, I am forever grateful.

To Fiona, the greatest sister a brother could ever have—you have put up with me for forty-plus years and your love knows no bounds, thank God.

To Tom, the greatest brother—you're the solid one in this family. Thank you for being you.

To all my old pals that have been there right from the start of this kaleidoscope of a life:

Tom—God bless that Renault 4.

Marius—your advice didn't fall on deaf ears.

Aidan—your prayers paid off.

Niall—Durty Nellie's will never be the same.

Keith—your notes never got such abuse.

Liam—there is nothing like Clonakilty black pudding.

Mick, Alan, and Paul—my appreciation for Guinness will never change.

Debbie and Deirdre—you two could run a hospital.

To all the wonderful consultants, doctors, and nurses who were in full support when I switched to music (maybe you were all just delighted I moved on, who knows?)—thank you for believing in me.

To Ronnie, who had the patience to work with a late starter and show me how to be passionate about singing.

To all the great and talented singers I've met along the way, the women who stood by me when things got rough: Marie Walshe, Cara O'Sullivan, Majella Cullagh, and Virginia Kerr—you are the best.

To Sherry and Gerry Laveroni—my older adopted brother and sister.

To Feinstein's at the Regency Hotel, Park Avenue—what a blast.

To all my friends in the U.S.A.—you have no idea the joy and happiness you have brought to me in the last three years.

To Rodger Lawson and Prudential—to say thank you for being such a good friend is not nearly enough.

To Mike and Cathy Doorley and Gerry, Jean, and Olivia Custer—you're just like family to me.

To Pronnsias O'Dunn. You will never know how grateful I am to you for giving me the extra push to go ahead. Thank you.

To Jim and Ali Henschel, who persevered with me along the way when I seemed to be losing my head—I'm still no better.

To Debbie Coleman—thank you for your help.

To Kathleen and Dennis Mullins—thank you for coming to my aid.

To Shay Healy—hang in there. You did a great job.

To Tony Roden—what time we spent singing together will shape my voice forever. Tony, "You're great."

To Lisa Drew—thank you for all your wonderful work, your committment, and your patience.

To Bill Hughes for having the confidence and belief in me in ninety-four and planting the seeds of singing in my heart and soul and coming back in ninety-eight to set me on my way.

Finally, to any person that I have forgotten to mention—it's not an oversight. It's just that there are so many of you. If I didn't stop now, I would have to write another book made up entirely of acknowledgments.